# Working Creatively with Obstacles to Client Change in Rational Emotive Behaviour Therapy

Productive therapeutic change is facilitated when the therapist and client have a good therapeutic relationship, share views on salient therapeutic matters, agree on goals to enhance client well-being, and understand what they each have to do to achieve the goals of therapy. This book will address the obstacles to client change that both client and therapist bring to Rational Emotive Behaviour Therapy (REBT).

Addressing these obstacles to client change head on, the book enables both the client and practitioner to move beyond problems in the consulting room and build a more productive relationship, resulting in more effective sessions and assisting in the resolution of underlying problems for which the client has sought help. This updated second edition will move beyond the language of 'resistance' in the first edition to instead reposition the term through the lens of barriers to change. A further emphasis will be placed on online therapy and barriers such as clients not attending as many sessions as a therapist might expect or recommend.

This book is essential reading for any practitioner hoping to use REBT more effectively in their day-to-day practice.

**Windy Dryden** is in clinical and consultative practice and is an international authority on Single-Session Therapy and Rational Emotive Behaviour Therapy. He has worked in psychotherapy for more than 45 years and is the author or editor of over 275 books.

T0383767

# Working Creatively with Obstacles to Client Change in Rational Emotive Behaviour Therapy

## A Practitioner's Guide

Second Edition

Windy Dryden

Routledge
Taylor & Francis Group

LONDON AND NEW YORK

Second edition published 2025
by Routledge
4 Park Square, Milton Park, Abingdon, Oxon, OX14 4RN

and by Routledge
605 Third Avenue, New York, NY 10158

*Routledge is an imprint of the Taylor & Francis Group, an informa business*

First edition published by Routledge 2012

*British Library Cataloguing-in-Publication Data*
A catalogue record for this book is available from the British Library

*Library of Congress Cataloging-in-Publication Data*
Names: Dryden, Windy, author.
Title: Working creatively with obstacles to client change in rational emotive
behaviour therapy : a practitioner's guide / Windy Dryden.
Description: 2nd edition. | Abingdon, Oxon ; New York, NY : Routledge, 2025. |
Includes bibliographical references and index. |
Identifiers: LCCN 2024021776 (print) | LCCN 2024021777 (ebook) |
ISBN 9781032729947 (hbk) | ISBN 9781032729923 (pbk) | ISBN 9781003423379 (ebk)
Subjects: LCSH: Change (Psychology) | Rational emotive behaviour therapy.
Classification: LCC BF637.C4 D79 2025 (print) | LCC BF637.C4 (ebook) |
DDC 616.89/142–dc23/eng/20240603
LC record available at https://lccn.loc.gov/2024021776
LC ebook record available at https://lccn.loc.gov/2024021777

ISBN: 9781032729947 (hbk)
ISBN: 9781032729923 (pbk)
ISBN: 9781003423379 (ebk)

DOI: 10.4324/9781003423379

Typeset in Times New Roman
by Newgen Publishing UK

# Contents

# Preface

This book addresses the manifold difficulties both clients and therapists experience in Rational Emotive Behaviour Therapy (REBT). As usual, Albert Ellis (1985, 2002), the founder of REBT, led the way with his book, originally titled *Overcoming Resistance: Rational Emotive Therapy with Difficult Clients*. Ellis stated that the psychotherapy literature on difficult and resistant clients is extensive, but 'much less attention has been given to the difficult and resistant therapist' (Ellis, 1985: 161). The most challenging client to deal with, Ellis suggests, is the therapist. To present a balanced view of who creates the most problems in therapy, I have divided the book into two equal parts: 'Client Obstacles to Client Change' in Part 1, followed by 'Therapist Obstacles to Client Change' in Part 2.

You will notice from the above that I have used the term 'obstacles to client change' rather than the term 'resistance' and have done so throughout this book. The reason I have made this change is because I have concerns about the meaning of the word 'resistance' in the context of psychotherapy. Oxford Languages defines resistance as 'the refusal to accept or comply with something'. Its synonyms are 'hostility to' and 'aversion to'. I hold that the term 'obstacles to client change' does not mean 'refusal to accept', 'hostility to' or 'aversion'. Instead, the term indicates that the client comes to therapy to experience a change of some sort but, along the way, encounters certain obstacles to this change. In this book, I will discuss two sources of obstacles to client change: those emanating from the client in Part 1 and those emanating from the therapist in Part 2. I will address problems emanating from the therapist–client relationship in both parts of the book where appropriate.

Throughout the book, I have used the 'working alliance' framework that Bordin (1979) developed as a generic perspective on obstacles to client change in psychotherapy. Bordin introduced this concept as a tripartite perspective on why psychotherapy works and why it stalls. He argued that there are three domains of the alliance:

- *Bonds* – the interpersonal connectedness between therapist and client.
- *Goals* – what both therapist and client are aiming to achieve in psychotherapy.
- *Tasks* – what therapist and client do to achieve the latter's goals.

Later, I added a fourth domain – *Views* – which points to the fact that both therapist and client have particular views about salient aspects of psychotherapy not covered by the three other domains (Dryden, 2006, 2011).

From a working alliance perspective, productive therapeutic change is facilitated when the therapist and client:

- Have a well-bonded therapeutic relationship.
- Share similar views on salient therapeutic matters (e.g., the conceptualisation of the client's problems and how best they can be addressed).
- Agree on goals of therapy that will enhance the client's well-being.
- Understand what each has to do to achieve therapy goals and be able and prepared to undertake such tasks.

The working alliance perspective on obstacles to client change is that difficulties can occur in one or more domains of the alliance, but both parties can tackle these if there is the will to do so.

While this is a book on obstacles to client change in REBT and how to address them creatively, I have drawn on working alliance theory in the way I have structured the book in that I hold that this more generic theory brings coherence to the way REBT therapists need to intervene to get the therapeutic wagon moving in the right (i.e. therapeutic) direction.

Given this more generic perspective, my aim in this book is to offer ways of tackling difficulties in REBT that will assist their resolution and thereby help to build a productive and less stressful working alliance. As I do so, I hold that the following therapist qualities are useful in helping them address such difficulties: creativity, persistence, ingenuity, energy and persuasion. This book obviously cannot focus on every problem or difficulty in REBT, so some readers may be disappointed not to see their particular problems dealt with. Therefore, I suggest to those readers that they consult other REBT texts (such as Dryden, 2024) as well as apply or develop their problem-solving abilities.

One of the continual pleasures and challenges in REBT is increasing therapists' stock of techniques and strategies to address obstacles to client change. Such a process keeps therapists on their therapeutic toes and prevents psychotherapy from degenerating into an assembly line. I hope that I have communicated my enthusiasm for such problem-solving to the readers of this book.

Before we begin, two points. The first concerns my use of gender language. As far as possible, I have used gender-neutral language when referring to therapists and clients in this book. The exceptions are when, in a few examples, the narrative specifies the client's gender. My second point concerns the dialogues between therapists and clients and supervisors and supervisees. These are constructed rather than real to protect confidentiality, but they are representative of the kinds of dialogues that happen in REBT practice and supervision.

Windy Dryden
London and Eastbourne
February 2024

# Part 1

# Client Obstacles
# to Client Change

# Chapter 1

# Rational Emotive Behaviour Therapy in Brief

## Introduction

To get the most out of this book, you need to know the nature of Rational Emotive Behaviour Therapy (REBT). This introductory chapter aims to present a brief overview of the main features of this psychotherapy approach.

### REBT Is a Form of Cognitive Behaviour Therapy

An important distinction must be made between a therapy approach and a therapy tradition. The former is a specific form of therapy delivery that can be placed under the umbrella of the latter. Thus, in my view, REBT is a specific therapy approach that is located under the Cognitive Behaviour Therapy (CBT) umbrella.[1] There is no single therapy approach called CBT.[2] However, several different approaches form part of the tradition of CBT.

From this perspective, REBT was the first approach within the CBT tradition to be developed. Albert Ellis, a New York clinical psychologist originated it in the late 1950s (Ellis, 1958).[3]

## REBT Theory

In this section, I will begin by outlining REBT's *Situational ABC* framework which explains the factors that explain psychologically disturbed and healthy responses to life's adversities. Then I will discuss REBT's stance on negative emotions. Finally, I consider REBT's position on the role of attitudes as the key determinant of psychological disturbance and health and detail the shared and distinguishing components of rigid and flexible attitudes, on the one hand, and of extreme and non-extreme attitudes, on the other.

### REBT's Situational ABC Framework

REBT has a distinctive view of psychologically disturbed and healthy responses to life's adversities. It argues that when a person experiences psychological disturbance at $C$,[4] this occurs within a given situation and it is crucial to discover what the

DOI: 10.4324/9781003423379-2

person is most disturbed about. When discovered, this represents the *A* or adversity. *A* may represent an actual event, but it more often represents an inference the person makes about the situation.

Perhaps the most singular aspect of REBT is that it is based on an attitudinal view of psychological disturbance and health. Thus, when a person is disturbed, it is not because of the adversity that they are facing (or think they are facing) at *A* but because of the basic attitudes that they hold at *B* towards the adversity. The primary characteristic of these disturbance-creating attitudes[5] at *B* is that they are rigid and extreme. The primary goal of the REBT therapist in this circumstance is to help the person respond healthily to this adversity at *A*, and they do so by helping the person develop health-creating attitudes at *B*. The primary characteristic of these latter attitudes is that they are flexible and non-extreme.

When people hold rigid and extreme attitudes at *B* towards adversities at *A*, they will experience unhealthy negative emotions (UNEs) at *C*. The nature of these unhealthy negative emotions at *C* will be determined by the adversity at *A* (to be discussed later). They will also act (or tend to act) unconstructively and think in highly negatively distorted and ruminative ways at *C*.

Conversely, when these people hold flexible and non-extreme attitudes at *B* towards the same adversities at *A*, they experience healthy negative emotions (HNEs) at *C*. The nature of these healthy negative emotions at *C* will again be determined by the nature of the adversity at *A* (to be discussed later). They will also act (or tend to act) in various constructive ways and think in realistic and non-ruminative ways at *C*.

Table 1 represents graphically the *Situational ABC* framework described above.

*Table 1* REBT's *Situational ABC* Framework

| Situation | |
|---|---|
| Adversity (A) | |
| **Basic Attitudes: Rigid and Extreme (B)** | **Basic Attitudes: Flexible and Non-Extreme (B)** |
| **Disturbed Consequences of AxB (C)** | **Healthy Consequences of AxB (C)** |
| • **Unhealthy negative emotions**<br>• **Unconstructive behaviour**<br>• **Highly negatively distorted and ruminative thinking** | • **Healthy negative emotions**<br>• **Constructive behaviour**<br>• **Realistic and non-ruminative thinking** |

### REBT's Stance on Negative Emotions

I mentioned in the previous section that REBT distinguishes between unhealthy negative emotions and healthy negative emotions, the former stemming from rigid/ extreme attitudes and the latter from flexible/non-extreme attitudes. This distinction is vital because it helps clients see that specific emotional responses to adversities can be negative and healthy and can be set as therapeutic goals (e.g., 'I want to feel concerned, but not anxious'). As such, they do not have to aim for i) a less intense version of an unhealthy negative emotion ('I want to be less anxious'), ii) the absence of an unhealthy negative emotion ('I don't want to be anxious'), the presence of a positive emotion ('I want to feel calm') or the absence of an emotion ('I don't want to feel anything').

I mentioned above that a person's attitude at $B$ towards an adversity at $A$ (e.g. threat) determines the healthiness of the negative emotion experienced at $C$ (e.g. anxiety when the person holds a rigid/extreme attitude towards the threat; concern when the attitude held is flexible/non-extreme). However, the adversity at $A$ determines which emotion paring is experienced, as shown in Table 2.

*Table 2* Adversities and Emotions

| Emotion (UNE and HNE) | Adversities |
| --- | --- |
| Anxiety/Concern | Threat; danger |
| Depression/Sadness | Loss; loss of value; failure; undeserved plight |
| Guilt/Remorse | Moral violation (sin of commission and omission); hurting others |
| Unhealthy Regret/Healthy Regret | Taking action in the past you wished you hadn't; failing to take action in the past you wished you had; facing uncertainty about taking action now or in the future in case you make a mistake |
| Shame/Disappointment | Public disclosure of weakness; falling very short of one's ideal, negative judgment of self or of a reference group with which the person closely identifies by others |
| Hurt/Sorrow | Others treat you badly (and you consider that you do not deserve such treatment); others less invested in your relationship with them than you are |
| Unhealthy Anger/Healthy Anger | Frustrated; transgressed against; ego attacked, disrespected |
| Unhealthy Jealousy/Healthy Jealousy | Threat to present relationship posed by another person; facing uncertainty in relation to the aforementioned threat |
| Unhealthy Envy/Healthy Envy | Others experience good fortune which you lack and covet |

*Table 3* Rigid and Flexible Attitudes (Foundation) and Extreme and Non-Extreme Attitudes (Derived from Rigid and Flexible Extreme Attitudes)

| **Rigid/Extreme Attitudes** | **Flexible/Non-Extreme Attitudes** |
|---|---|
| *(Underpinning Psychologically Disturbed Responses to A)* | *(Underpinning Psychologically Healthy Responses to A)* |
| **Rigid Attitudes [Foundation]** | **Flexible Attitudes [Foundation]** |
| <br>\|<br>\|<br>\|<br>V | <br>\|<br>\|<br>\|<br>V |
| **Extreme Attitudes** | **Non-Extreme Attitudes** |
| *(Derived from Rigid Attitudes)* | *(Derived from Flexible Attitudes* |
| - Awfulising Attitudes | - Non-Awfulising Attitudes |
| - Attitudes of Unbearability | - Attitudes of Bearability |
| - Self-/Other-/Life-Devaluation Attitudes | - Self-/Other-/Life-Unconditional Acceptance Attitudes |

### Basic Attitudes: Rigid/Extreme vs. Flexible/Non-Extreme

I mentioned earlier that REBT holds an attitudinal view of psychologically disturbed and healthy responses at *C* to life's adversities at *A*. As Table 3 shows, of the rigid/extreme attitudes deemed to determine psychologically disturbed responses to adversities, the rigid attitude is regarded as the foundation from which three extreme attitudes are derived. Similarly, of the flexible/non-extreme attitudes deemed to determine psychologically healthy responses to the same adversities, the flexible attitude is regarded as the foundation from which three non-extreme attitudes are derived.

According to REBT theory, rigid and flexible attitudes have shared and distinguishing components, as do extreme and non-extreme components, which are detailed and exemplified in Table 4.

### REBT's Preferred Order for Dealing with Client Problems

A distinctive feature of REBT is that it outlines a logical order for dealing with clients' problems.

#### Disturbance before Dissatisfaction

REBT argues that unless there are good reasons to the contrary, therapists should address their clients' emotional problems before their dissatisfaction problems (Dryden 2021). The reasoning is as follows. If therapists try to deal with their clients' dissatisfaction issues before dealing with their emotional disturbance, their

*Table 4* Shared (Underlined) and Distinguishing Components of Rigid/Extreme and Flexible/Non-Extreme Attitudes

| Components of a Rigid/ Extreme Attitude | Components of a Flexible/ Non-Extreme Attitude |
|---|---|
| **Rigid Attitude** | **Flexible Attitude** |
| 1. *Preference* <br> 2. *Demand Asserted* <br><br> 'I want you to like me and therefore you must so' | 1. *Preference* <br> 2. *Demand Negated* <br><br> 'I want you to like me, but you don't have to do so' |
| **Awfulising Attitude** | **Non-Awfulising Attitude** |
| 1. *Evaluation of Badness* <br> 2. *Awfulising* <br><br> 'It would be bad if you don't like me and therefore it would be the end of the world' | 1. *Evaluation of Badness* <br> 2. *Non-Awfulising* <br><br> 'It would be bad if you don't like me, but it would not be the end of the world' |
| **Attitude of Unbearability** | **Attitude of Bearability** |
| 1. *Struggle* <br> 2. *Discomfort Intolerance* <br><br><br><br><br> 'It would be hard to bear if you don't like me and therefore, I could not bear it' | 1. *Struggle* <br> 2. *Discomfort Tolerance* <br> 3. *Worth It* <br> 4. *Willingness* <br> 5. *Going To* <br><br> 'It would be hard to bear if you don't like me, but I could bear it, it is worth bearing, I am willing to bear it, and I am going to do so' |
| **Devaluation Attitude** | **Unconditional Acceptance Attitude** |
| 1. *Negatively Evaluated Aspect* <br> 2. *Asserted Devaluation (of self/other/life)* <br><br><br> 'If you don't like me, that would be bad and would prove that I am an unlikeable person' | 1. *Negatively Evaluated Aspect* <br> 2. *Negated Devaluation (of self/ other/life)* <br> 3. *Asserted Unconditional Acceptance (of self/other/life)* <br><br> 'If you don't like me, that would be bad but would not prove that I am an unlikeable person. It would prove that I am a fallible human being capable of being liked and disliked' |

disturbed feelings will get in the way of the therapists' efforts to change directly the adversities about which their clients are dissatisfied.

For example, let's take the example of Paul, who is dissatisfied with his wife's spending habits. However, he is also unhealthily angry about her behaviour. Whenever he talks to her about it, he makes himself angry, raises his voice to his wife and makes pejorative remarks about her and her spending behaviour. Now what is the likely impact of Paul's expression of unhealthy anger on his wife? Does it encourage her to stand back and look objectively at her behaviour? Of course, it doesn't. Paul's angry behaviour is more likely to lead his wife to become unhealthily angry herself and/or to become defensive. In Paul's case, his anger had, in fact, both effects on his wife. Let's suppose that Paul *first* addressed his unhealthy anger and then discussed his dissatisfaction with his wife. His annoyance at her behaviour, but his acceptance of her as a person, would help him to view her behaviour perhaps as a sign of emotional disturbance. His compassion for her would have very different effects on her. She would probably be less defensive and because Paul would not be unhealthily angry, his wife would also be less likely to be unhealthily angry. With anger out of the picture, the stage would be set for Paul to address the reasons for his dissatisfaction more effectively.

## Disturbance before Development

In the late 1960s and early 1970s, I used to go to several encounter groups. This was the era of personal growth or development. However, there were several casualties of these groups. When these occurred, it was because attendees were preoccupied with issues of emotional disturbance. They were being pushed too hard to go into areas of development that warranted greater resilience.

In general, it is tough for clients to develop themselves when they are emotionally disturbed. To focus on areas of development when someone is emotionally disturbed is akin to encouraging that person to climb a very steep hill with hefty weights attached to their ankles. First, help the person remove their ankle weights (i.e., address their emotional disturbance) before discussing the best way to climb the hill!

## Dissatisfaction before Development

Abraham Maslow (1968) is perhaps best known for his work on self-actualisation. The relevance of this concept for our present discussion is this. It is challenging for clients to focus on their higher-order 'needs' when they are preoccupied with issues concerning lower-order 'needs'. Thus, if clients face a general dissatisfying life experience that cannot be compartmentalised and also want to explore their writing ambitions, they should address the former first unless this life dissatisfaction will help them write a better book!

While I have outlined REBT's preferred order in dealing with clients' issues, it also values flexibility. Thus, if clients want to deal with their problems in a different order, they should do so and observe the results. If it works, that is fine. If not, REBT's preferred position may prove to yield better results. The proof of the pudding is in the eating.

Having outlined REBT's position on dealing with a range of clients' issues. I will outline REBT's approach to helping clients with their emotional problems.

## The Working Alliance in REBT

Most approaches to therapy are a blend of relationship factors and technical factors. This section will discuss the working alliance that REBT therapists strive to develop and maintain with their clients. In doing this, I will draw on the work of Ed Bordin (1979) who proposed that the alliance between therapist and client comprises three domains: 'bonds', 'goals' and 'tasks'. Later, I added a fourth domain I termed 'views' (Dryden, 2006, 2011).

### Bonds

'Bonds' refer to the interconnectedness between the therapist and client. Like most therapists, REBT practitioners strive to show their clients that they a) understand them from their frame of reference, b) accept them as unique, fallible human beings, and c) strive to have an authentic relationship with them. They regard these 'core conditions' (Rogers, 1957) as important, but neither necessary nor sufficient for therapeutic change to occur.

Concerning therapeutic style, REBT therapists generally adopt an active-directive style. They actively participate with their clients while encouraging them to be actively involved in the therapeutic dialogue. While active, they direct their clients' attention to their problems and help them use REBT's *Situational ABC* framework (see above) to understand them and have a structure for dealing with them. REBT therapists use Socratic and didactic methods during the REBT process. At every stage, alliance-minded REBT therapists explain the purpose of their interventions and get their clients' permission to proceed. When working well together, REBT therapists and their clients have an excellent collaborative bond.

### Views

'Views' refer to the therapist and client's understandings concerning the practical and therapeutic aspects of their working together. In brief, shared views are therapeutic. Thus, ideally, therapist and client should agree on the practicalities of their partnership (fees, confidentiality, cancellation policy etc.) and on the therapeutic aspects of their partnership (e.g., what accounts for the client's problem, how they are both going to address these problems and what are the responsibilities of each participant) (see the section on 'tasks' below).

### Goals

'Goals' are the raison d'être of the therapist and client coming together. The client is in some psychological pain and is seeking help from the therapist for that pain. The client may have well-formed goals ('I want to feel concerned, but not anxious about drying up when giving presentations at work') or a vague sense of what they want from therapy (e.g., 'I want you to ease my pain'). One of the therapist's tasks (see below) is to help the client set achievable goals, which they both work towards. In brief, shared goals are therapeutic. When therapists have more ambitious goals than clients, this can create a sense of tension in the work.

## Tasks

'Tasks' refer to what the therapist and client do in therapy which is in the service of the client's goals. Ideally, the therapist and client understand their mutual tasks and agree to carry out those within their purview. Tables 5 and 6 present a diagrammatic overview of the therapist's and client's tasks, respectively, in REBT.

In this book, as you will see, I have used the working alliance framework to discuss client obstacles and therapist obstacles to client change.

## The Process of REBT

This section will provide an overview of the REBT therapy process.

### Assessing the Nominated Problem

The therapist asks the client for a specific example of the problem and uses the *Situational ABC* framework to assess the problem so that they both understand

*Table 5* The Therapist's Tasks in REBT

**The beginning phase**
  • **Establish a therapeutic alliance**
  • **Socialise your client into REBT**
  • **Begin to assess and intervene on the nominated problem**
  • **Teach the *ABCs* of REBT**
  • **Deal with your client's doubts**

**The middle phase**
  • **Follow through on the nominated problem**
  • **Encourage your client to engage in relevant tasks**
  • **Work on your client's other problems**
  • **Identify, examine and help change your client's core rigid and extreme attitudes**
  • **Deal with obstacles to change**
  • **Encourage your client to maintain and enhance gains**
  • **Undertake relapse prevention and deal with vulnerability factors**
  • **Encourage your client to become their own therapist**

**The ending phase**
  • **Decide on when and how to end**
  • **Encourage your client to summarise what has been learned**
  • **Attribute improvement to client's efforts**
  • **Deal with obstacles to ending**
  • **Agree on criteria for follow-ups and for resuming therapy**

*Table 6* The Client's Tasks in REBT

---

• **Specify problems and set goals**
• **Be open to the therapist's REBT framework**
• **Apply the specific principle of emotional responsibility**
  **- The client accepts that they disturb themself by holding rigid/
    extreme attitudes towards life's adversities**
• **Apply the principle of therapeutic responsibility**
  **- The client accepts that in order to reach their therapeutic goals,
    they need to implement REBT methods of change to develop and
    deepen their conviction in their alternative flexible/non-extreme
    attitudes towards the same life's adversities**
• **Disclose doubts, difficulties and blocks to change**
• **Become their own REBT therapist**

---

i) the client's primary unhealthy negative emotion at *C*, together with its main behavioural and cognitive concomitants; ii) the client's adversity at *A*; and iii) the rigid/extreme basic attitudes at *B* that underpin their disturbed responses at *C* together with the alternative flexible/non-extreme basic attitudes that will underpin their healthy responses to the adversity which are also clarified.

## Clarifying the Two B-C Connections

The therapist helps the client to understand the two *B-C* connections: i) the relationship between their rigid/extreme attitudes (at *B*) and their disturbed responses (at *C*) to the adversity (at *A*) and ii) the relationship between the alternative flexible/non-extreme attitudes (at *B*) and the healthy responses (at *C*) to *A*; responses that can serve as the client's problem-related goals.

## Preparing the Client to Examine Their Attitudes

The therapist then helps the client understand that the next step is for them to stand back and examine both sets of attitudes (rigid/extreme and flexible/non-extreme) and the purpose of doing so.

## Helping the Client to Examine Their Attitudes

Once the client has understood the rationale for the attitude examination process, the therapist begins to help them examine both sets of attitudes until they have understood that their rigid/extreme attitudes are false, illogical and generally yield poor results and that their flexible/non-extreme attitudes are true, logical and generally yield good results. In particular, it is crucial that the client fully understands that developing flexible/non-extreme attitudes will help them achieve their goals related to their nominated problem. Once the client has achieved this understanding, they are deemed to have achieved what Albert Ellis (1963) called *intellectual insight*. Here, the client may say things like, 'Yes, I understand why my rigid/extreme attitudes are false, illogical and unconstructive, but I still believe them' or 'Yes, I understand in my head why my flexible/non-extreme attitudes are true, logical and constructive, but I don't believe them in my gut'. Intellectual insight does not positively impact the client's emotions, behaviour and thinking. By contrast, having *emotional insight* (Ellis, 1963) means that they have 'gut' belief in their flexible/non-extreme attitudes and that these positively impact their emotions, behaviour and thinking.

### Helping the Client Understand the Change Process: From Intellectual Insight to Emotional Insight

Before embarking on the process of change from intellectual insight to emotional insight, it is important that the client understands what this journey involves. This is akin to having a map to see how to get from Point A (intellectual insight) to Point B (emotional insight).

### The Importance of Acting and Thinking in Ways Consistent with the Client's Developing Flexible/Non-Extreme Attitudes

As well as continuing to examine their attitudes, it is vital that the client acts and thinks in ways consistent with their developing flexible/non-extreme attitudes and inconsistent with the rigid/extreme attitudes they seek to leave behind. Like other approaches to CBT, this is traditionally done by clients carrying out homework tasks negotiated at the end of therapy sessions. The important thing that the client needs to appreciate here is that emotional change will occur during this process, but it is not predictable when this change will occur. The client needs to continue to think and act in ways that are consistent with their developing flexible/non-extreme attitudes until emotional change occurs.

### Helping the Client to Generalise Their Learning from Problem to Problem

Once the client has made progress on their nominated problem, they can transfer their learning to other problems they may have, and the therapist needs to help them do that. In my experience, most clients are not good at generalising their learning this way without the therapist's active help.

### Identifying and Helping the Client to Change Their Core Rigid/Extreme Attitudes in Favour of Core Flexible/Non-Extreme Attitudes

As the client and therapist work together on the former's problems, they will likely identify one or more core rigid/extreme attitudes. One such attitude will underly a number of the client's problems and is usually expressed in general terms (e.g., 'I must be approved by people I deem to be significant, and I am worthless if I am not'). The therapist needs to help the client formulate an alternative core flexible/non-extreme attitude and help them use this to underly the work to be done when facing actual or predicted situations where disapproval from others may be experienced.

**Helping the client to become their own therapist.** Perhaps the ultimate goal of REBT from the therapist's perspective is to help the client become their own therapist so that they learn to help themself in the future. This involves the client learning the skills of REBT such as assessing their problems, examining their attitudes, setting themself tasks to strengthen their conviction in their flexible/non-extreme attitudes and learning to identify and deal with obstacles to change. To do this, as therapy unfolds, the therapist adopts a less active, more prompting role so that the client gradually takes the lead to initiate therapeutic tasks that the therapist initiated in the earlier phases of REBT. Not all clients are interested in becoming their own therapists, but this should not prevent the therapist from raising the issue with clients since some of them will have this interest and should be encouraged to actualise it.

## Identifying and Dealing with Obstacles to Client Change

I have discussed the working alliance in REBT and the REBT process above when ideal conditions exist. In reality, such conditions infrequently exist, and therapists and clients will likely encounter various obstacles to client change. This forms the subject matter of this book and it is to this topic we will turn.

In the following chapters, I will discuss a variety of obstacles to client change across the four domains of the working alliance. In Part 1 of this book, I will focus on client obstacles to client change and in Part 2, I will highlight therapist obstacles to client change. I will put forward ways that these obstacles can be creatively worked with in therapy. However, please regard the suggestions found here as just that – suggestions. They should aid rather than replace your creativity as a therapist as you embark with your clients on the satisfying but sometimes rocky journey towards making a difference in their lives.

## Notes

1  I edit a series of books for Routledge entitled the 'CBT Distinctive Features' series. The purpose of this series is to show the distinctive features of several therapy approaches within the CBT tradition.
2  Aaron Beck's approach to CBT was originally known as 'Cognitive Therapy'. However, the 'Beck Institute of Cognitive Therapy' changed its name to the 'Beck Institute of Cognitive Behavior Therapy' in 2012 thus muddying the waters as to whether CBT is a therapy tradition or an attempt to rebrand Cognitive Therapy as Cognitive Behaviour Therapy.
3  When he first originated REBT, Ellis (1958) called it 'Rational Therapy' to emphasise its cognitive features. He changed its name to 'Rational-Emotive Therapy' in the early 1960s to show that it did not neglect emotion and changed it again in 1993 to show that it did not neglect behaviour.
4  $C$ stands for consequences of holding basic attitudes at $B$ towards adversities at $A$. There are three sets of such consequences: emotional, behavioural and cognitive.
5  When formally discussing the $ABC$ framework, I will use the term 'basic attitude' to preserve the $B$ in this framework. At other times I will use the term 'attitude'.

Chapter 2

# Dealing with Client Obstacles to Client Change in the Bonds Domain of the Working Alliance

Developing and maintaining a working alliance is one of the biggest challenges in psychotherapy. As I stated in Chapter 1, Bordin (1979) argued that the bond between therapist and client (which is what most people in the field mean by the therapeutic relationship) is one of a number of domains of the working alliance.

This chapter focuses on tackling those obstacles and difficulties primarily created by the client which block or impair the creation of a successful relationship and its maintenance.

### When Clients Struggle to Form a Therapeutic Bond

An appropriately bonded therapeutic relationship will encourage clients to carry out their goal-directed tasks. Therefore, it is important for REBT therapists to pay attention to their clients' anticipations (what the client predicts) and preferences (what the client wants) in this domain. Concerning preferences, for example, one client desires a formal relationship based on the therapist's expertise and authority within their field, while another client seeks an informal 'chat' and a more relaxed approach to therapy.

However, some clients' preferred bonds will reinforce rather than help them overcome their emotional problems. For example, a female client who saw one of my colleagues said she could not stand much stress or pressure in her life, so said to him, 'Could you be very gentle with me?' My colleague did not speak for ten minutes, and she enquired if he was going to ask her questions. He replied: 'I don't want to put you under any pressure'. She laughed, but the serious point was that if the therapist wrapped her in cotton wool, the client stood little chance of tackling her anxiety and social avoidance. This therapist's explanation of his clinical rationale for not 'tiptoeing' through therapy with the client opened the way for her to develop greater resilience towards life's vicissitudes.

Clients who exhibit dire needs for love and approval (e.g., 'I must be approved, and if I'm not, I am worthless') may expect the therapist to meet these needs. While REBT therapists offer clients unconditional acceptance as fallible human beings, they are cautious about giving clients excessive warmth for two reasons (Dryden and Ellis 1997). First, clients may feel better in the short term if they think

DOI: 10.4324/9781003423379-3

their therapist greatly approves of them. However, they will not necessarily get better in the long term because their disturbance-creating attitudes remain largely unexamined and, therefore, continue intact. It is far better to teach such clients unconditional self-acceptance irrespective of what the therapist thinks about them, for example:

> *Therapist:*    When you're no longer anxious about whether or not I like you, it will probably be the time to end therapy. Then you'll be much stronger to deal constructively with the inevitable rejection or disapproval that occurs in life.

Second, therapists may strengthen their clients' attitudes of unbearability (e.g., 'I can't face my problems on my own. It's too hard. I need lots of support from my therapist'). Thus, such clients avoid taking the primary responsibility for bringing about change in their lives and believe they cannot be happy without the continual support of others. The therapist can repeatedly counter with the self-defeating nature of this outlook, for example:

> *Therapist:*    If I have to hold your hand throughout therapy, how will you learn to walk on your own? When I let go of your hand when therapy is finished, what happens to you if there is no one else to grasp it?

Therefore, REBT seeks 'to help them [clients] become independent, to think for themselves and acquire self-helping habits rather than to remain needy of therapeutic succouring' (Albert Ellis, quoted in Dryden 1991: 52). However, as REBT is opposed to dogmatism, therapists may decide to display undue warmth for limited periods if it is deemed to be clinically justified (e.g. with suicidal clients or with those recently bereaved).

To determine the type of bond which is clinically effective at any given time in therapy, Kwee and Lazarus (1986) advocate therapists adopting the stance of an authentic chameleon, that is 'the therapist mak[ing] use of the most helpful facets of his or her personality in order to establish rapport with a particular client' (Kwee and Lazarus 1986: 333). The role of an authentic chameleon should not lead to a lack of genuineness on the therapist's part (trying to be all things to the client but without any apparent sincerity or conviction). Properly applied, the therapist as an authentic chameleon is a flexible device which allows the therapist to adapt themselves to and blend in with the requirements of the bond domain whenever necessary.

Therapists can develop this role by asking clients to specify how therapists should ideally interact with their clients and what personal qualities they should possess. If clients have had previous therapy, they can be asked what they found helpful and unhelpful about it with particular emphasis on the kind of bond that facilitated therapeutic progress, e.g. 'He was firm with me. If he had been soft with me, I would have run rings round him'. In a similar vein, clients can be encouraged to examine those individuals in their lives who have or have had positive or adverse effects on their personal development. Such an examination 'may provide the therapist with important clues concerning which types of therapeutic bonds to promote actively with certain clients and which bonds to avoid developing with others' (Golden and Dryden 1986: 370). All the methods mentioned above can help therapists to forge a productive and enduring bond with clients.

## When Clients' Interpersonal Style Serves as an Obstacle to Client Change

Other difficulties in the bond domain relate to clients' interpersonal styles. Such interaction styles may include passivity, over-excitability, and being overly intellectual or dominant. Therapists who reinforce these interpersonal styles risk failing to construct a working alliance that promotes client learning.

### Clients Who Are Passive

Clients who are passive need to be encouraged to participate so that gradually their 'brains take more of the strain' of therapy (Dryden and Neenan 2021), e.g. 'You might be expecting me to do most of the work in therapy but, in fact, we can't make much progress unless you also lend a helping hand'. REBT therapists may need to 'tone down' their active-directive approach to draw increased activity from passive clients. Therapists who increase their active style to provoke or arouse clients into action may have the opposite effect of encouraging greater passivity on their part.

### Clients Who Are Over-Excitable

Clients who tend to be over-excitable are not usually able to examine productively their problems if the therapeutic relationship or milieu is emotionally charged, e.g. through the use of cathartic or abreactive techniques. With these clients, therapists should employ more cognitive techniques such as looking at the short- and long-term consequences of their rigid and extreme attitudes to encourage a more contemplative approach to life. Therapists can adopt a 'quieter' interpersonal style to reduce the level of emotional arousal in the sessions.

### Clients Who Are Overly Intellectual

Clients who present with an overly intellectual style of interaction may provide seemingly plausible and 'rational' explanations of their problems and thereby avoid or bypass talking about their emotional reactions to these problems, e.g. 'My wife's infidelity was the natural consequence of our deteriorating relationship. Therefore, suggesting I was upset over this when it was bound to occur is absurd'. With such clients, Dryden and Yankura (1993: 239) suggest that 'counsellors should preferably endeavour to inject a productive level of affect into the therapeutic session and employ emotive techniques, self-disclosure and a good deal of humour' for clients to release their feelings.

### Clients Who Are Dominant

Clients who like to dominate or take charge of relationships need to be treated with caution by REBT therapists. Because of the persuasive and active-directive approach of REBT, such clients may believe that their authority and sense of control are being threatened or undermined and, therefore, 'fight back' to re-establish their control. This can lead to a power struggle between the therapist and client resulting in an impasse in therapy. Therapists should be mindful to employ strategies that preserve such clients' sense of control and authority and thereby emphasise that they are in charge of their thoughts and attitudes and whether to change them, e.g. 'If you decide to change your attitude of never showing any weakness, what attitude would you choose to put in its place that you consider would be more helpful?'

The choice of which interpersonal style to employ should be based on clients' accounts of which factors produce the best learning environment for them. Dryden and Yankura (1993: 239) advise that we should 'try to develop a learning profile for each of our clients and use this information to help us plan our therapeutic strategies and choose techniques designed to implement these strategies'.

### Problems in Client–Therapist Matching

Client–therapist matching refers to bringing together a corresponding or suitably associated pair of individuals to create a working bond. Poor matching in REBT (e.g. the client thinks the therapist is too old, the wrong gender or race, or too confrontational) can lead to obstacles to client change as they become more preoccupied with what they dislike about the therapist rather than focusing on their problems. The therapist should ask the client what particular quality or characteristic that they have blocks therapeutic progress. For example, a client might reply: 'You're a man. How can you possibly know what it is to be raped? Therefore, you can't help me'. The therapist can state (if he has worked with survivors of rape):

| | |
|---|---|
| *Therapist:* | It's perfectly true I've never been raped. I've counselled individuals, both male and female, who have been. What I do with these individuals is to help them tackle their attitudes, among others, of worthlessness or self-blame and their feelings such as shame and guilt. Do you want to commit to a few sessions and see if I can help you? |

If the client agrees but the poor matching continues, the therapist should respect her preferences and refer her to a female counsellor. Another tack that the therapist can use is to compensate for their client-perceived 'flaws' and adopt some of the client's recommendations (e.g. 'My therapist should relax more and let things unwind at a gentler pace') to form a good working alliance. Alternatively, the therapist may wish to maintain their hard-working stance (e.g. 'This is the best and quickest way to overcome your problems'). Through such sincerity, the client may naturally overcome their dislike of or aversion to certain of the therapist's qualities.

## When Clients Believe that Therapists Can't Help Them Unless They Know What It's Like to Have Their Problems

Matching problems can occur when clients think that their therapist should have had the same problem and recovered from the problem with which they are struggling. This frequently occurs with clients with substance misuse. An REBT colleague of mine who worked with this client group was frequently asked if they had a drink or drug problem. When they replied that they hadn't, clients usually responded: 'If you haven't been there yourself, then you won't know what it's all about. You haven't got a clue what heroin withdrawals feel like.' The therapist pointed out that medication could be used to moderate the severity of the withdrawals. Still, therapy is not about endlessly discussing the drugs they have used and swapping lurid anecdotes with the former addict-turned-counsellor. Therapy is focused on looking at the emotional and behavioural problems clients are attempting to keep under control through drug use. This rationale persuaded most of my colleague's clients to stay in therapy with a non-addict. For those few who were not convinced, the therapist gave them the contact details of local self-help groups such as Narcotics Anonymous or Alcoholics Anonymous. Therapists who deal with clients who devoutly believe in the 'You need to have been there to be able to help me' stance need to develop convincing arguments to maintain credibility in their clients' eyes, e.g. 'Do you expect your GP to have experienced your problems before they can help you?'

## When the Working Alliance Becomes Too Cosy

Different problems may emerge if the client and therapist have an enjoyable relationship and avoid the hard work and discomfort usually associated with therapeutic change. Suppose the client eventually tackles their problems. In that case, this may lead to a deterioration in the 'feel good' atmosphere of the relationship; therefore, there is a tacit agreement to prevent this from happening. Dryden and Yankura (1993: 238) suggest that this 'problem can be largely overcome if counsellors first help themselves and then their clients to overcome the philosophy of low frustration tolerance implicit in this collusive short-range hedonism'.

## When Clients Have Doubts about the Therapist's Credibility and/or Trustworthiness

Obstacles to client change in REBT can occur if the client doubts the therapist's credibility as a helper or the therapist's trustworthiness.

### Doubts about the Therapist's Credibility

The main goal of REBT therapists is to help clients let go of their rigid/extreme attitudes and develop an alternative set of flexible/non-extreme attitudes. Such an ambitious aim may engender doubts in some clients as to whether the therapist has the clinical competence or expertise to help them achieve such a goal, particularly if the problems are long-standing. For example, a client might say: 'Have you dealt with these types of problems before? Have you helped others to address these problems successfully? I'm not sure anyone can help me'. To convey credibility, therapists can present composite, not actual, examples of past successes, training qualifications, accreditation to a professional body, and articles and/or books written.

Grieger and Boyd (1980: 54) suggest that once therapy gets underway, the therapist's behaviour can quickly confirm or contradict the impression of expertness that they have been trying to create. Confirmation is much more likely when,

> by getting right to work [in the first session], the client is sensitively yet firmly led into a productive diagnostic exploration of the problem(s) ... there is no fumbling around, prolonged and unnecessary chit-chat, or sparring back-and-forth in terms of the relationship.

The therapist's manner and actions imply to the client: 'I know how to help you overcome your problems, so let's get going'. If some clients are still sceptical about the therapist's ability to help them, the therapist can suggest some trial psychotherapy sessions as a means of establishing their credentials.

### Doubts about the Therapist's Trustworthiness

Trust in the therapist enables clients to disclose often intimate problems secure in the knowledge that they will not be humiliated or ridiculed, their problems will not be trivialised and the therapist will not make any personal gains from their disclosures. However, not all clients will automatically trust their therapist, so therapists need to create a milieu in which it can develop. Clients can be congratulated whenever they make a disclosure and assured that it is safe to do so (the information will not leak out of the psychotherapy room). Therapists can use their own clinically relevant self-disclosure as an example of 'how to open up' or offer encouragement to the client to make initial or further disclosures. If the client is slow to respond to these techniques, it is vital that therapists display patience and do not put the client under pressure through their unvarying active-directive style. Walen et al. (1992: 44) point out that it is important to 'take some time to get to know the client and get a feel for their thinking. The patient is more likely to discuss personal problems if he or she believes that the therapist is truly interested in listening'.

REBT therapists also need to be alert to the dysfunctional aspects of some clients' difficulties in developing trust with them, e.g. 'Because I've been hurt badly in the past, I absolutely must be sure that you won't let me down. I couldn't stand it if this happened again'. Therapists need to probe for examples where their clients believe their trust has been betrayed to understand their current wariness, e.g. do they place absolute trust in others and therefore demand unimpeachable behaviour from them? Have they been too quick to trust others and feel easily hurt when things go wrong? Why do they see this as the final straw if they are let down again? As well as tackling some of these ideas, therapists can suggest that they be granted a small measure of provisional trust as a means of testing them out while acknowledging the uncertainty involved.

## Other Forms of Relationship-Focused Client Obstacles to Client Change

### When Shame Prevents Self-Disclosure

Fear of personal disclosure resulting in feelings of shame may lead clients to be reluctant to talk about the full extent of their concerns. Thus, a client who thinks, for example, that he can't admit to the therapist that he has sexual feelings towards his sister as it is disgusting, and therefore he is disgusting, will withhold disclosure for fear of being shamed by the therapist.

By offering clients a general stance of unconditional acceptance as fallible human beings, therapists can encourage them to reveal their 'shameful' thoughts and feelings and engage in the examination of their associated self-defeating ideas and attitudes (e.g. having sexual feelings towards siblings does not mean that you are going to have sex with them or that such feelings mean you are a bad person). Through such methods, clients can learn to be more open in therapy 'and get at the source of some of the things they find most bothersome' (Ellis 1985: 12).

### Dealing with Transference and Non-Transference Issues

A client may find it difficult to create a productive relationship with their therapist due to an issue of transference, i.e. clients displace on to therapists the feelings and attitudes they have towards significant others in their lives. For example, a client who believes they must defer to authority figures in their life tells the therapist: 'I will work hard in therapy because you know what's best for me'. The client will probably make good progress in this case but for non-therapeutic reasons. The therapist can applaud their determination to work hard but question their obeisance, e.g. 'It's more important that you independently decide what's best for you from a position of self-acceptance rather than automatically accepting wisdom from on high'. The client might agree with this viewpoint but again for the wrong reason – because the therapist told them. To overcome this problem, the therapist needs to leave most of the decisions involving therapeutic progress to the client without confirming that they are making the right ones. By developing independent thinking, the client can examine their 'worshipful' attitudes towards others.

Clients may develop non-transference feelings for the therapist whereby, for example, a female client falls in love with her therapist because he embodies certain qualities she finds highly desirable in a man, and not because he represents a father figure to her. Thus, obstacles to client change can develop as the client impedes her progress to stay in therapy as long as possible. The therapist needs to tackle this problem sensitively but firmly: first, by revealing and helping her to examine the rigid/extreme attitudes underlying her strong feelings, e.g. 'As I've fallen in love with my therapist, I must stay in therapy indefinitely. I couldn't bear not to see him again'; second, while pointing out to the client that he is flattered by her feelings for him, therapy aims to work hard to tackle her presenting problems and not to foster a romantic relationship. Such a straightforward approach may dampen her romantic ardour and refocus her attention on why she originally came to therapy. However, if her feelings are unabated, a referral to another counsellor may need to be effected.

### When Clients Fight with the Therapist

Ellis (1985, 2002) described clients who deliberately fight against therapy and frequently attempt to initiate and win power struggles with the therapist as wilfully resistant. While I disagree with the language 'wilfully resistant', I do accept that some clients struggle to be in therapy and may fight with the therapist.

To make the therapeutic relationship more productive and less obstructive, the therapist can point out to such clients how self-defeating their behaviour is:

| | |
|---|---|
| *Therapist:* | It seems that everything I say about your depression and this theme of failure in your life is immediately shot down in flames by you. Wouldn't it be better if you considered some of the points I'm making? Some of them might even help you. |
| *Client:* | Nothing you've said has been remotely helpful. I don't think you're going to be any help at all. You therapists are all the same – bloody useless! |
| *Therapist:* | How many therapists have you seen in the last year? |
| *Client:* | About six. |
| *Therapist:* | You don't stay long in therapy then? |
| *Client:* | What's the point if no one's helping me? |

*Therapist:*   What sort of help are you looking for?

*Client:*   I don't know. You therapists are supposed to be the experts. That's a joke.

*Therapist:*   Well, I don't know what those other therapists did with you, but I will help you locate some attitudes that you have which contribute to your depression, and we'll work together to replace those attitudes with more constructive ones. This therapy will require much work from you, particularly outside of sessions.

*Client:*   I'm supposed to do your work for you then? I thought I was the client. You're supposed to tell me what's wrong and get me better.

*Therapist:*   I don't have a magic wand to make you better. If you don't do any work then therapy will be a waste of time for you, like your previous encounters in therapy.

*Client:*   And for you. If you fail with me you won't be able to tell everyone how great you are.

*Therapist:*   Can I level with you? Or shall I beat around the bush?

*Client:*   Level with me.

*Therapist:*   I have no personal interest in whether your problems are sorted out, but I will do my professional best to help you if you commit yourself to change. The decision is yours.

*Client:*   What are you trying to do – scare me? You're just trying to be tough. If I tell you you're 'crap' and walk out right now; it'll be a different story then. I wonder how you handle failure?

*Therapist:*   I handle failure reasonably well. I don't get depressed over it. I don't put my ego on the line because I have to get you better, not to feel worthless or useless. Whether we make a lot of progress or whether you emerge victorious from therapy having beaten me down is irrelevant to me personally. If you remain miserable and depressed, which is highly likely, it certainly won't stop me from enjoying my life. So, if you want to waste time or leave, please go ahead.

*Client:*   All right. There's no need to be like that. You might be able to help me after all. I just wasn't sure about you, that's all. OK, so how are you going to get me over my depression?

*Therapist:*   As I said earlier, we (emphasises word) are going to do it, not just me. I think one of your major problems is what is called in REBT 'an attitude of unbearability'. This means that you don't do any sustained hard work to overcome your problems because you believe it is too difficult or uncomfortable. Instead, you just waste time in therapy playing games, sabotaging progress, that sort of thing. This time, you could behave differently if you choose to.

> *Client*
>   *(reluctantly):*    All right, I'll give it a go, but I'm not promising anything.
>   *Therapist:*        OK. Let's see how we get on then.

By not engaging in a power struggle with the client or desperately trying to persuade them to stay in therapy, the therapist shows that they have kept their ego out of the psychotherapy room and, therefore, will not be crestfallen if no progress is made or if the client abruptly terminates or continues to act unpleasantly. The therapist's forthright approach starkly illustrates to the client the likely consequences of their behaviour – they will remain emotionally disturbed. The therapist hypothesises that this disturbance is partly maintained by the client's attitude of unbearability, which leads them to waste therapy time rather than confront their problems. By persistently and forcefully maintaining a clinical focus and thereby not getting 'sucked into' the client's attempts to undermine therapy, the therapist eventually secures the client's tentative agreement to participate constructively in it.

### When Clients Are Involuntary

Clients who are involuntary are those who reluctantly come to therapy at the insistence of others (e.g. parents, partners, courts, employers) and claim that they have no emotional or behavioural problems. The following techniques can be employed with such clients. First, agreeing with clients that others are probably wrong about them but examining their claims anyway, e.g. 'I'm sure your wife does exaggerate how much you drink, but as we have this hour together, shall we try and see why she's upset about it?' Second, agreeing with clients that others have probably 'got it in for them' but that still does not solve their problems, e.g. 'It must be very bad living at home with your parents on your case all the time, but your behaviour in response to theirs is making life more difficult for you than it has to be'. Third, agreeing with clients that therapy is probably a waste of time and even though they have to be here, they still retain the upper hand, e.g. 'I know being here is part of the probation order, but you still have the choice whether to cooperate. In that sense, you have more power than the courts or myself. So why not use that power in a way that might help you?'

Such methods may turn clients who are involuntary into being voluntary and thereby entice them into the orbit of therapy. For other approaches with clients who are involuntary see Young (2024).

### When Clients Have Hidden Agendas: The Importance of Accepting Clients

Hidden agendas are the covert but real reasons why some clients enter therapy rather than the apparent ones they disclose to the therapist. For example, a client who is addicted to drugs enters therapy 'to get off drugs for good' but seeks to sabotage it to prove he is a 'hopeless addict' and thereby continue his drug use; a woman attends couple psychotherapy to save her relationship although, in reality, she wants to end it but guilt prevents her from doing so.

By offering all clients an attitude of unconditional acceptance as fallible human beings, Ellis (1985, 2002) suggested that REBT therapists can provide a thera-peutic milieu which encourages the development of an honest and open alliance that makes it more likely that clients will reveal their hidden agendas. After that, helping them to examine their attitudes can be undertaken. In the above examples, the therapist tackles the hopelessness of the client addicted to drugs, 'I'll always be a junkie. I was born one', and the woman's self-devaluation attitude, 'I would make him so miserable if I left him. I would be such a terrible person for doing that to him'. It is vital that therapists remain alert for clues that clients might offer as to their real motives for being in therapy, e.g. the woman's frequently stated worries about her partner's inability to cope on his own if she left him rather than focusing on how she can help to save the relationship.

### When Clients Want to Argue

Some clients may turn the therapy room into a place for an argument. Whatever the therapist says, they will argue with it. They hold that therapy will not be able to help them, that they will never change or that the therapist does not understand 'real life' problems. They argue with every response the therapist makes to them. Here, it is important that therapists do not argue with clients over such issues because it may help to create a power struggle that results in an impasse in therapy. Dryden and Neenan (1995: 7) suggest the following possible resolution to this problem:

> If you win the argument, you also lose it because you will remain emotion-ally disturbed. If I win the argument, you will also win because I can help you to overcome your emotional disturbance. Now, who do you want to win the argument?

Clients usually suggest the therapist and then therapy can constructively pro-ceed. Suppose some clients state that they want to win. In that case, they are likely to find they have secured a Pyrrhic victory, i.e. won at considerable emotional cost to themselves (see the section of this chapter on dealing with clients who fight with the therapist, above).

### When Clients Want Their Therapist as a Friend

Sometimes clients can make the mistake of viewing the therapist as another (or the only) friend in their life and therefore expect the therapist to 'indulge' them, e.g. meet them outside of sessions, allow them to turn up for therapy only when they feel like it, lend them money, be a taxi service for them, allow them to bring alcohol to the session. Clients can become indignant, hurt or rejected when the therapist turns down their requests, e.g. 'I thought you're supposed to be on my side'. As Walen et al. (1992: 44) point out: 'the basis for the therapeutic relationship is not friendship but professional competence, credibility, respect, and commitment to help the client change'. Therefore, the therapist in their role as a concerned professional can respond:

| | |
|---|---|
| *Therapist:* | If I behave like your friend, how much real progress do you think you are going to make? The business of therapy is lots of hard work to overcome your problems. So, let's sort out what our respective roles are. |

The earlier this is done in therapy, the less misunderstanding will occur.

The preceding account of clients' difficulties in forming a productive relationship with the therapist is not meant to be exhaustive; these and other problems can occur at any time during therapy rather than all appearing in its early stages. Therefore, the therapist should be prepared to monitor continually the bond domain of the working alliance. The strength of the bond will be tested, often severely so, as the therapist introduces the client to the *ABC* framework of self-created disturbance, which is discussed in Chapter 3.

# Dealing with Client Obstacles to Client Change in the Views Domain of the Working Alliance

In my opinion, effective REBT is based on a number of agreed understandings between therapist and client. If both disagree on any aspect of the process, a potential obstacle to the client's progress exists and needs to be identified, explored and resolved. Such disagreements that therapists and clients may have about therapy are often based on different views that they respectively hold about this activity.

As this is a book on working with obstacles to client change in REBT, I will concentrate on client obstacles to client change in the views domain of the alliance with particular reference to how REBT conceptualises client problems and their amelioration. It is to be noted that client obstacles to client change in the views domain may occur in more generic areas. Thus, clients and therapists may disagree on the practicalities of therapy (i.e. fees, how long therapy should last, how long sessions should last and how often they should meet) and on the issue of confidentiality and its limits (for a discussion on these more general points, see Dryden 2011).

Whatever the issue is concerning possible discrepant views on therapy held by therapist and client, therapists need to be explicit with clients about the views they hold about different aspects of therapy and encourage their clients to be explicit about their views as well. Therapists are advised to engage their clients in an honest and open discussion of their respective views when these are at variance with one another. If these differing views cannot be reconciled and this fact makes therapy non-viable, at least this decision has been made on the explicit exchange of information, and the therapist may effect a suitable referral.

## When Clients Hold Views about Therapy that Are Very Different from Those Inherent in REBT

Clients may come to psychotherapy expecting to be the passive recipients of the therapist's insights into their problems and, through this osmotic process (absorption of the therapist's wisdom), leave therapy 'cured'. As REBT is a collaborative endeavour in emotional problem-solving, clients are quickly disabused of their ideas of inaction or minimal effort by frequent use of the words 'us' and 'we', e.g. 'Let us put our heads together and see what we can do to overcome your problems'.

DOI: 10.4324/9781003423379-4

This theme of a hard-working, collaborative partnership often needs to be repeated throughout therapy.

Some clients may protest that this places too much responsibility on them, e.g. 'You're supposed to be helping me, not the other way round!' To make some headway with their problems, clients need to develop a philosophy of effort ('There's no gain without pain'). The client's expected role in therapy can be outlined, e.g. an early problem-solving focus, learning a particular framework of largely self-induced emotional disturbance, and carrying out homework tasks to emphasise the work the client will have to do (see also Chapter 1). If the client still insists on the gain without the pain, the likely results of this attitude can be spelt out: 'If you put nothing into therapy, it's hardly surprising if you get nothing out of it. Therefore, you're going to remain emotionally disturbed'. This message is best conveyed Socratically rather than didactically and baldly stated. Frequent encouragement from the therapist that hard work pays off, supported by composite case examples of clients who had similar problems and eventually overcame them, can motivate such clients to adopt a problem-solving role.

## When Clients Think that Therapy Is about Venting Feelings or Open-Ended Exploration of Problems

Some clients think that in therapy, all they need to do is express their feelings and talk about their problems. Such clients believe therapy is where they can 'get it all out'. Any infringement on their right to do this might impair the development of a productive alliance. However, as REBT advocates an early problem-solving focus, client (or therapist) long-windedness usually interferes with therapeutic efficiency.

Many REBT therapists argue that it is important to socialise clients into REBT at the outset. Here is how I approach this task (see Dryden 2011).

> *Windy*: Well, now, there are many approaches to therapy, and it is important that you understand something of the one that I practise, which is known as Rational Emotive Behaviour Therapy. REBT is based on an old idea attributed to Epictetus, a Roman philosopher who said, 'Men are disturbed not by things, but by their views of things.' In REBT, we have modified this and say that 'People are disturbed not by life's adversities, but rather they disturb themselves by their rigid and extreme attitudes that they hold towards these adversities.' Once they have disturbed themselves, they try to get rid of their disturbed feelings in ways that ultimately maintain their problems.
>
> As an REBT therapist, I will help you to identify, examine and change the rigid and extreme attitudes that we argue underpin your emotional problems and to develop alternative flexible and non-extreme attitudes. I will also help you to examine how you have tried to help yourself that hasn't worked and encourage you

to develop and practise more effective, longer-lasting strategies. At the beginning of therapy, we will consider your problems one at a time, and I will teach you a framework that will help you break them down into their constituent parts. I will also teach you various methods for examining and changing your rigid and extreme attitudes and a variety of methods to help you consolidate and strengthen your alternative flexible and non-extreme attitudes. As therapy proceeds, I will help you to take increasing responsibility for using these methods, and my ultimate aim is to help you to become your own therapist. As this happens, we will meet less frequently until you feel you can cope independently.

As will be reiterated in Chapter 8, a socialising statement such as the one in the box is presented and discussed piece by piece. Presenting a block of material without giving your clients an opportunity to share their understanding of it and discuss it is likely to engender client obstacles to client change rather than dilute it.

The above statement can also be sent in writing by email attachment to potential clients who want to consider whether or not to become a client of REBT before giving their informed consent to proceed. This information can be considered the 'informed' part of informed consent.

It may also be necessary to make a compromise between the client's view concerning venting feelings and the therapist's view on the importance of being explicit about the nature of REBT. Wessler and Wessler (1980) suggest that before introducing such clients to the *ABC* framework of emotional disturbance, where clients' problems are conceptualised in REBT terms (see below), let them 'complain, whine,[1] emote, and generally say what concerns them ... [but] we would not ordinarily devote more than a half session to such expression of feelings' (Wessler and Wessler 1980: 69). As the socialising statement makes clear, REBT therapists are not interested in feelings per se but in the rigid and extreme attitudes underpinning them and this should be made clear to clients at the outset. By quickly identifying, examining and helping clients change these attitudes in favour of those that are flexible and non-extreme, clients' emotional problems can be ameliorated as rapidly as possible.

Another way to staunch clients' tendencies to discuss their feelings at length without necessarily upsetting the developing working alliance is to ask for permission to interrupt them, e.g. 'If you are giving me more information than is necessary to gain an understanding of your problems, can I have your permission to step in and stop you?' If this is given – which it invariably is – the therapist can then ask the client how they can best do this. In this manner, therapists can communicate to clients that action is required from them rather than more talk. Interrupting without permission can create the impression of the therapist's rudeness or insensitivity.

Some clients may want immediate help with practical problems rather than following the REBT approach of tackling emotional problems first and then their practical aspects next. For example, a client wants to discuss a career move because they have to give an answer to their boss within 24 hours of the first therapy session. The client may not realise or admit how anxious they are about making a decision. The therapist can discuss the pros and cons of such a move, the client's vocational expectations, etc., to help them decide. In this way, the therapist addresses both the client's immediate needs as well as developing hypotheses about their anxiety, which the therapist can present in subsequent sessions. Some REBT therapists might declare, 'We don't do it that way!' with respect to addressing a practical problem before an emotional problem. These therapists should address their intransigence so they realise that clients' requirements take precedence in therapy over their rigid adherence to REBT protocol.

## When Clients Have Difficulties Accepting the *ABC* Framework

The *ABC* framework of emotional disturbance is the cornerstone of REBT theory and practice (Dryden 2024). It is also known as the *ABCs* of REBT (see Chapter 1). This framework sets out a primarily attitudinal-orientated theory of emotions. *A* stands for adversities, which are aspects of situations about which clients are most disturbed and are often inferential in nature. They are mediated by basic attitudes (at *B*), which, in turn, largely determine the emotional, behavioural and cognitive consequences clients will experience at *C*. Clients are taught that *B*, not *A*, lies at the foundation of their emotional reactions to events, e.g., 'It's not being rejected that accounts for your depression but rather the attitudes that you hold towards being rejected that are mainly responsible for your current state'. For many clients, the disturbance-creating *B-C* connection represents a paradigmatic or radical shift in their understanding of emotional causation, e.g. 'You mean to tell me that I upset myself over my neighbour's obnoxious behaviour and he doesn't have much to do with it?' Hence, the many difficulties clients experience in accepting the *ABC* framework, which I will now examine.

## When Clients Think that *A* Causes *C*

*A-C* thinking refers to clients' statements which place primary responsibility for their emotional problems (at *C*) on others, external events, or the world (*A*), e.g., 'My boss makes me angry'; 'The weather makes me depressed'; 'Life makes me feel ashamed of myself'. There is no clue in these statements of any sense of personal involvement in helping to create these emotional reactions. Probably the majority of clients who enter therapy will subscribe to this type of *A-C* thinking, which will have been reinforced by family, peer and cultural teaching, e.g. 'My parents always told me that without a good job, you're nothing in life'; advertising which equates a 'beautiful body' with being happy and worthwhile. Because the *A* and *C* components are usually so inextricably linked in the client's mind, the therapist has to prise them apart for clients to see the presence and importance of their basic attitudes (at *B*). This is necessary to teach clients the general and specific principles of emotional responsibility (Dryden, 2024). This usually involves a two-stage process whereby clients are taught how their thoughts influence their feelings before focusing on the disturbance-producing properties of rigid and extreme attitudes. Understanding the thought–feeling link is a vital part of clients' induction into REBT, and often more time is spent on establishing this general connection, thereby 'opening the way' for them to grasp the specific role of rigid and extreme attitudes in their emotional disturbance.

Some REBT therapists, including myself, argue that by teaching clients the specific principle of emotional responsibility (i.e., that rigid and extreme attitudes underpin emotional problems), they are also being taught the general principle of emotional responsibility (i.e., that thinking determines feeling). Hence, it is more efficient to teach the specific concept at the outset than to teach the general concept before teaching the specific concept. However, since many REBT therapists first begin by teaching the general principle of emotional responsibility, I will now discuss how to respond when clients have difficulties with this general principle.

## When Clients Have Difficulties with the General Principle of Emotional Responsibility

The general principle of emotional responsibility states that you feel as you think. Therefore, clients' thought patterns are elicited to show how they largely disturb themselves over adverse or unpleasant life events. As some clients might be keen to tell their 'He/she/it makes me miserable' stories, therapists can, if it seems clinically relevant, get their point of view across first as in the following:

| | |
|---|---|
| *Therapist:* | Just before we come to your problems, you seem very anxious. Is that because you got here ten minutes late? |
| *Client:* | Yes, that's right. I rushed all the way here. I was desperate not to be late. |
| *Therapist:* | What were you anxious about in getting here late? |
| *Client:* | That you would think very poorly of me. I want your help, but I can't get here on time. That would make me more inadequate than I already am. |
| *Therapist:* | Let me ask you this: is it simply getting here late that makes you anxious or your thinking that it would reveal more of your inadequacy? |
| *Client:* | Both? |
| *Therapist:* | Well, if you got here late and you didn't care at all, would you be anxious? |
| *Client:* | I suppose I wouldn't have been. I didn't want to appear more screwed up than I already am. |
| *Therapist:* | Can you see what point I'm trying to make? |
| *Client:* | Well, I suppose I wouldn't have been anxious if I didn't have that idea. |
| *Therapist:* | Good. That our ideas and thoughts primarily create our emotional problems is a point I will keep returning to. OK, what problem would you like to talk about? |

In this example, the therapist immediately orientates the client towards *B-C* thinking, thereby establishing a reference point they can repeatedly bring the client back to, to help attenuate the latter's *A-C* thinking. Throughout therapy, therapists need to be mindful of employing only *B-C* language to reinforce the *ABC* framework they are teaching and 'wean' their clients away from *A-C* language.

Some clients might agree that lateness per se is not the cause of their anxiety, but the meaning they attach to their lateness is the real culprit. However, even though they acknowledge the instrumental role of their thinking in this example, they are not persuaded it has any relevance to the real problems they want to discuss in therapy – problems where, in their view, *A* really does cause *C*. For example, clients may state that losing their job made them very depressed. Here, therapists can use a technique known as contrasts (Wessler and Wessler 1980) to demonstrate that clients' thinking still plays a primary role in their emotional problems:

| | |
|---|---|
| *Therapist:* | Would fifty people, all in the same position and salary as you, all be depressed about losing their jobs? |
| *Client:* | Well, they wouldn't be happy about it. |
| *Therapist:* | Probably not, but would they all be depressed? |
| *Client:* | I expect a few of them wouldn't be too upset. Their job might not mean everything to them like it does to me. |
| *Therapist:* | And that's the point – different ideas about the same situation lead to different emotional reactions to it. Was there a time in your life when you lost a job but didn't become depressed about it? |
| *Client:* | Yeah, when I was a lot younger. But it wasn't important to me unlike this job. |
| *Therapist:* | Then it didn't matter so much; now it's everything to you. |
| *Client:* | That's true. I wasn't so wound up about it then. |
| *Therapist:* | With this present job, have you always believed that it means everything to you? |
| *Client:* | I've always considered it to be very important to me, but I suppose I became wrapped up in it after the divorce and my social life began to disappear. |
| *Therapist:* | If you had lost your job before the divorce, would you have been so depressed? |
| *Client:* | I would have been irritable and miserable for a while, but nothing like I am now. |

In this illustration, the therapist employs three different ways to demonstrate to the client that *B* (thinking), not *A* (losing their job), is mainly responsible for their *C* reactions to losing the job:

1. By asking the client if a large number of people (fifty in this example) would all react in the same way to the same event. The client grudgingly concedes that a few might not. It is advisable at this stage of therapy not to push for a higher number who would have reacted differently; it is enough that they make the concession. The client then unwittingly answers why these few would not become depressed – 'their job might not mean everything to them as it does to me'; in other words, it is the reason for their existence.
2. By seeking evidence from earlier in the client's life when they did not become depressed about losing their job. This evidence contradicts their *A-C* statements because their thinking then towards their job was more relaxed than their current all-or-nothing thinking.
3. By showing the client that, even in their present job, their thinking about it has not remained constant, producing different emotional reactions pre- and post-divorce.

It is important when teaching the general *B-C* connection not to create the impression or state as a fact that thinking totally produces feeling and that unpleasant life events are of no significance in the development of emotional disturbance. As well as being contrary to REBT theory and practice, the potentially destructive effects upon the working alliance hardly need spelling out. Therefore, therapists are strongly reminded not to minimise the impact of clients' adversities on their feelings. For example, 'Your girlfriend running off with your best friend must seem like the ultimate betrayal, but isn't your view of yourself as now completely worthless because of this betrayal the most devastating act of all?' Here, the therapist is trying to be strongly empathic yet challenging at the same time. Some clients will insist that *A* does cause *C* and rest their case with the horror of the Nazi concentration camps, an example that clients frequently use to demolish the therapist's arguments. This issue will be considered later in the chapter.

Another means of conveying *B-C* thinking to sceptical clients is to teach them that they feel as they think (Burns 1980):

| | |
|---|---|
| *Therapist:* | How would you feel if you believed your life was empty, boring and friendless? |
| *Client:* | I expect I'd feel pretty bad. |
| *Therapist:* | If you were to be more precise, which emotion in particular would 'pretty bad' refer to? |
| *Client:* | I'm not sure what you mean. |
| *Therapist:* | Well, would you feel depressed, angry, hurt, for example? |
| *Client:* | Oh, I see what you mean. Er, depressed. Yeah, that's it, depressed. |

| | |
|---|---|
| *Therapist:* | OK. How would you feel if you were going to a job interview, believed all the other applicants would perform better than you and that this proved you were inferior? |
| *Client:* | I'd feel bloody anxious. Who wants to be judged as inferior? |
| *Therapist:* | You've just reinforced my point. One last example. How would you feel if you believed that you had acted like a drunken fool at a party and made an unwanted pass at a friend's wife? |
| *Client:* | If I did behave like that, I would feel very ashamed and avoid both of them for a while. But surely not everyone would feel like that? I know someone who definitely would not have felt like that. |
| *Therapist:* | Because he would have told himself …? |
| *Client:* | Probably because he couldn't care less and that parties are for enjoying yourself. |
| *Therapist:* | And that's why he would have felt very differently about it. |

In this therapy excerpt, the therapist is teaching the client to note how his thoughts precede and influence his feelings. Important points to consider are the following:

1.  In response to the therapist's first question, the client says he would feel 'pretty bad'. REBT practice requires that the client specify an unhealthy negative emotion (e.g. anxiety, guilt, depression) to make explicit the cognitive content of that particular emotion. By accepting 'pretty bad' as an emotion, both therapist and client would remain stranded at a level of vagueness and uncertainty – which emotion(s) is the client referring to? – which would diminish both the educational and therapeutic aspects of REBT.
2.  The client has provided more grist for the cognitive mill by emphasising the anxiety-provoking nature of being seen as inferior in others' eyes.
3.  While the client says he would feel ashamed of his drunken behaviour, it occurs to him that not everyone would feel the same way, thereby implying a challenge to the therapist's thesis. However, he strengthens the therapist's arguments because his friend would think very differently about the same situation and, therefore, not become emotionally disturbed about it.

Therapy provides many examples where clients can be repeatedly shown that they feel as they think (e.g. strong emotion or signs of physical tension in the session) in order for them to identify and examine their disturbance-producing ideas.

## When Clients Believe that Others Make Them Upset

In the minds of many clients, other people are undoubtedly the source of their emotional problems, which is reflected in their use of language, e.g. 'You make me angry by asking all these questions'; 'My wife makes me feel guilty because I forgot her birthday'. Such statements imply that clients have no control over their feelings and, therefore, cannot be held responsible for them. Other people not only cause these problems but also usually have the solution to them, e.g. 'If my wife would stop going on about how much her birthday means to her, then I wouldn't feel so guilty'. The therapist's task is to teach clients that they largely disturb themselves over others' behaviour. This will be revealed by examining their internal statements or self-talk; so, concerning the first example, the therapist might say to the client, 'Let's see what you're saying to yourself that gets you angry about these questions I'm asking you'. The idea that clients disturb themselves and thereby need to restructure their statements accordingly is often met with disbelief and sometimes downright hostility.

---

*Client:*      What do you mean that I upset myself? You're making me angry by saying that.

*Therapist:*   I am not expecting you to agree with me, but why do you get angry about me expressing a point of view?

*Client:*      Because you shouldn't talk such crap. No one goes around saying 'I upset myself'.

*Therapist:*   Let me ask you this: if you were sitting there thinking, 'My therapist is talking rubbish, but I couldn't care less what he says', would you get so steamed up about it?

*Client:*      If I didn't care what you say, I'd probably laugh at you.

*Therapist:*   And am I responsible for making you laugh as well?

*Client:*      Yes, because you're still talking rubbish.

*Therapist:*   OK. So, I have this tremendous power over you to make you angry or make you laugh. So, are you just a puppet manipulated by others?

*Client:*      No one controls me.

*Therapist:*   I apparently do.

*Client:*      No, you certainly don't!

*Therapist:*   Well, you can't have it both ways. So, who controls your thinking and decides how to respond to things?

*Client:*      I do.

*Therapist:*   Therefore, who makes you angry?

*Client:*      I suppose the answer is me, but I'm still unconvinced.

---

In this excerpt, the client is still very doubtful about the therapist's arguments, but at least the therapist has made small inroads into the client's thinking, which the therapist can now seek to widen and deepen. Other clients may see lack of emotional control as a way of life because they believe others have deprived them of it.

| | |
|---|---|
| *Client:* | I've felt depressed on and off for about fifteen years. My husband has made me like this. |
| *Therapist:* | How has he been able to do that? |
| *Client:* | Getting at me all the time. Putting me down, telling me I'm useless at everything. That sort of thing. |
| *Therapist:* | Do you agree with him? |
| *Client:* | It's not that I agree with him. He makes me feel like that. It's been going on for so long. |
| *Therapist:* | How did you see yourself before you met him? |
| *Client:* | I didn't have much confidence in myself, low self-esteem, that sort of thing. I was grateful that he married me and took me off the shelf. |
| *Therapist:* | I understand how difficult it must be living with all that verbal abuse, but don't you agree with his put-downs because these ideas are already in your head? Do you know who put them there? |
| *Client:* | He did. |
| *Therapist:* | No, you did. You've already told me how you saw yourself before you met him. Because you have a self-devaluing philosophy, you easily agree with and apply what your husband says about you to yourself. |
| *Client:* | It's hard to believe what you say. I've thought it's him all these years, and you say it's mostly my fault. If it's true what you say, I must be pathetic for making myself so unhappy for all these years and not seeing it. |
| *Therapist:* | I certainly would disagree that you are pathetic, and we'll come to that in a moment, but if we don't agree with or believe what others say about us, then they can't make us depressed. What he is doing is unpleasant, but if you tell yourself that he is wrong and that you are an ordinary human being with good and bad points and nothing he could say to you could change that, would you feel depressed? |
| *Client:* | I guess not. |
| *Therapist:* | So, in therapy, do we need to focus on his attitude towards you or your attitude towards you? |
| *Client:* | My attitude towards me. |

Clients are ultimately responsible for their ideas and attitudes; others cannot put ideas into their heads unless they are allowed to in some way, e.g. a man who complains that his girlfriend's unkind comments make him feel worthless as a lover is shown that her comments are only adding to his considerable self-doubt about his sexual prowess. Other clients may say they are not responsible for the way they think as they have been 'brainwashed' by others or society, e.g. 'The reason I'm always on a diet is that everywhere you look, you see pictures of thin women. You can't feel good about yourself if you're not thin'. Rather than being brainwashed, clients are shown that they are insufficiently critical of the messages delivered by others, media, advertising, society, etc. Therapy can become the forum where clients restore their critical faculties by subjecting their 'brainwashed attitudes' to scrutiny.

Another problem that clients have with accepting emotional responsibility is that they confuse responsibility with blame and proceed to condemn themselves, as in the following therapy excerpt.

| | |
|---|---|
| *Client:* | I've been thinking it's him all these years, and you say it's mostly my fault.<br>*[The therapist never used the word 'fault'.]*<br>If it's true what you say, then I must be pathetic for making myself so unhappy for all these years and not seeing it. |

So, it is easy to understand clients' reluctance or refusal to acknowledge their self-induced emotional disturbance. The therapist's skill is to encourage clients to accept responsibility without blaming themselves for this disturbance.

| | |
|---|---|
| *Therapist:* | Let's be clear on the critical differences between responsibility and blame. Because you feel as you think, you are mainly responsible for the negative ideas that keep your depression going. Of course, your husband has significantly reinforced what you already think. If you accept responsibility for your emotional states, you can also decide not to condemn yourself for creating them. |
| *Client:* | What do I do if I don't put myself down? |
| *Therapist:* | You can learn to accept yourself with these problems, and I'll teach you ways of fighting back so you can gain greater control of your emotions. Can you put all that back to me in your own words? |
| *Client:* | Let me see if I've got this straight. I've mainly been messing myself up all these years. I don't have to put the boot in anymore – I'll leave that to my husband. I can be responsible for my feelings and remain nice to myself. And you will teach me how to deal with these bad feelings. |
| *Therapist:* | Very well summarised. Now, let's get to grips with your problems. |

## When Clients Believe that They Can't Escape Their Past

Many clients often state that past events dictate or shape their present feelings and behaviour and, therefore, they are prisoners of the past, e.g. 'He took all the money from our joint account and ran off with someone else. I was devastated. It still makes me very bitter after all these years and I'll never be free of it'. The client assumes that past, albeit grim, events have an iron grip on their present and future life. REBT therapists seek to show clients that it is not past events that determine present problems, but rather the attitudes they have constructed from these events and continue to repeat to themselves in the present. However, many clients want to explore their past, often at great length, to get at the roots of the problem. While acknowledging that a client's rigid/extreme attitudes have a developmental history, 'the crucial thing is for him or her to give up these currently held ideas so that tomorrow's existence can be better than yesterday's' (Grieger and Boyd 1980: 76–7). The following excerpt will clarify some of these points.

| | |
|---|---|
| *Client:* | My parents dumped me in a children's home when I was ten years old. Unwanted, unloved, abandoned. |
| *Therapist:* | And how do you feel today about being dumped in a children's home twenty years ago? |
| *Client:* | How do you expect me to feel – happy? I'm still angry and depressed, of course. My parents made me feel worthless by what they did to me. |
| *Therapist:* | Even if that was their intention, then why do you still believe you are worthless today? |
| *Client:* | Because of what happened when I was ten. What do you expect me to say to them as they hand me over to a children's home: 'It's OK, I forgive you?' If I could understand why they did it to me, I might feel a bit better about myself. |
| *Therapist:* | Let's say they did it because they couldn't cope financially with your upbringing. Would you feel happier? |
| *Client:* | No. Other parents managed it. |
| *Therapist:* | I understand how tough it must have been to see it any other way when you're 10, but when did you start to think for yourself – 16, 18, 21? |
| *Client:* | 18, I suppose. |
| *Therapist:* | OK. You've had twelve years to examine this attitude that you're worthless. Have you made any progress? |
| *Client:* | How can I make progress? It's their attitude, not mine. |

| | |
|---|---|
| *Therapist:* | Well, let's say you got the attitude from your parents, but you have been carrying it in your head ever since. You still choose to believe it. That's the point. |
| *Client:* | I never thought of it like that. Is it possible to see it any differently after all these years? |
| *Therapist:* | Yes, it is, and it certainly won't take twenty years to change and they will probably be much happier than the last twenty. |
| *Client:* | I'd like to try it then. |

The concept of free will can also be used to encourage clients to accept emotional responsibility. If they believe they have some freedom of choice in how they respond to past and present events in their lives, this can be contrasted with their 'chained to the past' arguments, e.g. 'We've already discussed how you chose not to be ground down by certain unpleasant past events, so why with this particular event, losing your job two years ago, do you believe you can't recover from it?' In this case, the client is not exercising their free will for whatever reason, and the therapist needs to discover why.

### Responding to the 'Concentration Camp Exception' Argument

Many clients may grudgingly accept that their thinking, rather than events, does play a significant part in creating their emotional problems but then counter with an argument that they believe will knock the wind out of the therapist's sails: 'It might be true in my case, but there's absolutely no way that argument can be used with those who suffered in the Nazi concentration camps. Their suffering was caused by others'. While agreeing with the client's last point, the therapist can point out that those not selected for immediate extermination were put to work in the camps under the most appalling conditions and that their attitude towards survival was crucial in determining how they coped with this inhuman treatment. Thus, some individuals were sustained by their religious faith, which meant that God was with them even (or particularly) in the camps; some Jews willed themselves to survive to bear witness to Nazi atrocities in the post-war reckoning. Others, like Viktor Frankl (the founder of logotherapy and a survivor of Auschwitz), showed themselves that only they, not the Nazis, could deprive themselves of their humanity. Whatever the foundation of their belief, it gave individuals the determination to stay alive and fight back in their way. Similar stories of incredible fortitude are described in Alexander Solzhenitsyn's *The Gulag Archipelago*, an account of the hardships and brutality of the Soviet prison camp system.

## When Clients Say: 'I Don't Think Anything'

Some clients protest that nothing passes through their mind when they experience, for example, anxiety or anger, e.g. 'One minute I'm fine, the next minute I'm a quivering jelly. It just came out of the blue'. Therefore, they claim the *ABC* framework does not apply to them. Beck (1976) points out that many of our thoughts and ideas are automatic; therefore, what we are thinking is not always immediately apparent to us. However, it is relatively easy to access our automatic thoughts and ideas as they usually lie outside of our awareness.

---

*Therapist:*   Just before you turned to jelly, did anything happen that you can remember?

*Client:*   Only that the phone rang. My sister answered it. It was only my girlfriend saying she'd be round later. So, it was good news.

*Therapist:*   Were you expecting bad news?

*Client:*   Well, I was a bit worried.

*Therapist:*   What about?

*Client:*   Honestly, we've been having trouble, rowing and stuff. I know this other guy has been sniffing around. I think she likes him. She was seen talking to him the other day.

*Therapist:*   How much do you care about her?

*Client:*   I'm very keen on her. I'd be devastated if she dumped me.

*Therapist:*   So, you were looking forward to her phone call, but at the same time, you were thinking …?

*Client:*   She'd ended our relationship and run off with him. I'm feeling a bit jelly-like again. Oh God!

*Therapist:*   Do you still believe that your anxiety came out of the blue?

*Client:*   No, but that doesn't make it any easier to deal with.

*Therapist:*   We'll come to that.

---

In this illustration, the 'way in' that the therapist was looking for to tease out the client's thinking was his remark that the telephone call 'was good news'. This enabled the therapist to test the hypothesis that the client was expecting the opposite. This revealed a string of anxious thoughts culminating in feelings of devastation at the prospect of being rejected. The client gave corroboration that the therapist was on the right track by the return of his 'jelly-like' symptoms while he was discussing the situation with his girlfriend.

Some clients can be insistent that there is no *B* between the *A* and *C*; therapists should not be discouraged by this and persevere (but not dogmatically) to reveal it to them. As Hauck (1980: 237) says: 'Don't lose faith in your theory'.

## When Clients Want to Explore Their Feelings, Not Their Thinking

Many clients assume that lengthy explorations of their disturbed feelings will somehow help to remove them. Their previous experiences with psychodynamic therapy, for example, may have strengthened such an approach to therapy. Therefore, they want to focus only on feelings and not get sidetracked into discussing the thinking that might be linked to their problems, e.g. 'I'm not interested in my thoughts. Feelings are what it's all about. What's down here, not up there' (the client pats their stomach, then taps their head). What is often implied in such statements is that thinking and feeling are separate processes. Ellis (1994) has consistently argued since he founded REBT in the mid-1950s that sustained feeling is usually accompanied by or the direct result of sustained thinking; in many respects, thinking and feeling are the same. REBT therapists, therefore, seek emotional change by scrutinising clients' disturbance-producing ideas:

| | |
|---|---|
| *Therapist:* | If you change your thinking, you can change your feelings. They are so closely tied together. |
| *Client:* | I thought they were miles apart. |
| *Therapist:* | Well, let's try an experiment. You talk about a feeling, and I'll stop you as soon as an idea emerges. Is that OK? |
| *Client:* | Yes, I'm willing to try that. Well, I get angry a lot in my life. I explode more than I care to admit. People seem to get in my way all the time, and … |
| *Therapist:* | Please stop. An angry idea seems to be that people are blocking and frustrating you somehow. I'm not saying it's the main one, but an idea did come up very quickly. |
| *Client:* | I thought I was still talking about my feelings. |
| *Therapist:* | Well, you are – through your ideas. Can we try another experiment? |
| *Client:* | OK. |
| *Therapist:* | Describe a recent event where you felt upset but don't identify the emotion. Leave that to me. |
| *Client:* | Well, my husband keeps promising to take me away for the weekend, and a few weeks ago, we were ready to go, but he cancelled it at the last minute due to business problems. I felt so let down, even betrayed by his behaviour. I was so looking forward to going. |
| *Therapist:* | OK. Was the feeling hurt? |
| *Client:* | Yes, it was. How did you know that? |
| *Therapist:* | By listening for the ideas underlying the feeling. Did you sulk? |
| *Client:* | For the whole weekend. How did you know I sulked? |

| *Therapist:* | Because particular behaviours are associated with specific emotions and I'm able to work out both by … |
|---|---|
| *Client:* | Would it be my ideas? |
| *Therapist:* | Exactly. Do you want to try this therapy as a way of changing some of the unpleasant feelings you've described? |
| *Client:* | OK. I'll give it a try. |

Clients need to be reminded frequently of the distinction between thinking and feeling and how the former significantly influences the latter so that they can understand within the *ABC* framework the origins and maintenance of their emotional problems. As we have pointed out, because this is a crucial task for the therapist to perform, establishing the general principle of emotional responsibility in the early stages of therapy is usually considered to be more important than focusing on the particularities of its specific REBT form (though not all REBT therapists would agree with this double-barrelled approach to self-created disturbance and therefore some teach only its specific form such as myself).

## When Clients Have Difficulties with the Specific Principle of Emotional Responsibility

REBT's conception of emotional disturbance is that it stems mainly from individuals' rigid attitudes in the form of musts, absolute shoulds, have tos, got tos and oughts, and the extreme attitudes that are derived from these rigid attitudes, e.g., 'I must have your love, and I am worthless without it'; 'You have to make things easy for me, and if you don't, I can't stand it'. Emotional health in REBT is seen as primarily underpinned by flexible attitudes and the non-extreme attitudes derived from them, e.g., 'I would greatly prefer your love, but I don't need it. It would be hard to accept if I don't receive it, but I can still accept myself.'; 'I hope you make things easier for me, but you don't have to do so. If you don't, it would be hard, but I can stand the struggle involved'. Clients are taught to detect and discriminate between their rigid/extreme attitudes and their flexible/non-extreme attitudes.

## Dealing with Clients' Use of the Word 'Should'

At first glance, the word 'should' may seem innocuous. Yet, its potentially pathological character can appear when clients transmute preferential shoulds into absolute ones, e.g. the healthy anger-inducing 'You (preferably) shouldn't talk to me like that' versus the unhealthy anger-producing 'You (absolutely) shouldn't talk to me like that!' In the following extract, the therapist shows the client how his self-created disturbance primarily arises from his emphasis on the rigid use of 'should' rather than directly caused by his girlfriend's non-compliance.

| | |
|---|---|
| *Client:* | My girlfriend makes me angry. She never listens to my point of view. |
| *Therapist:* | How does she make you angry? |
| *Client:* | I've just told you – she should listen to what I'm saying! |
| *Therapist:* | I want to put it the other way around: you make yourself angry by continually demanding how she should be behaving. |
| *Client:* | Well, she should listen. I listen to her. |
| *Therapist:* | You listen to her, so she should (stresses word) listen to you. |
| *Client:* | Exactly. Wouldn't you get angry if I didn't listen to you? |
| *Therapist:* | No, because there's no reason why you absolutely should (stresses word again) listen to me, but it would be desirable if you did because I'm here to help you. Look, every time you use the word 'should' in an absolute sense, you're setting yourself up as a dictator and demanding how your girlfriend should behave. You're also firing up your own boiler and ready to explode when she doesn't do what you demand. So you make yourself unhealthily angry, not your girlfriend. |
| *Client:* | OK. You might have a point there, but it would be nice if she did listen to me. You're not going to disagree with that, are you? |
| *Therapist:* | No, that's fine if you keep to that desire. Now, how would you feel if you believed that 'it would be very nice if she listened to me, but there is no reason why she absolutely should listen to me'? |
| *Client:* | I'd be pissed off but not unhealthily angry. My boiler wouldn't be at danger level. |
| *Therapist:* | Do you enjoy exploding in front of her? |
| *Client:* | No, I don't! I feel like a right idiot. |
| *Therapist:* | So, how can you stop behaving like a 'right idiot' as you call yourself? |
| *Client:* | Stop making myself unhealthily angry. |
| *Therapist:* | And how can you accomplish that? |
| *Client:* | Not using the word 'should'. |
| *Therapist:* | Only in its absolute form. There's nothing wrong with using it as a preference, but when you cross that dividing line … |
| *Client:* | I'll start exploding again. |
| *Therapist:* | Right. I'll show you how to keep on the non-exploding side of that 'should' divide. |

Points to note in this exchange from therapy are the following:

1. The therapist ties the client's absolute 'should' to his unhealthy anger and contrasts it with the preferential statement 'it would be nice if …' in order to produce a different emotional outcome (healthy anger or annoyance).
2. The therapist is modelling the specific principle of emotional responsibility by saying they would not disturb themself because they would not be insisting that the client listens to them; they do point out that they would adhere to their non-disturbed flexible attitude towards the client's attention.
3. By focusing on what the client does not like about his angry behaviour, the therapist hastens his acceptance of the specific principle of emotional responsibility but makes sure he puts it in his own words so that they both agree on the cognitive roots of his unhealthy anger.
4. The therapist emphasises that it is only absolute shoulds the client should steer clear of and not preferable shoulds.

## Responding to the 'It's Only a Word' Criticism

Karen Horney (1950) spoke of the 'tyranny of the shoulds' that people live by. 'Musturbatory' (musts) thinking plays a similarly totalitarian role in people's lives. Clients are usually unaware of the absolutist philosophies that lie behind their unconditional musts, which lead them to inflict emotional harm upon themselves. When the therapist helps the client to identify their rigid attitude in the form of a 'must', for example, the client may say that as must is only a word, it can't have so much power. In the interchange below, the therapist helps the client see that it is not the word 'must' that has the power to disturb her but the meaning that she invests in the word.

| | |
|---|---|
| *Client:* | I'm really anxious about the exam. |
| *Therapist:* | What are you anxious about? |
| *Client:* | Failing, of course. |
| *Therapist:* | And if you did fail, what then? |
| *Client:* | If I fail the exam, I'll be completely useless. |
| *Therapist:* | Are your friends as anxious as you are? |
| *Client:* | No one wants to fail, but some of my friends are OK with the exam. |
| *Therapist:* | And that's why it's not the exam itself that's making you anxious; it's the way you think about the exam that is the real problem. |
| *Client:* | What's my thinking? |
| *Therapist:* | Something like, 'I must pass this exam, and If I don't, I'm completely useless'. Does this sound familiar? |

| | |
|---|---|
| *Client:* | Yes, I can hear myself saying that. But how can that make me anxious? |
| *Therapist:* | Your use of the word 'must' puts you under tremendous pressure and drives your anxiety. It does not allow you any room to manoeuvre if things go wrong. |
| *Client:* | It's only a word. How can a word lead to anxiety? |
| *Therapist:* | It's a word that contains a self-defeating outlook and packs an emotional punch. What kind of outlook do you think your friends hold – the ones who are not stressed out about the exam? |
| *Client:* | That's easy: they say they will do their very best, but it's not the end of the world if they fail. They certainly wouldn't see themselves as I would. They can always retake it. |
| *Therapist:* | What do you notice between their attitude and yours? |
| *Client:* | They are not driving themselves mad like I am. |
| *Therapist:* | Are they studying any less than you are? |
| *Client:* | I don't think so. As we're talking about this, I realise I get so anxious that my brain freezes, and I can't take anything in. |
| *Therapist:* | Right. That won't help your studying. Do you now see how you make yourself anxious? |
| *Client:* | Yes. |
| *Therapist:* | How? |
| *Client:* | By saying to myself, 'I must succeed at all costs'. I'm not allowing myself the possibility of failing. It's beginning to sink in, so how do I eliminate this horrible word? |
| *Therapist:* | Well, it's not the word itself you want to get rid of but the self-defeating attitudes that lurk behind it. We could start by looking at the healthy and flexible attitudes some of your friends seem to have. Maybe you could learn to adopt and act upon some of these attitudes if you find them helpful. |
| *Client:* | I hope so. |

Once clients have accepted both the general and specific principles of emotional responsibility (though, as we have said, not all REBT therapists agree with this double-headed approach to teaching self-induced disturbance), they are now ready to formulate their goals for change.

### Note

1   Personally, I don't use such terms such as 'whine' which are, in my view, quite pejorative. However, it was a word favoured by Ellis and some of his followers continue to use it.

Chapter 4

# Dealing with Client Obstacles to Client Change in the Goals Domain of the Working Alliance

Goals for change are what usually bring clients to the therapist's office. Bordin (1979) suggests that agreement between the therapist and client on the latter's goals for change is one of the key components in developing a successful working alliance. However, what may seem like a relatively straightforward process is often filled with misunderstandings and pitfalls as both sides strive to agree on therapeutic change. REBT therapists like to establish treatment goals that are specific, clear and measurable so that progress or the lack of it can be determined. This chapter looks at some of the difficulties that clients experience in following or accepting such criteria for goal-setting.

## When Clients Want to Change C by Changing A Rather than by Changing B

Clients frequently state that their goal in therapy is to get others (e.g. partner, in-law, boss, neighbour) to change before they can do so, or that simply through others changing they will automatically feel better, e.g. 'If my husband pays more attention to me then I won't be so angry; so what can I do to get him to change?' This is what, in REBT, we refer to as changing the $A$. Such clients need to be socialised to REBT goal-setting methods to profit from this approach. REBT's position on this is that it is important for the client to target their disturbed feelings for change before trying to influence others to change. They do this, of course, by changing $B$. So, how can REBT therapists respond when clients want to change their disturbed feelings at $C$ by changing adversities at $A$? Here is an example:

| | |
|---|---|
| *Therapist:* | In REBT, the focus of change is squarely on the client. You are the one seeking therapy, not your husband. |
| *Client:* | But he's the one making me angry, so the focus should be on him. He should damn well pay more attention to me! |
| *Therapist:* | REBT is first and foremost about helping clients overcome their largely self-created emotional upsets – in your case, unhealthy |

DOI: 10.4324/9781003423379-5

|  |  |
|---|---|
|  | anger – and then deciding what practical steps can be taken to make life more pleasurable for or acceptable to them. |
| *Client:* | How can I agree to that when I'm not the problem? |
| *Therapist:* | You are the one that's unhealthily angry, not your husband. If I did agree with your goal, how am I supposed to change him when he isn't here, and, by what you say, wouldn't be interested in therapy? |
| *Client:* | I thought you could tell me how to change him. |
| *Therapist:* | I don't have such magical powers, but later in therapy, we can look at ways you might exert some influence on his behaviour. |
| *Client:* | Why can't we do that now? |
| *Therapist:* | Because it's doubtful that you will positively influence him while you're so angry. |
| *Client:* | How can you be so sure? |
| *Therapist:* | Because it hasn't worked so far. |
| *Client (wearily):* | OK, you win. What do we do then? |
| *Therapist:* | I'll show you how to stop making yourself unhealthily angry about his behaviour, and then … |
| *Client:* | Am I just supposed to put up with it then? Not care anymore? |
| *Therapist:* | No, you can express strong annoyance or disapproval of his behaviour while at the same time trying to get him to change. |
| *Client:* | What if that doesn't work? |
| *Therapist:* | Then you can decide not to go back to making yourself angry and consider other options. |
| *Client:* | Such as …? |
| *Therapist:* | How long you are prepared to continue to put up with it. |
| *Client:* | You mean leave him? |
| *Therapist:* | That could be a longer-term option if his behaviour doesn't change. |
| *Client:* | I couldn't do that. |

In this illustration, the following are important points to note:

1. The therapist repeatedly puts the locus of change within the client and does not let the therapeutic focus switch to her husband's behaviour. This is necessary if the client is to accept emotional responsibility for her anger.
2. If the therapist did focus on her husband, this would not only be a highly unrealistic goal to agree to but also smack of therapist arrogance (they can change people's behaviour without them coming to therapy). However, the therapist says there might be ways to influence her husband's behaviour as part of her goals after she has undisturbed herself. Therefore, they are linking the work the client has to do on herself with future potential benefits.

3. The client believes if she gives up her unhealthy anger, the only alternative is not to care any longer. The therapist shows her that she can display healthy negative emotions which express her disappointment while at the same time seeking constructive ways of attempting to change her husband's behaviour.
4. If the client's attempts fail, she has the choice of making herself unhealthily angry again or deciding on another course of action. When she says, 'I couldn't do that [leave him]', the therapist can make a mental note that she may be harbouring other disturbance-producing attitudes that require therapeutic attention, e.g. 'I couldn't bear living on my own, that's why he has to change'; 'Despite his behaviour, I need him to be happy'.

Clients who blame external events or circumstances (e.g., being stuck in a tedious job or noisy neighbours) for their emotional problems might understandably state that their goal is to get out of or away from these adverse *As* (activating events) as quickly as possible. This is a practical goal rather than an emotional one. However, if therapists accede to this goal, they will be helping clients to change the *A* rather than stay put and undisturb themselves in the face of these *As*. The therapist is not advocating that clients should 'just put up with it', but the danger in the practical solution is that their disturbance-creating attitudes will remain intact, e.g. 'I can't stand a job that isn't always interesting'; 'I'm moving away because I'm ashamed of myself for not being able to confront them about the noise'. If similar circumstances or events occur again, this will probably reactivate the clients' rigid/extreme attitudes. Once clients remove their emotional disturbances (putting up with their job so 'I can learn to stand it'; accepting themself for their perceived weakness and learning assertive techniques), they can then decide what productive course of action to pursue.

### Helping Clients Translate Behavioural Goals into Emotional Goals

Clients may present in therapy complaining of, for example, lack of confidence, procrastination or social avoidance, e.g. 'I'm fed up with always putting off writing this article. What I need from you is a good kick up the backside to get going'. While it might be tempting to offer the client a collection of behavioural techniques to overcome their procrastination, the real challenge for the therapist is to reveal to the client the emotional blocks behind it.

| | |
|---|---|
| *Client:* | I'd be really happy if I could get going on this article. |
| *Therapist:* | OK. Imagine that you're sitting at your desk, ready to start your article. Now, how do you feel? |
| *Client:* | I feel uncomfortable, a bit edgy. Not relaxed at all. |

| | |
|---|---|
| *Therapist:* | But what emotion are you experiencing? |
| *Client:* | I'd say anxiety. |
| *Therapist:* | What is anxiety-provoking in your mind as you sit there, ready to start? |
| *Client:* | I'm not sure if it will be good enough. |
| *Therapist:* | And let's assume it won't be. Then what? |
| *Client* *(very tense):* | The publishers might reject it. |
| *Therapist:* | Let's say that they do. Picture yourself reading the rejection slip. Then what? |
| *Client:* | That's it. The rejection slip means I'm a worthless failure. A fraud. |
| *Therapist:* | So, what you're most anxious about is having your article rejected by the publisher, which, if it happened, your attitude would be that this would prove that you are a failure and a fraud. Is that right? |
| *Client* *(sighs deeply):* | Yeah, that's the truth. I keep on trying to deceive myself into thinking that I'm a lazy person. It doesn't hurt as much. |
| *Therapist:* | OK. If I can help you feel concerned but not anxious about the possibility of failure and teach you self-acceptance whatever happens, will that help you tackle your procrastination? |
| *Client:* | It sounds all right in theory. |
| *Therapist:* | Well, it will help you put all your energy into writing a good article rather than wasting it on fear of failure. If it gets turned down, you can ask for constructive feedback and resubmit it. If you don't submit it, you definitely will fail in your bid to become a writer. |
| *Client:* | Yes, I know. That's the real goal – coping with failure. |
| *Therapist:* | If you're prepared not to let yourself be intimidated by it, you'll stand much more chance of becoming a professional writer through sustained and persistent effort. |
| *Client:* | OK. I'll give it a shot. I hope I don't have to put in too much effort. |

In the above extract from therapy, important points to consider are the following:

1. Procrastination is usually underpinned by anxiety, and the therapist demonstrates how to deal with it by first encouraging the client to imagine carrying out the avoided activity. Another way of identifying the underlying emotion would be a homework task for the client of actually sitting and starting to write the article.

2. The client's presenting problem as defined, avoiding writing an article, looks very different when assessed through inference chaining – fear of failure and subsequent self-devaluation.

3. The initial goal was for a 'good kick up the backside to get me going', which probably meant a stiff talking to from the therapist. The goal that emerged from the assessment was much more ambitious: overcoming the client's anxiety and replacing it with concern while learning to accept themselves in the face of possible rejection from the publishers. If the client does not strive for such goals, they will probably bring about what they fear – seeing themselves as a failure.

4. The client's parting comment, 'I hope I don't have to put in too much effort', may indicate the presence of an attitude of unbearability or discomfort intolerance ideas. Wessler and Wessler (1980: 104) state that discomfort intolerance is almost always involved in procrastination as the 'short-term discomfort of engaging in a task is avoided despite the potential long-term benefits of completing the task'.

5. Though it did not emerge in the therapy extract, procrastination is less commonly found in narcissistic anger that some individuals have about putting forward for judgement themselves or their work when their superiority or talent should be self-evident. The client also had this problem, and the therapist negotiated with them the following goal: to see themselves as a fallible and equal rather than a superior human being. Still, they might be a superior writer, and the only way to find out was to submit their work.

## When Clients Want to Set Indifference as a Goal

REBT therapists prefer clients to select healthy negative emotions and their associated constructive behaviours as therapeutic goals. However, clients often believe that indifference, passivity or resignation is the best way to deal with emotional distress, e.g. 'This is the third girlfriend to dump me in as many months. I feel down in the dumps about it. I want to feel completely indifferent about it all, then I'll be able to handle it'. The trouble with indifference as a goal is it implies that clients are trying to suppress their healthy desires for unpleasant events not to have occurred; indifference does not help clients pursue appropriate courses of action to prevent a bad situation from becoming worse. Also, indifference to unpleasant events often means living a life of pretence and usually leads to inner conflicts. These points will be illustrated in the following excerpt.

| | |
|---|---|
| *Therapist:* | If I teach you how to feel indifferent, how will that help you? |
| *Client:* | I won't give a damn about being dumped, and my depression will go. |
| *Therapist:* | Will you ask more women out? |
| *Client:* | No, I'll give that a rest for a while. |

| | |
|---|---|
| *Therapist:* | Is that what you want? |
| *Client:* | Not really. Not at all. |
| *Therapist:* | The big problem with indifference is that it gets you nowhere. You will still be miserable, but desperately trying to pretend otherwise, and you'll avoid the opportunity of changing some aspects of yourself that might be turning women off, which may lead to more successful relationships. And you can learn how to feel sad about being rejected without becoming depressed and withdrawn. How does that sound? |
| *Client:* | Well, they all said I was possessive, which turned them off. I don't want to be like that. I want to be more relaxed with women. |
| *Therapist:* | And be able to handle rejection? |
| *Client:* | Yeah, that too. |
| *Therapist:* | So how will pretending to be indifferent help you? |
| *Client:* | It won't. I'll be even more screwed up. |
| *Therapist:* | OK. What are your new goals, then? |
| *Client:* | To stop pretending that rejection doesn't hurt, make some changes and go out with more women. It sounds good as I say it. |

Clients often assume that if they surrender their rigid attitudes, the only alternative that the therapist is offering is to feel passive in the face of adverse life events, e.g. 'He is always insulting me. What am I now supposed to do – roll over and play dead!' The therapist may have partly created this problem by not quickly building up the self-helping alternative to unhealthy anger, namely, healthy anger (sometimes referred to as annoyance or irritation) and the flexible attitudes underpinning it. Clients can be shown that there is a middle way between demands and passivity – a set of flexible attitudes expressed in mild, moderate, strong or intense terms. Particularly with angry clients, it is usually important for them to feel strong or intense healthy negative emotions if they are to eliminate their unhealthy anger. In the above example, the client can confront his detractor with a quote from Voltaire, the eighteenth-century French philosopher: 'Sir, I dislike intensely what you say but will defend to the death your right to say it'.

### When Clients Want to Feel Happy in the Face of Adversity

Instead of seeking to feel indifferent to adverse events, some clients believe that meeting them head on will nullify them, e.g. 'I've been turned down yet again for another job. Let's go out and party and drink to failure – screw success. That's how I want to feel'. However, as a goal, this has a hollow ring to it and will probably become more apparent if the job rejections continue. Clients must have had some constructive purpose in seeking employment, which the therapist needs to tease out and contrast with their celebratory attitude to failure. A healthy negative emotion such as sadness or disappointment, underpinned by flexible and non-extreme attitudes, will help to keep clients focused on job hunting while acknowledging without despair the unpleasantness of repeated rejection. If clients want to celebrate something, they can toast the indomitability of their spirit enshrined in their new outlook.

## When Clients Want to Feel a Less Intense Version of a Disturbed Emotion

This goal implies that clients only want to diminish the strength of their unhealthy negative emotion(s) rather than remove them. Therefore, they will still hold on to lingering rigid/extreme attitudes, e.g., 'I still must have the other person's love, but I don't want to feel so uptight about it'. Albert Ellis has suggested that 'there is an emotional variable of intensity which goes with the must' (quoted in Dryden 1991: 20), which means that the client below wants to express their 'must' in less dogmatic ways to reduce their anxiety. However, this still makes them highly vulnerable to emotional disturbance:

| | |
|---|---|
| *Therapist:* | How does your anxiety interfere with the relationship? |
| *Client:* | Well, I'm always worried if they still love me, dread them going off with someone else, and would get very depressed if they left me because, without them, my life would be nothing; I would be worthless. Those are the things I get very anxious about. I want to feel less anxious. |
| *Therapist:* | It doesn't sound like your anxiety helps you enjoy the relationship. |
| *Client:* | Not much. |
| *Therapist:* | So, will reducing your anxiety rather than getting rid of it make much improvement? |
| *Client:* | It will probably help a bit. |
| *Therapist:* | But will you be substantially happier? |
| *Client:* | In all honesty, probably not. It's been going on for so long. |
| *Therapist:* | The real problem, as I see it, is you hanging on to that rigid attitude – 'I must have the other person's love because without them my life would be nothing, I would be worthless'. That statement keeps your anxiety going very powerfully. |
| *Client:* | Well, what else can I do or say? That's what I believe. |
| *Therapist:* | Imagine that a few months from now, your anxiety has gone because you have successfully examined your rigid anxiety-provoking attitudes and developed a set of flexible concern-based attitudes instead. You've become a new person: enjoying |

life rather than dreading it, savouring love rather than being a slave to it. How would you now feel in the relationship?

*Client:*      Like a tremendous burden has been lifted off my shoulders. It would be wonderful.

*Therapist:*   And how much would you now enjoy the relationship?

*Client:*      A tremendous amount … but it's all a pipe dream, isn't it?

*Therapist:*   It doesn't have to be if you can learn to feel un-anxious concern about losing the other person's love. At least it won't leave you tied up in emotional knots: Never really enjoying what you believe you desperately need.

*Client:*      What you say is very valid, but changing after all these years does seem very scary. However, I'm willing to give it a go.

*Therapist:*   So are we agreed that we're going to help you develop concern rather than reduce your anxiety if you want a fundamental change in the way you see the relationship and yourself within it?

*Client:*      Yes, I know I need more than a Band-Aid to sort this problem out. I want my self-respect back.

*Therapist:*   It will probably return when you've freed yourself from the ball-and-chain you call love. Or what has been called 'love slobbism'.

*Client:*      It sounds hideous, like some disease. Is there an antidote?

*Therapist:*   I will show you how to inoculate yourself against it.

Points to consider in this extract are the following:

1.  The therapist is reluctant to help perpetuate the client's emotional disturbance and shows them the negligible practical benefits to the relationship if they only reduce their anxiety. The therapist points out the crucial role of their rigid thinking in maintaining their anxiety about the 'dreadful' prospect of losing their partner's love.

2.  The client is stumped as to how to overcome their anxiety. Still, the therapist uses tantalising imagery to encourage them to commit themself to the possibilities of real change.

3.  The therapist offers the client different ways of feeling in the relationship that will help them to avoid the usual emotional havoc they experience: highly anxious about losing their partner's love, the prospect of deep depression if their fear is realised.

4.  The therapist renegotiates the new goals with the client to confirm they have understood and accepted the therapist's clinical rationale for change – 'Yes, I do know that I need more than a Band-Aid.'

5.  The therapist points out that the client's self-respect is more likely to come back through developing a healthier form of love and abandoning their 'love slob-bism'. This will be achieved by maintaining their strong desire for love while removing their dire necessity for it and by proving to themself that they can still survive and be happy even without love.

## When Clients State that They Never Want to Be Unhappy Again

Some clients state as a goal for therapy that they never want to be unhappy again. However, as well as flying in the face of human experience, such a goal may contain the seeds of future disturbance when the client experiences unpleasant events again. Even though REBT therapists encourage clients to strive for happier and longer lives and, if possible, achieve self-actualisation (realising one's potential), they are also aware that the human capacity for self-disturbance can be only minimised, not eradicated. Therefore, the therapist is wise to declare that the goal is unobtainable and probe for the client's reasons for choosing it, e.g. 'I've had five years of hell with this depression, and I never want to go through it again. I deserve every area of my life to be happy from now on'.

The therapist can point out they would be a very poor therapist if they agreed to such a goal and 'set out with you on the road to eternal happiness' because they would be colluding with the client's delusion that such a goal is obtainable. Also, there is no inherent 'deservingness' in the universe of permanent happiness, but hard work and determination will likely bring more than less happiness. Suppose the client is afraid of becoming depressed again. In that case, they can learn to develop an 'early warning system' based on cognitive, emotive and behavioural cues to respond and limit its impact. The client may have an implicit demand in their goal that needs to be isolated and examined: 'I must never become depressed again'.

Similar unrealistic goals are advanced by clients who want a particular problem not to reappear rather than seeking pervasive happiness in their lives, e.g. 'I hope that this therapy will get rid of my panic attacks for good'. As with all treatment goals, it is important to explain that change is a nonlinear process; therefore, clients can expect setbacks and relapses. Also, progress is usually measured along three dimensions:

1.  *Frequency* – are the panic attacks less frequent than before?
2.  *Intensity* – are the panic attacks less intense than before?
3.  *Duration* – do the panic attacks last as long this time?

REBT therapy has built-in relapse prevention methods if clients are prepared to forcefully and consistently examine their rigid/extreme attitudes and keep developing their alternative flexible/non-extreme attitudes.

## When Clients Set Vague Goals

When asked about what they want to achieve from therapy, many clients respond with quite vague goals (e.g. 'I want everything to be OK in my life' or 'I want to find out who I really am'). If this vagueness in goal-setting is not dealt with, 'both therapist and client are likely to end up frustrated when they look back to determine the utility of the therapy experience' (Walen et al. 1992: 52). Therefore, the above statements need to be refined to produce goal-setting clarity.

| | |
|---|---|
| *Therapist:* | What isn't OK in your life at the moment? |
| *Client:* | Everything. |
| *Therapist:* | Such as ...? |
| *Client:* | Well, my job is deadly dull, my relationship is going nowhere, and I seem to be falling out with my friends and arguing with my parents all the time. Do you get the picture? |
| *Therapist:* | So, it's one big mess then. |
| *Client:* | Right. |
| *Therapist:* | Well, let's start clearing up the mess. We can link each problem area to a clear and specific goal. |
| *Client:* | I don't follow. |
| *Therapist:* | What would you like to achieve with your relationship difficulties for example? |
| *Client:* | I want to leave my girlfriend, but I don't like living alone. |
| *Therapist:* | Because ...? |
| *Client:* | I'm no good at entertaining myself. I need company all the time. |
| *Therapist:* | Do you get depressed on your own? |
| *Client:* | Yeah, I do. |
| *Therapist:* | If I could help you overcome your depression, what effect would that have on your relationship? |
| *Client:* | I would definitely leave her and learn to stand on my own feet without rushing from one usually bad relationship to another. |
| *Therapist:* | Is that out of desperation to avoid loneliness? |
| *Client:* | Yes, I'm ashamed to say. |
| *Therapist:* | But you will probably start picking more suitable partners from a position of strength, not desperation. |
| *Client:* | I certainly hope so. |
| *Therapist:* | Right, we can apply this process to each problem, one manageable piece at a time. How does that sound? |
| *Client:* | Things are already much more straightforward. |
| *Therapist:* | That's because your initial goal of wanting everything to be OK was vague. We needed to find out what wasn't OK in your life. In |

> REBT, we pinpoint the specific problem areas we need to work on and then develop clear goals for change, like overcoming your depression. That's how we move from vagueness to clarity.

The therapist can liken their goal-setting role to looking through a camera viewfinder: if the picture is fuzzy, then bring it into focus. The other client statement, 'I want to find out who I really am', might suggest that the client sees therapy as a metaphysical journey of self-exploration while the REBT therapist expects to have a relatively clear idea of the destination before they set out. In this way, therapy remains structured and problem-orientated rather than letting the client ramble on in a disorganised fashion. Problem-solving training for this client begins with such questions as 'What prevents you now from knowing who you are?' or 'How will you know when you've found your true self?'

## When Clients Fail to See the Difference Between Short-Term and Long-Term Goals

REBT offers clients two forms of change: elegant and inelegant (Ellis 1980). Elegant change involves clients removing their goal-blocking rigid/extreme attitudes and replacing them with goal-attaining flexible/non-extreme attitudes. Elegant or attitude change in REBT can occur in specific events or towards life in general, but both forms aim to reduce self-created disturbance significantly. Inelegant change is usually concerned with symptom-removal, but without concomitant attitude change, e.g., a client is relieved that their partner is not going to leave them after all but avoids looking at their underlying attitude that 'my partner must not leave me, and my life would be over if they do'. Therefore, the client might feel better for superficial and palliative reasons, but it is unlikely they would get better because their disturbance-producing attitudes remain intact and ready for reactivation when the next relationship problem arises. Therapists would do a disservice to their clients if they did not specify the important differences between quick fixes and lasting changes.

| | |
|---|---|
| *Client:* | What I want from coming here is to learn relaxation and a bit of positive thinking to get me through these talks. I get so anxious about doing them. |
| *Therapist:* | Are they a regular feature of your job? |
| *Client:* | Yes, I do a lot of in-house presentations to colleagues. |
| *Therapist:* | What do you think you are anxious about? |
| *Client:* | Making mistakes, looking like a fool, having my colleagues think badly of me. Those sorts of things. |
| *Therapist:* | Out of that list, which one are you most worried about? |

| | |
|---|---|
| *Client:* | My colleagues thinking badly of me. I couldn't bear that. But what's that got to do with learning relaxation? |
| *Therapist:* | Well, if you're really worried about losing your colleagues' approval, relaxation won't make much impact on that. |
| *Client:* | But it will help me to calm down. |
| *Therapist:* | It might help you to some extent, but your need for their approval will continue to fuel your anxiety, and ... does it get in the way of giving a polished performance? |
| *Client:* | Yes, it could be better. |
| *Therapist:* | What I want to offer you then is the choice between tinkering with your problem and overhauling it. |
| *Client:* | An overhaul sounds pretty drastic. |
| *Therapist:* | Do you want the quick fix of a relaxation tape or to develop natural confidence, poise and polish in the long term? |
| *Client:* | Put like that – the overhaul. |
| *Therapist (chuckling):* | Well, step this way for an overhaul. |

In the above extract, the client accepted the therapist's persuasive rationale for fundamental change within a specific problem area. The therapist did not attempt to impose their view on the client – the client does not have to embrace the elegant solution to their problem(s). As it turned out, the need for approval underlay the client's workplace interactions and affected their social life. Eventually, the client chose to pursue attitude change in several areas of their life.

Some clients turn up for therapy wanting 'to kick around a few ideas'. This usually refers to their viewpoint that they have some understanding of the causes of their problems but hope therapy will clarify their thinking on these issues, e.g. 'I've always felt that I haven't done as much with my life as I'd like to because I lack confidence. If you could help me see more clearly why I'm like this, I know I can make more progress'. What they are seeking is insight into their problems. Once this is gained, they believe their problems will spontaneously resolve themselves.

Ellis (1963) distinguished between intellectual and emotional insight: the former is self-helping flexible and non-extreme attitudes lightly and intermittently held, while the latter refers to those same attitudes ideas deeply and consistently held (see also Chapter 1). To move from intellectual to emotional insight, clients usually need to work hard to ameliorate their problems. However, many clients believe that intellectual insight alone is sufficient to bring about such change and, therefore, want to terminate therapy when they believe such insight has been gained. The therapist needs to point out the short-term nature of this option – seeing the reasons for one's problems is not the same as doing something about them. Unless the client, as in the above example, examines and changes their confidence-draining attitudes in favour of confidence-building attitudes in various situations, they will remain isolated at the level of intellectual insight and will not achieve significant change in the long term.

## When Clients Have Conflicting Goals

Sometimes, a client will present in therapy with a list of goals that conflict, but they remain unaware of their inherent contradictions. This may occur, among other reasons, because the goals reflect their disturbance or they have not considered sufficiently their longer-term aims. While the therapist does not want to dismantle the client's goals in a brusque manner for fear of damaging the working alliance, the therapist does need to demonstrate their essential incompatibility.

| | |
|---|---|
| *Therapist:* | If I've understood you correctly, you want to learn to be more self-accepting and, at the same time, feel better about yourself by making people like you. |
| *Client:* | Yes, that's right. I won't be so hard on myself and have lots of friends. |
| *Therapist:* | Why are you so hard on yourself? |
| *Client:* | Well, I get depressed because I don't have any friends ... well, one or two, but not close friends. |
| *Therapist:* | You appear to want self-esteem, not self-acceptance. |
| *Client:* | Aren't they the same thing? |
| *Therapist:* | In REBT, we see self-acceptance as just that, irrespective of whether or not you have friends. Of course, having friends is very nice – I wouldn't argue with that. Self-esteem depends on things going right in your life, like having friends, and when things go wrong, your self-esteem usually goes down. So, self-acceptance and feeling better about yourself by making people like you are contradictory and, therefore, won't work. |
| *Client:* | But can't I be self-accepting and have friends? |
| *Therapist:* | You can have both as long as you have a healthy desire for friendship, but as soon as you convert that desire into a desperate need for friendship, you destroy your base of self-acceptance. Your goals are continually in conflict with each other. |
| *Client:* | I understand what you say, but self-acceptance without friends is a lonely existence. |
| *Therapist:* | I'm sure it is, but I didn't say that. You can learn to stop putting yourself down while at the same time changing those aspects of yourself which might be turning people off. Can you think of anything? |
| *Client:* | Well, I have been told – quite often, actually – that I pour out my problems within a few minutes of meeting someone. |

> *Therapist:*  Right, so you can learn to develop self-acceptance and build a circle of friends. Now, your goals will be compatible.
>
> *Client:*  What happens if I don't make any friends? Am I still supposed to accept myself?
>
> *Therapist:*  Yes, and persist in uncovering the blocks to friendship. But let's take it one step at a time.

In this illustration, the therapist is teaching the client the following:

1. Self-esteem is conditional on having friends while self-acceptance is not; however, the therapist is careful to support the client's desire, but not their dire need, for friendship.
2. Self-acceptance does not mean splendid isolation but the starting point for a non-damning examination of those attributes which may be keeping potential friends at bay.
3. The client's goals for change are now complementary rather than contradictory. Their last comments indicate that they have a lot of hard work ahead if they want to internalise the principle of self-acceptance, as they are still making it conditional on having friends rather than unconditional.

## Dealing with Other Problems in Goal-Setting

Some clients may be so emotionally disturbed that they are unable to discuss with the therapist any constructive goals for change, e.g. 'My life is a complete and utter shambles. I can't see it any other way'. At this point in therapy, it would be unwise for the therapist to persist in their attempts to focus the client's vision beyond their present problems when they are 'myopic'. The therapist should tackle first the client's immediate disturbances (e.g. depression and anger) and help them to create order out of chaos. From a non-disturbed viewpoint, the client can decide what longer-term therapeutic goals to pursue (their vision has now been restored, so to speak).

Switching from an unhealthy to a healthy negative emotion may 'seem unattainable to clients because they cannot conceptualise the new emotion and may not agree that it is adaptive and more functional' (Walen et al. 1992: 53). For example, a man who beat up his wife said the only way to prevent him from doing it again was to feel guilty – 'I need to keep on reminding myself what a bad person I am'. Initial attempts to encourage him to feel remorse for his actions but avoid self-condemnation proved fruitless as he believed this would 'let me off the hook'. However, seeing himself as a bad person led to heavy drinking and further assaults upon his wife. After admitting the self-defeating nature of his guilt, he agreed to the new emotional goal of remorse. This would enable him to examine the reasons for his violent behaviour (which he was much less likely to do while feeling guilty) and learn non-violent methods of dealing with his frustrations. Also, he was encouraged to examine frequently the effects of his violence upon his wife so that he would not minimise her suffering through self-absorption in analysing 'my dysfunctional behaviour'.

Other clients are caught in a cleft stick over emotional change. While acknowledging that their present feelings engender personal distress, they still consider these the right feelings to retain rather than relinquish.

| | |
|---|---|
| *Client:* | I know I'm going to burst a blood vessel or have a heart attack if I don't stop all this unhealthy anger, but I know I'm right over this issue. I must be right because otherwise, I wouldn't be unhealthily angry, would I? So how can I give up my anger? That will mean defeat. |
| *Therapist:* | Being unhealthily angry doesn't automatically mean you're right. On the other hand, you can be right without being unhealthily angry. Have your displays of anger produced any tangible benefits? |
| *Client:* | The other person knows I'm angry. |
| *Therapist:* | But have they stopped parking in your reserved space? |
| *Client:* | No, they bloody well haven't! |
| *Therapist:* | Do you think they get pleasure from seeing you so angry? |
| *Client:* | Probably. I often see the person smirking. |
| *Therapist:* | You say you don't want to be defeated, yet you're the one losing your cool and parking elsewhere. Is that how you define winning? |
| *Client:* | What else can I do? At least I haven't lost my anger and turned into a wimp. That would be the ultimate humiliation. |
| *Therapist:* | Look, you've tried it your way for several months, and they haven't budged. How about leaving to cool down for a while and calmly considering a range of options you probably haven't seen because of that red mist in front of your eyes? |
| *Client:* | Will it work? |
| *Therapist:* | I don't know yet, but your way certainly hasn't. If my approach doesn't work, you can always return to your anger and put your heart and arteries under tremendous stress. Do we have a deal? |
| *Client:* | OK, I'm willing to give it a whirl. |

The therapist shows the client that even if they have right on their side, their unhealthy anger has not produced any practical returns, and therefore, they have 'lost' the struggle so far. By letting go of unhealthy anger, the client can channel their energy into a hoped-for constructive resolution of this problem. As a further means of encouraging therapeutic movement, the therapist is careful to retain the anger option for future use if the planned strategy does not work. Also, the therapist reminds the client of the adverse physical effects of prolonged anger. The idea of a 'deal' allows the client to sheathe their sword of anger while retaining their dignity.

Once clients have identified and agreed upon their outcome goals and thereby committed themselves to the change process, the next stage is for them to execute the necessary tasks to realise these goals. Between the desire and reality of change falls the long shadow of hard work, which is examined in Chapter 5.

# Chapter 5

# Dealing with Client Obstacles to Client Change in the Tasks Domain of the Working Alliance

In Chapter 3, I discussed the principle of emotional responsibility whereby clients accept that they largely disturb themselves with rigid/extreme attitudes towards adverse events. This principle allows them to gain insight into their problems. Therapeutic responsibility encourages clients to take action to tackle their problems. This aspect of therapy requires clients to have a highly active role, which is spelt out to them by the therapist, for example:

> *Therapist:* I can teach you how to play chess, but I can't play the game for you. Similarly, with your problems, I can teach you what accounts for and maintains them, but you have to undertake the hard work to overcome them.

This chapter examines the difficulties clients experience when attempting to translate REBT theory into everyday practice by undertaking various tasks.

## When Clients Have Hidden Agendas: Offering Constructive Alternatives

Clients who bring hidden agendas into therapy construct two sets of goals: the therapist works on the ostensible goal advanced by the client while the client pursues the real one. Needless to say, this involves a lot of wasted time and effort on the therapist's part. However, it is important that therapists do not display any anger when they discover their clients' real motives for coming to therapy and, instead, try to encourage a constructive course of action.

> *Therapist:* So, all that stuff about staying off drugs forever and becoming a model citizen wasn't true. You're really here because you want a court report from me, which you hope will keep you out of prison. Is that right?

DOI: 10.4324/9781003423379-6

| | |
|---|---|
| *Client:* | Yes. I don't want to go to prison. |
| *Therapist:* | There's no guarantee that a court report from me will keep you out of prison. |
| *Client:* | Every little bit helps, though. |
| *Therapist:* | I'm not going to write one for you because you're here for opportunistic reasons and have not shown any real evidence that you are committed to therapy. I don't turn out court reports like an assembly line. |
| *Client:* | There's no point in staying then. |
| *Therapist:* | Let's say you don't go to prison; what then? |
| *Client:* | I don't know. |
| *Therapist:* | Come on, I know your track record. Back to drugs, crime and the occasional overdose. How long before you're back in court yet again? I know you've been in prison before. |
| *Client:* | It might be different this time. (irritated) Well, what else is there for me? Everything's messed up in my life. |
| *Therapist:* | I can arrange admission to a drug rehab. It might be the answer. You've shown many times that you can't stay off drugs on your own. |
| *Client:* | Yes, I know, but rehab, it's just like a prison. |
| *Therapist:* | I would disagree. You'll have to work much harder in rehab. You can leave any time you want, which requires a lot of motivation to stay there. Will you at least consider it? |
| *Client:* | I'll think about it, but I'd rather have a court report. |
| *Therapist:* | As I'm not going to write one, does this mean this will be our last session? |
| *Client:* | More than likely. |
| *Therapist:* | OK. Let's spend the rest of the session then looking at the advantages for you, one by one, if you go to rehab. Agreed? |
| *Client:* | All right, it won't hurt. |

In this extract, the therapist has revealed the client's hidden and real agenda without agreeing to it. After explaining their reasons for not writing a court report, the therapist attempts to interest the client in a longer-term goal, which may help the person to become and remain drug-free. The client's response suggests they are only interested in things that serve their immediate interests and will probably not remain in therapy. However, the therapist does not resign themself to the client's likely termination and seeks to keep them in therapy by itemising the longer-term benefits of a drug rehabilitation centre.

## When Clients Say I've Tried Examining My Attitudes, But ...

Clients are expected to examine their rigid/extreme attitudes and flexible/non-extreme attitudes in various contexts to reduce their emotional problems significantly. This is one of their primary tasks in REBT. Ellis (1979) pointed out that clients need to use commitment and energy to examine their attitudes if they wish to develop flexible/non-extreme attitudes. Also, examining attitudes should be undertaken in a sustained manner so that clients are systematic in working towards attitude change rather than sporadically or haphazardly. However, clients frequently engage in examining their attitudes in a tepid, intermittent or lacklustre fashion, which results in little or no relief from their emotional distress.

| | |
|---|---|
| *Client:* | Examining my attitudes doesn't work. |
| *Therapist:* | In what way? |
| *Client:* | Well, I tried examining my attitudes a couple of times and nothing happened. |
| *Therapist:* | What was supposed to have happened? |
| *Client:* | My anxiety was supposed to go, wasn't it? |
| *Therapist:* | I don't believe I ever said you would be cured in a few weeks. What attitudes were you examining? |
| *Client:* | I think it was something about not showing any weaknesses to friends. |
| *Therapist:* | The actual attitude was, 'I must not show any weaknesses to friends'. I suggest you write it down. |
| *Client:* | OK, I will. |
| *Therapist:* | You told me last week that you've had this rigid attitude for about fifteen years. Now, how deeply do you believe it? |
| *Client:* | Very deeply. |
| *Therapist:* | So, fifteen years of the old attitude versus two weeks of the new flexible attitude, which was ...? |
| *Client:* | Oh, something like preferring not to show any weaknesses. |
| *Therapist:* | Well, you missed out '... but there's no reason why I must not show any weaknesses ...'. That statement cuts the heart out of your rigid attitude. You'll also need to write down that attitude for it to sink in. Now, fifteen years versus two weeks. What were you expecting to happen? |
| *Client:* | A lot. It sounds silly now you put it in perspective. I know it's going to be more challenging than I thought. |
| *Therapist:* | How much effort did you put into examining those two sets of attitudes? |

*Client:*       Not much – I was watching television at the same time. Doesn't matter, does it?

*Therapist:*   Unless you inject a great deal of passion, energy, force, power and persuasion into the examination of your attitudes, you are hardly likely to get much benefit from doing so. And not in front of the television but where it counts – in front of your friends while revealing a weakness.

*Client:*       I know what you say is true, and I suppose I'll have to try harder.

In this excerpt from therapy, the therapist is teaching the client the following important points:

1. Real change does not occur after a few stabs at examining attitudes. The client's misunderstanding regarding the process of change is compounded by their vagueness about their rigid attitude.
2. Contrasting the client's fifteen years of habituation to their rigid attitude with their first tentative steps at examining both sets of attitudes is designed to show them the hard work that lies ahead.
3. Unless the client clearly understands their newly acquired flexible attitude expressed in its complete form (the therapist fills in the gap), it is unlikely to have much therapeutic impact upon them.
4. Examining attitudes should be carried out persistently with force and energy in those situations where the client experiences anxiety – just anywhere will not do, and certainly not in front of the television!
5. The client's last comment 'I suppose I'll just have to try harder' may indicate that they have not yet grasped what is expected of them or they have attitudes of unbearability, e.g., 'I want to change, but it must be easier, and I won't do anything if it is going to be too hard'. The therapist would seek evidence to support or discredit such hypotheses.

### When Clients Want to Try Rather than Do

It is important that clients commit to undertaking an activity in contrast to only attempting it. When clients agree to carry out homework assignments, they frequently say, 'I'll try to do them' rather than 'I'll do them'. The former attitude implies a good chance of failure or, at best, only half-hearted attempts. In contrast, the latter attitude suggests that the tasks will be carried out with the probability of making faster progress and more profound change. Therefore, it is important that therapists elicit a commitment to 'doing' rather than to 'trying'. These points are illustrated in the following excerpt:

| | |
|---|---|
| *Therapist:* | Now, we've negotiated this homework task of you asserting yourself with a work colleague. Will you carry out this task? |
| *Client:* | OK. I'll try to. |
| *Therapist:* | Let me ask you this: will you try to leave the session when it's finished? Will you try to drive your car home? Will you try and eat this evening? In other words, you're going to do these things. So, will you try to carry out your homework task, or will you do it? |
| *Client:* | These other things are easy to do; that's why I do them. Now this other business of asserting myself, that's different. |
| *Therapist:* | Did you try to learn to drive and cook for yourself? Were they easy to do when you first started? |
| *Client:* | I know what you're getting at – I did them, and they weren't easy at first. |
| *Therapist:* | How much progress did you make by doing these things rather than trying to do them? |
| *Client:* | I made quick progress. OK, I'll do (emphasises word) the homework task. Satisfied? |
| *Therapist:* | You are not doing the task for me; it's for your benefit. You've identified unassertiveness as a problem you wish to overcome. |
| *Client:* | You don't give up, do you? I'll do the task because it's going to help me. |
| *Therapist:* | Good. |

## When Clients Have Issues about the Place of Homework in Therapy

Some clients believe that just talking to their therapist will produce constructive change within them. This viewpoint may have been strengthened by their previous experiences with therapeutic approaches that did not emphasise the importance of homework tasks or did not assign any. Pondering therapeutic ideas between sessions might bring a greater understanding of their problems. Still, an armchair philosophy to problem-solving remains just that – clients can glimpse the exciting possibilities of change but do not realise them because they fail to act on their emerging flexible and non-extreme attitudes. Clients need to realise that what happens outside of therapy is usually considered more important in REBT than what happens inside it as they learn to develop confidence and competence in facing their problems. Therefore, an hour-long weekly session is the starting point for change, with the other 167 hours outside therapy providing its driving force. Such increasing independence as a problem-solver reduces the potential for dependence upon the therapist, e.g., clients carry out their homework tasks only to gain approval from the therapist rather than see the tasks as a means of standing on their own feet. Such arguments can help clients see that homework is essential to effect deep and enduring change in their lives.

## When Clients Think that They Have to Go Slowly with Homework Tasks

When some clients reluctantly agree to undertake their homework tasks, they then insist that these tasks have to be done slowly or piecemeal, e.g. 'I have to take it one tiny step at a time doing this exposure work. If I'm any quicker, I'm going to feel terrible. I can't stand feeling like that'. Ellis (1983a) criticised gradualism in therapy for creating the impression that change can be brought about only in a slow and painless way, thereby reinforcing clients' attitudes of unbearability (that they cannot bear much or any discomfort in facing their problems). Gradualism can, from this perspective, increase the degree of difficulty clients will experience in tackling their problems. Ellis encouraged clients to use implosive (flooding) methods to confront their fears immediately and fully to achieve rapid amelioration and significantly increase their tolerance level for discomfort. However, many clients will be unlikely to favour this method of change. As a therapeutic compromise between implosion and gradualism, several years ago, I suggested negotiating challenging, but not overwhelming tasks with clients (Dryden, 1985). These points will be clarified in the following excerpt.

| | |
|---|---|
| *Therapist:* | If you take tiny steps in overcoming your agoraphobia, how long before you can, for example, walk to and go into a supermarket alone? |
| *Client:* | I don't know, but certainly many months, even a year or more. |
| *Therapist:* | Would you like to make faster progress? |
| *Client:* | I suppose I would, but I feel dreadful when I go outside. I get so panicky. It's so bad I can't bear it. That's the real problem. |
| *Therapist:* | That statement 'I can't bear it' is so common among people with anxiety problems. The 'it' usually refers to the tremendous discomfort they experience in facing their fears. |
| *Client:* | I know how they feel – it's the same for me. |
| *Therapist:* | Do you believe you can overcome your problems without discomfort? |
| *Client:* | I know that is impossible but it's got to be kept to an absolute minimum. |
| *Therapist:* | What would be the effect on your progress if you say to yourself every time you do a homework task, 'I can't bear it! I can't bear it'? |
| *Client:* | I'll have a ball-and-chain around my ankle. Probably stop doing the tasks or find endless excuses not to do them. |

| *Therapist:* | There is a very dramatic and rapid way to overcome what we in REBT call 'discomfort anxiety', which is what you suffer from. |
|---|---|
| *Client:* | I don't think I'm going to like this … |
| *Therapist:* | This involves jumping in at the deep end. This means walking to and staying in the supermarket and learning to bear the significant discomfort you will experience. So, you stay in the situation until the discomfort passes. In this way, you make rapid progress and learn that you can bear it but without liking it one bit. |
| *Client:* | You're either joking or you're mad! |
| *Therapist:* | Neither. I'm serious. I would teach you various techniques that will help you stay in the situation. Some clients are amazed at their progress when they do it this way. |
| *Client:* | I will tell you now. I'm not going to do that. |
| *Therapist:* | OK. There is a middle way between tiny steps and jumping in at the deep end and it's called 'challenging, but not overwhelming'. |
| *Client:* | That sounds ominous … |
| *Therapist:* | Well, the task would be harder than you like, such as walking to the end of your road rather than the front gate, but would fall short of the terror you imagine if you went to the supermarket straight away. So, you would learn to tolerate the discomfort quite quickly without being paralysed by it. |
| *Client:* | That might be something I'm prepared to try but I want more discussion about it first. |
| *Therapist:* | Certainly. Where shall we begin? |

## When Clients Fail to Carry Out Homework Tasks

Some clients may be eager to carry out their homework tasks yet come back to therapy the following week feeling despondent over their failure to execute them, e.g. 'I'm completely useless. I felt so confident, and nothing happened'. As well as accepting themselves for not undertaking their tasks, clients could learn the 'win-win' formula of homework tasks: that if they did the task, they would have won, and if they failed to do the task, they also would have won because they learn which factors blocked or interfered with task execution. If they haven't done the task, the client and therapist renegotiate it, with the client committing to taking the required remedial steps. This formula emphasises that clients are always on a learning curve for tackling their problems.

## When Clients Do Not Carry Out Homework Tasks as Agreed

REBT homework assignments require clients to face adversities (at *A*) to examine and change their rigid/extreme attitudes and get experience in developing their alternative flexible/non-extreme attitudes. This is seen as the most efficient and enduring method of constructive change. However, clients may agree to such a homework approach in therapy, yet at the next session, declare 'success' but for different reasons.

---

*Client:*      Homework went very well. I feel much more relaxed now in queues.

*Therapist:*   What was the rigid/extreme attitude you were examining?

*Client:*      'I must not waste my time being stuck in queues and I can't bear it if this happens.' God, I used to get so angry about bloody queues.

*Therapist:*   It seems you've had great success. What happened?

*Client:*      Well, I was in this queue, listening to music, and I got to the checkout as calmly as possible.

*Therapist:*   When you say 'listening to music', were you wearing headphones?

*Client:*      Yes, I was.

*Therapist:*   What was the homework task we agreed on last week?

*Client:*      For me to stand in queues, examine my rigid/extreme attitude, and practise my flexible/non-extreme attitude.

*Therapist:*   Can you see how you've changed, perhaps in a subtle way, the task?

*Client:*      Oh, the headphones. I thought they would help me.

*Therapist:*   They are a good idea if you're looking for a short-term solution. However, in REBT we encourage clients to look for longer-term ones and this involves facing adversities; in your case, examining and changing your rigid/extreme attitudes and rehearsing your flexible/non-extreme attitudes when in queues. What you did was to distract yourself from your anger.

*Client:*      I see what you mean, but aren't you going over the top on this issue?

*Therapist:*   Well, imagine distraction with music is the only technique you use, then one day you're in a long queue and your music fails to play. Then what?

*Client:*      I hadn't thought of that. I suppose if I'm honest, I'll get angry over the music not playing because I can't block out with music my anger about being stuck in bloody queues!

| | |
|---|---|
| *Therapist:* | Will you do the homework task we originally agreed then: to face the frustration of being stuck in queues and practise your new flexible/non-extreme attitude? |
| *Client:* | Yes, I will. No distractions this time. |
| *Therapist:* | Good. Once you've overcome your unhealthy anger, then you can choose from a non-disturbed viewpoint if you wish to wear headphones. |

In this extract, important points to consider are the following:

1. The therapist elicits details of the homework task from the client to determine if they carried out what was agreed upon at the previous session.
2. Feedback from the client shows they altered the homework task by distracting themself from the adversity at *A* (being stuck in the queue) rather than facing it.
3. Wearing headphones is a practical solution to the client's problems rather than an emotional one favoured by REBT therapists, i.e. their attitude of unbearability is being held at bay by the music rather than examined and changed.
4. The therapist encourages the client to point out the limitations of the practical solution through the 'music not working' example. This convinces the client to do the original homework task. The therapist, who does not want to appear a killjoy, suggests a possible return to the headphones once the client's unhealthy anger has gone.

## When Clients Say I'll Do It Tomorrow

Clients can employ many excuses and delaying tactics to avoid carrying out their homework tasks. Underpinning the 'I'll do it tomorrow' syndrome is usually an attitude of unbearability, e.g., 'These tasks involve too much hard work. I shouldn't have to work this hard to sort my problems out. There must be an easier way?' For some clients, this syndrome becomes a way of life as they search for the easy solution to their problems, which proves to be continually elusive. With clients who routinely avoid homework, REBT therapists can point out that if they put nothing into therapy, they will get nothing out of it and thereby remain emotionally disturbed. Estimates can be made of the time clients are likely to spend in therapy (and money paid if they are private clients) as an inducement for them to start carrying out their homework tasks, for example:

| | |
|---|---|
| *Therapist:* | You've successfully avoided your assignments so far. At this rate, you'll be in therapy for the next couple of years instead of doing what you want to – going out with a woman. You'll be as lonely then as you are now because you won't push yourself. |

Confronting such clients needs to be done regularly so they are not 'let off the hook', but confrontation in REBT means being assertive, not aggressive or abrasive. One method that can be used is the 'but-rebuttal' (Burns, 1980):

---

| | |
|---|---|
| *Client:* | Yes, you're right – I don't want to be in therapy for years but I'm not ready yet to ask someone out. |
| *Therapist:* | You haven't been ready yet for several months and I doubt you ever will be if you keep on defining rejection as an awful experience, the end of your world. |
| *Client:* | Yes, I know it sounds so silly, but I'll feel devastated if it happens. |
| *Therapist:* | As I've been explaining, your feelings are based on your attitudes, so feeling devastated is not brought about by rejection but by how you evaluate rejection. So, rejection doesn't bring your world crashing down; your 'awfulising' about it does that. Now, if you can learn to see rejection as unpleasant but not awful … |
| *Client:* | Yes, I know believing that would probably help me, but, on the other hand, I don't think it will work for me. |
| *Therapist:* | How can you know that when you haven't asked anyone out yet? |
| *Client:* | Yes, I haven't tried it, but when will I know it's the right time to start? |
| *Therapist:* | There's no perfect time to start. We've done a lot of preliminary work: rehearsal through imagery and behaviour, expressing forceful flexible and non-extreme coping statements, learning assertiveness techniques and so on. Now would be a good time to leave the laboratory and try these things out in the real world. |
| *Client:* | Yes, I suppose it is but you never know; she might say 'Yes' rather than 'No'. |
| *Therapist:* | That might be nice, but it wouldn't help you. Do you know why? |
| *Client:* | I'm not sure, but it would make me feel much better. |
| *Therapist:* | Only in the short term because you'd be continually anxious about being dumped and how would you feel if you were? |
| *Client:* | Devastated. Utterly depressed. |
| *Therapist:* | Back to square one. So, you need several rejections first to cope constructively with them, and then you'll enjoy your first 'Yes' much more. Now will you agree to face your first rejection? |
| *Client:* | There's a woman I fancy, but she wouldn't give me the time of day. I'll try to ask her. |

| | |
|---|---|
| *Therapist:* | Now we've been over this trying versus doing several times … |
| *Client:* | I meant I'll do it. I've got to do it if I want to stop living my life as if I'm afraid of the dark. |

The therapist wears down the client's 'Yes, but' statements until the client commits themself to carry out the homework task. The therapist's rebuttals underscore REBT principles to motivate the client. Even when the client becomes hopeful that the first woman they ask says 'Yes' rather than 'No', the therapist does not shrink from pointing out the self-defeating nature of their optimism. REBT therapists prefer to negotiate homework tasks that will bring about enduring rather than superficial changes in clients' lives, so they are alert to the short-term effect implicit in the assignments that many clients suggest. As pointed out earlier in this chapter, there is an important distinction between 'trying' and 'doing', which the client is reminded of. Clients can learn the but-rebuttal technique to resolve their doubts or ambivalence about change.

## When Clients Wonder about the Relevance of Tasks to Their Goals

Some clients become confused or are unsure about how some of the tasks they are expected to carry out relate to their goals, e.g. 'How has acting foolishly in public got anything to do with helping me to speak up in meetings?' Such perplexity on the client's part may have been partly engendered by the therapist not making the link between task and goal explicit. Whatever the cause, the therapist can help the client to make the connection between shame-attacking exercises (Ellis, 1994) and their inability to express their opinions at meetings.

| | |
|---|---|
| *Therapist:* | Now let's go over this again: what are you most anxious about at these meetings and thereby prevent yourself from speaking up? |
| *Client:* | I'm afraid of saying something stupid and looking a fool in the eyes of others as well as my own. |
| *Therapist:* | What do you lack that I keep stressing with you? |
| *Client:* | Self-acceptance. I won't allow myself to look like a fool in the eyes of others. |
| *Therapist:* | You're assuming you can control how they see you. But what do you think you look like by staying silent at meetings? |
| *Client:* | I know that doesn't look good either. |
| *Therapist:* | So, you've trapped yourself. Now what is the point of a shame-attacking exercise? |

| | |
|---|---|
| *Client:* | To learn to accept myself for saying or doing something foolish in public. |
| *Therapist:* | To accept yourself in the face of what …? |
| *Client:* | Others' criticism, laughter, disapproval, ridicule, whatever. |
| *Therapist:* | So, how will these exercises help you at meetings? |
| *Client:* | Well, if I accept myself, then I'll be able to speak up instead of being struck dumb by my anxiety. |
| *Therapist:* | So, you can contribute to the meeting now more than just silence. |
| *Client (laughs):* | I certainly hope so! |
| *Therapist:* | Do you now see the link between the task and your goal? |
| *Client:* | Yes, walking backwards down the road will help to set me free from my self-imposed restraints. |
| *Therapist:* | Watch out for lamp posts. Seriously, you'll probably find in time that these exercises will also liberate you in other areas of your life. |
| *Client:* | You're right. It's not just at meetings that I have problems speaking up. |

As well as clarifying the task–goal link, the therapist needs to ensure that the homework task logically or naturally follows on from the work done in the session, e.g. 'stay-in-there' activities (Grieger and Boyd, 1980) would be typical tasks to negotiate if the session discussion focused on the client's attitude of unbearability which led them to avoid emotionally fraught situations. When clients agree to carry out a task, it does not automatically mean that they have sufficient skills to accomplish it; therefore, therapists need to ascertain if their clients have any task-relevant skills deficits or if they have a skill in their repertoire but subjectively believe that they are unable to use this skill in a particular setting. For example, a client may say they have no idea how to start a conversation with a person they are attracted to or knows how to do it with other people but lacks confidence with this particular person. The therapist can employ behavioural and imaginal rehearsal to teach the client the necessary task skills and elicit and challenge any assignment-blocking attitudes. Such preliminary work increases clients' confidence in carrying out their homework tasks successfully.

Once the above considerations have been dealt with, the therapist needs to pin down clients to when, where and how often they will undertake their tasks rather than a vague assurance that 'I really will do it in the coming week'. The therapist can applaud the client's determination and add that specificity with homework tasks will help the client concentrate more on the work ahead. Both therapist and client can keep a written record of the homework task to reduce or eliminate ambiguity or disagreement when it is reviewed at the next session. Being transparent and specific during homework negotiation enables the therapist to whittle down clients' excuses for not carrying out their assignments.

## Troubleshooting in Advance Obstacles to Clients Undertaking Homework Tasks

Therapists need to help clients identify and remove the potential or actual obstacles that might prevent them from undertaking their agreed assignments, e.g. 'Is there anything you can think of that might interfere with or block you from completing this task?' Clients' responses may include the following: i) there is a possible obstacle, e.g. 'I don't think I'm going to have enough time'; ii) 'Nothing springs to mind' but actually they foresee one or two obstacles but reveal them only at the next session as a reason for not doing their tasks, e.g. 'My friend suddenly turned up and stayed the week'; iii) they genuinely do not see any obstacles to homework completion. Therapists can offer their hypotheses to jog clients' awareness of potential difficulties or suggest additional ones they have overlooked.

| | |
|---|---|
| *Therapist:* | You say you can't think of anything, but you haven't done the homework task yet as it always seems to slip off your agenda for the coming week. |
| *Client:* | Well, I always mean to do it but after a hard day at the office, I look forward to relaxing in the evening. |
| *Therapist:* | Well, you could relax for part of the evening and then start writing that report. What will happen at work if you keep on relaxing but don't do the report? |
| *Client:* | The you-know-what will hit the fan if it's not finished by the end of the month. |
| *Therapist:* | Three weeks to go then. It seems that the attitude getting in the way is something like: 'As I've worked hard all day, I must relax in the evening, and I can't bear it if I can't relax when I deserve to'. Can you hear yourself saying something like that? |
| *Client:* | Yes, that sounds familiar. I can't seem to shift that idea at the moment. I've got to get that report done, though. |
| *Therapist:* | OK. What would be a good strong statement to get you going and respond to that motivation-draining idea? |
| *Client:* | What I found helpful in the past when I've been shirking is to imagine being back in the army and the sergeant yelling at me: 'Get bloody moving or you'll get my boot up your backside!' |
| *Therapist:* | Use that image, and let's throw in some rewards and penalties. Now what do you enjoy doing? |
| *Client:* | Relaxing. |
| *Therapist:* | No relaxing until after you've worked on the report. How long do you need to work on it for each night? |
| *Client:* | About two hours. |

| | |
|---|---|
| *Therapist:* | Work for two hours first and then relax. What don't you like doing apart from the report? |
| *Client:* | I hate doing DIY. There are shelves waiting to go up around the house, and my wife keeps on telling me to put them up. |
| *Therapist:* | If you don't work on the report, no relaxing. Two hours of DIY instead. |
| *Client:* | Anything but that. |
| *Therapist:* | Do you agree to do the homework task using rewards and penalties? |
| *Client:* | Yes, I do. |
| *Therapist:* | OK. Let's write that all down in a homework contract and hope you will apply the penalties if you don't keep to it. |
| *Client:* | I've no excuse for letting the report slip off my agenda. |

The use of rewards and penalties (not punishments), also known as operant conditioning or contingency management, helps clients to shape new goal-directed behaviours (writing a vital report) and reduce or extinguish goal-blocking ones (procrastination underpinned by attitudes of unbearability). Operant conditioning methods can teach clients the pitfalls of short-term hedonism or instant gratification because avoiding hard work and discomfort takes them further away from their goals rather than closer to them. Grieger and Boyd (1980: 145) suggest that rewards and penalties provide 'the extra incentive that makes the difference between avoiding or completing it [homework]'. Ellis (quoted in Dryden, 1991) added that if clients fail to administer their rewards and penalties, they can ask a friend, relative or partner to act as a monitor and help them adhere to their contingency management programme; in the above example, the client can ask for his wife's assistance if he breaks his homework agreement.

### When Clients Don't Know What Homework Tasks Will Help Them

REBT therapists offer clients various homework assignments to help them tackle their emotional problems. These assignments can be placed within four main categories:

- *cognitive* – e.g. reading REBT self-help books, completing *ABC* forms.
- *imagery* – e.g. rehearsing in the mind's eye carrying out a particular task.
- *behavioural* – e.g. staying in an unpleasant situation until habituation occurs.
- *emotive* – e.g. shame-attacking exercises, which allow the client to experience disturbed emotions to change them.

Some clients claim that none of the above modalities appeals to or will be able to help them and cannot offer any alternative tasks they might be able to accomplish.

| | |
|---|---|
| *Therapist:* | Now you say you want to develop more confidence, particularly at work and with women. Right? |
| *Client:* | Yes, that's right. |
| *Therapist:* | And would you agree that the two of us just talking about your problems every week is not going to bring about much change in your life? |
| *Client:* | It hasn't done so far. |
| *Therapist:* | So what else needs to be done besides talking? |
| *Client:* | I've got to get myself moving in some way. |
| *Therapist:* | Good. Now you said you're not interested in reading anything … |
| *Client:* | I can barely get through the newspaper. I only really read the sports section. |
| *Therapist:* | And the idea of imagining yourself as being more assertive at work won't help either. |
| *Client:* | My mind goes blank. I've never been any good at visualising things. |
| *Therapist:* | The shame-attacking exercises would help to teach you self-acceptance which would then form the base to develop greater confidence in your life. |
| *Client:* | I don't fancy deliberately acting foolishly. I can do without that task. |
| *Therapist:* | What about a relatively straightforward behavioural task like asking for the money back you lent to a friend in your office? |
| *Client:* | I couldn't do that; he might think I'm a Scrooge. |
| *Therapist:* | What task do you want to do that you think will help you? You know yourself best. |
| *Client:* | I can't think of anything. It seems we're both stuck. |
| *Therapist:* | Well, let me suggest that your first homework task is to think of one. |
| *Client:* | What if I can't? |
| *Therapist:* | Then, at the next session, we'll examine how you blocked yourself from coming up with one. This will provide more information on the nature of your problems. So, we will both learn from it. I haven't been able to interest you in anything so far. Maybe you'll do a better job. |
| *Client:* | I'll see what I can do. I'm not making any promises, though. |
| *Therapist:* | OK. At the end of each session, it is important that you have a homework task to carry out. My task is to make sure that you have one. So, we both have to work hard in therapy and you outside of it as well, if you're to make progress. |

The above extract shows that the client's homework avoidance is linked to their presenting problems. Still, the therapist defers to the client's superior self-knowledge to try to tease out a task. When this proves fruitless, and the client believes they have outmanoeuvred the therapist, the latter suggests that the first homework task 'is to think of one'. Even if the client cannot think of a task, this will provide critical cognitive data, which will be examined at the next session. Therefore, the client will not return to therapy empty-handed in the way they might imagine. The therapist points out that both have tasks to perform if the client is to make progress and emphasises the 'hard work' theme to alert them to what lies ahead for them in and out of therapy.

### When Clients Are Apprehensive about Being Their Own Therapist Once Therapy Ends

The ultimate aim of REBT therapy is for the therapist to become redundant and for clients to develop into their own self-therapist. Therapy moves towards termination when clients have shown proficiency in using the REBT to conceptualise and tackle their problems. Formal therapy may be over, but self-therapy requires life-long practice to maintain therapeutic gains and deal effectively with future problems. Clients may be apprehensive that they will falter and not be able to carry out their REBT-based tasks on their own.

| | |
|---|---|
| *Client:* | I like the idea of being my own therapist, but I'm not sure if I will be totally successful on my own. |
| *Therapist:* | Being a self-therapist is not about achieving total success but managing your problems in a way that will significantly reduce your level of disturbability. |
| *Client:* | I know that's more realistic, but I'm not sure if now is the right time to leave therapy. |
| *Therapist:* | How can we put that to the test? |
| *Client:* | I knew you would ask me that. Leave therapy and find out, I suppose. |
| *Therapist:* | That will provide you with the best information to answer your question. Whenever you start upsetting yourself over problems in your life or start slipping back, what do you need to do? |
| *Client:* | Put the problem within the ABC framework to find out what I'm telling myself. |
| *Therapist:* | When you've located your rigid and extreme attitude, then what? |
| *Client:* | Examine it and the flexible and non-extreme alternative using the 'which is logical, true and helpful' mode of questioning. |
| *Therapist:* | And then? |

*Client:*      Set myself several tasks to think, feel and act in ways consistent with my flexible and non-extreme attitude so I can strengthen it. That's the theory, anyway.

*Therapist:*   And the practice. You have been doing it throughout therapy. Why should you behave differently when you leave therapy?

*Client:*      Well, I suppose it's because you are no longer there.

*Therapist:*   I'm only there one hour a week. Who did the hard work of change? Was I with you when you faced your panic in the supermarkets?

*Client:*      I did those tasks all on my own. You were the last thing on my mind when I was panic-stricken!

*Therapist:*   That's my point – you did them, not me. You are the agent of your own change. I was acting as your consultant or adviser.

*Client:*      OK. I accept that. I remember you saying that self-therapy is a lifelong task, but surely, there will come a time when things will be taken care of themselves and I can put my feet up?

*Therapist:*   With lots of practice, responding to your rigid and extreme attitudes and developing your flexible and non-extreme attitudes will become much easier, but you can never stop being a therapist to yourself otherwise you might find those old attitudes creeping back. Would your physical well-being look after itself if you stop having baths or brushing your teeth?

*Client:*      Obviously not. So, looking after your physical and mental health are equally important.

*Therapist:*   Exactly. Now, if you do get stuck on your own, you can come back to therapy, and I'll be your adviser again for a brief period.

*Client:*      Thanks. That's good to know.

In the above therapy excerpt, important points to note are the following:

1. The client's doubts about becoming 'totally successful' as a self-therapist may reflect implicit rigid and extreme attitudes, e.g., 'I must never be upset again'; 'I must be healthy at all times'. The therapist will need to probe for and deal with these ideas if they are present before therapy is terminated.
2. The therapist maintains a problem-solving focus to the end of therapy by suggesting that the client's question will be answered only through leaving therapy.
3. The therapist encourages the client to go through again the REBT framework of change to keep on reminding themself of what needs to be done when they are emotionally upset. Repeating the *ABCs* of REBT aids the process of constructive change.
4. When the client assumes that the therapist's absence in their life will adversely affect their progress, the therapist points out that they were always absent

during the real test of therapy – when the client faced their problems on their own – and this did not undermine their progress. The therapist mentioned that they advised the client on problem-solving, but the client did all the work.

5. The client wonders if lifelong self-therapy is necessary as they believe their mind will eventually self-regulate. The therapist makes an analogy with physical hygiene to show them that lifelong maintenance of their REBT skills is required if they want to keep them.

6. If the client develops serious difficulties as a self-therapist, they can return to therapy for further problem-solving. The therapist uses the word 'brief' to indicate that 'fine-tuning' of the client's new role is probably required rather than a wholesale reappraisal of it. The latter strategy may lead the client to feel discouraged about and deskilled in their new role.

## Dealing with Clients' Other Task-Related Difficulties

A crucial task for clients is to be receptive to and eventually accept the general and specific principles of emotional responsibility. Little, if anything, can be accomplished in therapy if clients continually blame others or events for their emotional problems. For an extensive discussion of encouraging emotional responsibility, see Chapter 3.

Setting an agenda in REBT allows each session to be focused on a specific set of items so that the most is made of therapy time. Agenda-setting keeps both therapist and client on track to realise the latter's goals for change. However, some clients may object to what they perceive as a therapy straitjacket and an infringement of their right to talk about whatever comes to mind, e.g. 'Who are you to say what should be discussed?' The therapist needs to point out that each session agenda is negotiated and not imposed, but it must have clinical relevance to the client's presenting problems. This means that idle chit-chat, endless pleasantries, meandering conversations, etc., are banished from the agenda in the drive for therapeutic efficiency, e.g., 'We are not here to discuss the weather or television programmes but to help you overcome your guilt feelings as quickly as possible. The session agenda ensures that we both never lose sight of that goal'. Clients can be assured that agenda-setting is a flexible procedure and can be suspended if a crisis or other significant event supervenes, e.g. the client becomes suicidal.

For some clients, the word 'homework' is reminiscent of their schooldays and may have negative or unpleasant connotations for them, e.g. detention for not doing it, parental pressure to 'do your homework otherwise you'll end up bottom of the class'. Some clients may also assume that the therapist is patronising them. Such reasons might lead to homework avoidance or rebellion against it. To forestall these problems, a different term can be agreed upon, e.g., self-help tasks or outside therapy activities, which is more acceptable to and beneficial for the client.

The first four chapters of Part I looked at client difficulties in each of the four domains of the working alliance: bonds, views, goals and tasks. The final chapter in Part I explores client obstacles to client change in the various stages of the therapeutic process.

# Chapter 6

# A Process-Orientated View of Client Obstacles to Client Change

The REBT therapy process can be divided into beginning, middle and ending phases with their own distinctive features and client obstacles to client change. Though these phases may seem artificially contrived, they can provide yardsticks of a client's progress; for example, in the middle phase, clients should preferably have greater confidence in tackling their emotional problems and identifying core rigid/extreme attitudes. This chapter deals with client problems typically experienced within these phases.

## Dealing with Client Obstacles to Client Change in the Beginning Phase

In this phase, therapist and client develop a working alliance, an early problem-solving focus is established, the client is taught the *ABCs* of REBT and homework tasks are negotiated. Client obstacles to client change arising from these activities have been dealt with in earlier chapters.

Other problems clients experience include what Grieger and Boyd (1980: 79) call 'the "cathartic cure" myth'. Because suppressed emotions (e.g. anger) have finally been released, clients can understandably feel a tremendous sense of relief and happiness at the end of the first session, concluding that therapy is finished. From the REBT perspective, talking about one's disturbed emotions is, on its own, seen as a superficial remedy as clients have not yet identified, examined and changed the rigid and extreme attitudes that largely create disturbed emotions. In the above example, if clients leave therapy prematurely, they are likely to find that their relief is short-lived, as their underlying attitudes will stir up further anger. Such a rationale will help to disabuse clients of their 'I thought airing my feelings would get rid of them' notions and encourage them to stay longer in therapy to seek enduring methods of change.

### When Clients Want It All Sorted Out Today

Some clients come to therapy with the expectation that a couple of sessions will solve all their problems, and when this does not occur, rapid demoralisation can

DOI: 10.4324/9781003423379-7

take place. Such clients need to be inducted into the realities of REBT and its goal-setting procedures.

---

*Therapist:*   Where did you get the idea that I had a magic wand?

*Client:*   I thought you therapists knew the answers to everything. You're supposed to be able to sort me out.

*Therapist:*   I hope I can sort you out, but only with your considerable help. I certainly don't have the answers to everything, but I certainly do have an explanation of and solution to your emotional problems. I can't produce a magic wand; instead, I can offer you two very different words – hard work.

*Client (sarcastically):*   Great, that's cheered me up. I thought I was coming here for help, and I feel even more depressed now.

*Therapist:*   Because ...

*Client:*   Because now it seems I'll never get over this depression. You're not going to be of any help.

*Therapist:*   That's because you're placing all the responsibility for change on my shoulders. If I had a formula for an instant cure, I'd be a millionaire by now. The instant cure formula is unrealistic. It seems to me that part of your depression stems from a sense of helplessness, and that's why you look to others to pull you out of it.

*Client:*   Well, I certainly can't do it. I'm a failure.

*Therapist:*   You haven't had much success so far, but I do have a tried-and-tested formula for tackling depression that brings results.

*Client:*   What is it?

*Therapist:*   Your depression is created by certain attitudes you hold, and if you examine and change these attitudes both inside and outside of therapy, you'll probably be surprised how quickly you improve.

*Client:*   Sounds like a lot of hard work.

*Therapist:*   Yes, those two words again. Are you willing to take a risk and forget all about magic wands and instant cures?

*Client:*   Reluctantly, but I'll have a go.

*Therapist:*   Good. Now, let's find out what you are making yourself depressed about in the first place and start sorting it out.

---

The client's reply, 'reluctantly', indicates they still hope for an instant solution to their problems. As well as self-devaluation attitudes ('I'm a failure') regarding their inability to pull themself out of their depression, the client is probably also holding attitudes of unbearability, e.g., 'I can't bear the hard work and struggle involved in facing my problems. There's got to be a quick and easy solution somewhere'. The solution offered by the therapist (though the client is not keen to hear it) is that hard work based on shared responsibility for change is the most effective way to lift their depression.

The therapist encourages the client to accept a 'tried and tested' formula by suggesting the likelihood of an early improvement in their mental state. Once the client is superficially persuaded by this rationale, the therapist then switches them to a problem-solving focus to discover their primary depression-inducing attitudes. With this type of client, the therapist will need to keep emphasising the self-defeating nature of the instant cure versus the self-helping nature of hard work to deepen the client's commitment to constructive change.

### When Clients Have Misconceptions about REBT

Some clients' wariness about committing themselves to REBT stems from misconceptions they hold about its theory and practice. These misconceptions may have derived from, among other sources, critics of REBT (often those who have seen Albert Ellis work with the eponymous client in the film *Gloria*), former clients who have had negative experiences or outcomes with this approach and have laid the blame entirely at REBT's door, or some REBT therapists themselves who provide poor role models for the flexible/non-extreme attitude system they purportedly teach. Whatever their source, the therapist's task is to elicit clients' doubts, reservations and objections (DROs) about REBT and discriminate them from genuine misunderstandings about its practice, e.g. 'Will I be in therapy for a long time?' and 'I'm afraid you're going to brainwash me' respectively (Dryden 2022). The following list includes three major misconceptions clients have about REBT and provides answers to them.

#### REBT Is a Form of Brainwashing

Leaving aside clients' assumptions that they have no control over their thinking, the brainwashing fear is that REBT therapists will 'implant' their point of view in their clients' minds, and they will leave therapy as an REBT clone. What therapists seek to do is encourage clients to think for themselves by subjecting their self-defeating attitudes (e.g. 'I'm worthless and miserable without a partner in my life') to logical, realistic and functional examination as well as their self-enhancing alternatives (e.g. 'I would prefer a partner in my life, but I don't need one and can be happy and self-accepting without one'). Clients are also urged to scrutinise REBT similarly. Albert Ellis (1983b), the founder of REBT, long argued that scepticism towards all things in life is an important feature of mental health. Therefore, therapists work towards clients emerging from therapy as independent thinkers, not REBT robots.

A final point is that some clients confuse the force and energy therapists employ to examine their views with indoctrination. Such forceful examination has been found to be effective and rapid in helping clients respond effectively to their rigid/ extreme attitudes and develop flexible/non-extreme attitude alternatives. Still, this approach might initially overwhelm clients, hence their suspicions about 'being brainwashed'. The therapist can allay such suspicions by explaining the rationale for such methods.

### REBT Cares Nothing for People's Feelings

One criticism of REBT contends that it advocates a purely cognitive approach to understanding oneself and the world and, therefore, is devoid of emotion. Negative connotations associated with the word 'rational'[1] conjure up images of cold, logical individuals who view others with icy detachment. However, this is a caricature of REBT and not its actual practice. Though REBT is a primarily cognitively orien-tated approach to understanding emotional disturbance, it does use other senses to effect constructive change in an individual's life. In fact, thinking, feeling and behaving are given equal prominence in the name of this therapy. However, to be accurate, thinking would be seen as first among equals because the other two modalities are used in the service of cognitive change.

Clients' emotions are almost always at the centre of the therapist's attention as therapists seek the most efficient way to replace their clients' unhealthy negative emotions (e.g. depression) with healthy negative ones (e.g. sadness, the self-helping alternative to depression). The most efficient way, as far as REBT is concerned, is for clients to identify, examine and change through a variety of multimodal meth-ods the rigid and extreme attitudes underpinning their unhealthy emotions to create a flexible/non-extreme and emotionally stable outlook. The word 'rational' has no sinister meaning nor implies a lack of emotion. It simply refers to whatever con-structive means will help clients attain their therapeutic goals and live happier and longer lives.

### REBT Teaches to Be Selfish

Individuals who act selfishly pursue their pleasures and goals in life at the expense of others. Their preoccupation with their well-being makes them oblivious to or indifferent to the effects of their actions upon others. While REBT does urge cli-ents to prioritise achieving their goals – after all, who else will do it for them? – it advocates a policy of enlightened self-interest (or self-care), not selfishness. This policy reminds clients, when planning their goals, to take into account the concerns and wishes of others and thereby avoid acting in socially irresponsible or harm-ful ways; not to do so may rebound upon them and undermine their own goals, e.g. someone who wants a wide circle of friends but believes they should exploit them when necessary eventually finds themself rejected, alone and despised. REBT contends that if individuals choose personally and socially responsible goals, they are more likely to realise them and help produce a more equitable and congenial society in which to live.

### Clients' Concerns about the Interactional Style of Their REBT Therapists

Another source of some clients' hesitancy in committing themselves to therapy is that they confuse REBT with the therapist's interactional style. Therefore, it is 'important for therapists to make enquiries which will help them to determine whether client objections are focused on issues pertaining to the therapy or the therapist' (Dryden and Yankura 1993: 197). If the therapist's style is the issue, e.g. 'You are asking too many questions' or 'You'll have to go more slowly if I'm to understand what you're saying', the therapist will need to modify it for therapy to proceed.

### When Clients Won't Be Honest about Negative Reactions to Therapy

Eliciting feedback from the client on each session is part of agenda-setting. REBT therapists seek positive and negative comments to help them tailor therapy to the individual client's requirements. While many clients might be ready to offer both types of feedback, some clients in the initial stages of therapy will need to be encouraged to provide critical comments. In contrast, others will avoid doing so altogether. Such avoidance is often reflected in this last group's presenting problems.

| | |
|---|---|
| *Therapist:* | This is our third session of therapy. Was there anything I did today that was unhelpful, rude or insensitive? |
| *Client:* | No, you were wonderful as always. You are helping me so much. |
| *Therapist:* | Well, thank you for those comments, but you haven't voiced any criticisms yet about our three sessions. |
| *Client:* | They have all been excellent. |
| *Therapist:* | Did you notice what I did halfway through today's session? |
| *Client:* | Do you mean when you read the newspaper for a few minutes? |
| *Therapist:* | Yes. What did you think about me doing that? |
| *Client:* | Well, you're the expert. I'm sure you had a good reason for doing it. |
| *Therapist:* | I think most clients would see that as downright rudeness. In what way did you see it differently? |
| *Client:* | I don't think you're rude. I think you are a very nice person. |

| | |
|---|---|
| *Therapist:* | Let me suggest something: If you comment negatively about me, you're afraid I'll reject you or won't like you. This links in with your anxiety about losing the approval of significant others in your life. |
| Client *(hesitantly):* | Well, I am a bit afraid of you not liking me if I say something that might not be nice. I'm always afraid of being rejected by everyone. |
| *Therapist:* | Well, we've shed more light on your problems now. From my point of view, I will not reject you no matter what you say in therapy. But more importantly, I can teach you how to develop self-acceptance irrespective of whether people like you or not, including myself. |
| *Client:* | If only I could be like that … |
| *Therapist:* | I assure you that such a goal is possible. |

The newspaper reading exercise confirmed the therapist's hunch about the client's dire need for the therapist's approval, militating against the client and providing negative feedback.[2] This was linked to a broader pattern of approval-seeking in the client's life. The goal of achieving self-acceptance was offered to the client as the most effective way of overcoming these problems.

## Dealing with Client Obstacles to Client Change in the Middle Phase

During this phase, the therapeutic focus is on strengthening clients' flexible/non-extreme attitudes and weakening their rigid/extreme ones. This is achieved by clients using multimodal methods of examining these attitudes in various problematic situations to internalise a new and effective philosophy of living. This phase is often called rational emotive behavioural working-through and 'constitutes the heart of RE[B]T' (Grieger and Boyd 1980: 122). Client resistances encountered in this stage are now described.

### When Clients Lack a Criterion for Coping

Some clients may want to discuss in each session what bothered them most in the preceding week rather than continue to work on a problem they wish to overcome. Such a lack of continuity from session to session may result in the fragmentation of therapy as both therapist and client lose their clinical focus, and no real progress is made. Therefore, it is important for the therapist to underscore the need for a coping criterion for each problem, i.e. a method of assessing when clients have reached the stage of managing a problem but not always smoothly or easily. The coping criterion can be used to determine the right time to switch from one client problem to another.

However, if circumstances warrant it, the therapist should be flexible and switch to another problem before the coping criterion is attained on the previous one, e.g. a crisis in the client's life or another issue on the client's problem list is deemed to be of greater clinical importance than the one initially selected. Once the switch has been made, a coping criterion should be reached on the new problem before moving to another one. Suppose the therapist believes the client is 'hopping' between problems. In that case, the therapist can explore the cognitive dynamics involved in problem avoidance and the self-defeating nature of such behaviour with the client.

### When Clients Fear Losing Their Identity if They Change

Clients frequently complain of feeling 'strange' or 'unnatural' as they work towards attenuating their deeply held rigid/extreme attitudes and internalising a newly emerging flexible/non-extreme. This state is often called cognitive-emotive dissonance. Such a clash between old and new ways of thinking and feeling often leads to inner conflict or turmoil as 'they [clients] see a better way, but cannot yet actualise it, so they conclude that they cannot possibly overcome their disturbance' (Grieger and Boyd 1980: 161). The 'alien' and uncomfortable feelings that clients encounter in this stage of change often prompt them to leave therapy to feel 'natural' again. The 'I won't be me' syndrome is an example of cognitive-emotive dissonance.

| | |
|---|---|
| *Client:* | I don't want to be the submissive partner in my relationship any longer. I'm completely fed up with seeing myself as unworthy and grateful for anyone taking an interest in me. |
| *Therapist:* | So, is striving for self-acceptance and being assertive helping to change this view of yourself? |
| *Client:* | It's helping a lot, but it's such a weird feeling – it's as if I'm in someone else's body. This can't be me doing these things; it just isn't me. Sometimes, the feeling is so uncomfortable I want to give up therapy. |
| *Therapist:* | I assure you these feelings belong to you and no one else. This feeling of a stranger inhabiting your body is widespread when individuals are shedding one self-image and acquiring another. Moving through this transitional phase requires much persistence, tolerating these feelings until the strangeness fades. When it does eventually fade, will you still believe that you are a stranger to yourself? |
| *Client:* | I expect to feel more relaxed and comfortable with my new image. |
| *Therapist:* | A year from now or less, you may well see your old ideas and feelings as alien to you. |

| | |
|---|---|
| *Client:* | I sincerely hope so. |
| *Therapist:* | Have you ever been through a similar experience? |
| *Client:* | I was a heavy smoker once and couldn't function without a cigarette. I couldn't imagine myself without one. |
| *Therapist:* | And when you stopped? |
| *Client:* | A lot like now: quite frightening, uncomfortable, felt like I'd lost my identity, silly as it seems. |
| *Therapist:* | So why did you persist? |
| *Client:* | Because of the health benefits I wanted. |
| *Therapist:* | And can you apply those same lessons today? |
| *Client:* | Yes, I think I can. I do want very different things for myself now. So, the quicker I cope with this strange period in my life and see it as a natural part of change, the quicker I will come out of it. |
| *Therapist:* | Exactly. |

In the above therapy extract, important points to consider are the following:

1. The therapist explains that cognitive–emotive dissonance is a phenomenon common to clients undergoing therapeutic change to put the client's disturbing feelings of unreality and depersonalisation into perspective.
2. To get through this 'transitional phase', persistence or tackling the client's discomfort disturbance is required to tolerate the above feelings.
3. The therapist encourages the client to look beyond this phase to the expected successful integration of the client's new thoughts and feelings; the old self-defeating ways will probably be experienced as alien.
4. The therapist locates a previous episode of cognitive–emotive dissonance that the client overcame to apply the same lessons to the present one.
5. Though not mentioned in the above dialogue, the 'I won't be me' syndrome can be named and understood to undermine its potentially adverse effects.

### When Clients Don't See the Differences Between Attitude Change and Non-Attitude Change

During the middle phase of therapy, REBT therapists seek to determine the nature of clients' progress in tackling their emotional problems. The therapist's preferred solution (but not always the client's) is the attitude change approach, whereby clients change their attitudes from rigid/extreme to flexible/non-extreme. Non-attitude change solutions involve changing distorted inferences but not the underlying rigid/extreme attitudes from where they derive, effecting behaviourally based change, or changing unpleasant activating events (*A*s) rather than confronting them.

Some clients want the enduring benefits of an attitude change yet employ non-attitude change methods to achieve it. For example, someone who decides their inferences were wrong about their work colleagues' dislike of them fails to focus on the implicit rigid/extreme attitude that 'They must like me and if they don't I can't accept myself'. The danger here is that the disturbance-producing attitude has been left intact, and the client has not learned any coping strategies if their inferences eventually turn out to be accurate. Also, inferentially based change, like the other two non-attitude forms of change, has limited generalisability to the client's other problems as it does not usually provide the attitudinal context in which to understand which critical attitudes link their manifold problems, e.g. in the above example, the need for others' approval. Revealing and examining these underlying attitudes provides the most efficient means of tackling clients' problems rather than proceeding ponderously on a case-by-case basis.

This discrepancy between desiring attitude change but using non-philosophical methods to achieve it may arise because clients, among other reasons, repeat parrot-fashion REBT concepts or mechanically examine their rigid/extreme attitudes without realising what consistent and forceful action is required of them or want lasting change with little effort. To deal with these difficulties, the therapist can clearly outline the steps involved in achieving attitude change and contrast these with the clients' lack of commensurate effort in attaining it.

### When Clients Don't Realise that Change Will Be Hard

Dryden and Neenan (2004) argue that it is during the middle stage of REBT that clients demonstrate the most obstacles to change. Clients may have had an initial surge of progress or optimism in tackling their problems but now have experienced setbacks, faltering progress or the sheer grind of overcoming a long-standing problem. Such obstacles can lead to disillusionment or despair over the realities of change, usually underpinned by attitudes of unbearability, e.g., 'If I had known how hard it was going to be, I wouldn't have bothered in the first place'; 'I expected change to be difficult but not this hard!' Therapists need to make explicit clients' attitudes of unbearability beliefs and encourage them to examine them forcibly and change them. e.g. 'Change should be hard, not easy, so stop wasting valuable time and energy moaning about it'; 'I'm going to stop complaining and see this through to the bitter end'. Such determination will enable clients to acquire attitudes of bearability and thereby help them realise their therapeutic goals.

### When Clients Feel Overwhelmed with Their Many Problems

As clients move into the middle phase of therapy, they may begin to realise how many problems they have and may become discouraged. While struggling to identify, examine and change the rigid and extreme attitudes associated with each of their problems, clients may fail to notice the emergence of a particular theme which links these attitudes and coalesces into a core rigid/extreme attitude because they feel overwhelmed by the number of problems piling up. Core attitudes lie at the deepest level of cognitive awareness and are the most difficult to reveal. However, once tapped into, they allow clients the opportunity for a significant change of attitude in their lives. Helping clients to identify and work with these core attitudes often re-energises them because they realise that awareness of such attitudes brings order into chaos.

| | |
|---|---|
| *Therapist:* | We've unearthed quite a few rigid 'shoulds' in your various problems. With your boss … |
| *Client:* | He absolutely shouldn't overload me with work. |
| *Therapist:* | Stuck in queues, traffic jams, et cetera … |
| *Client:* | I absolutely shouldn't have to put up with the inconvenience of these things. |
| *Therapist:* | When things start going wrong for you … |
| *Client:* | I absolutely shouldn't have to work hard to put things right. You don't need to go on; I get the picture. I seem to have many problems, and they overwhelm me. |
| *Therapist:* | I understand that, but the good news is that there is probably a theme which ties all these attitudes together. |
| *Client:* | I'm not sure what you mean. |
| *Therapist:* | When we sift through these attitudes, they always seem to involve you complaining about something. What do you think is the essence of these complaints? |
| *Client:* | I suppose if I'm honest with you, I'm always moaning when I have to struggle in any way or work hard, especially with something I don't like. |
| *Therapist:* | The theme seems to be having a smooth life path. Would you agree? |
| *Client:* | Yes, I would. That does feel right. |
| *Therapist:* | So, what might be the core attitude from which these ideas stem? |
| *Client:* | That other people, life itself, absolutely should make things easy and trouble-free for me. |
| *Therapist:* | And when things aren't made easy for you? |
| *Client:* | I can't bear all the hassle and discomfort involved. That's why I'm always getting angry or depressed over it. |
| *Therapist:* | Now that we've revealed this core attitude, we can be more ambitious in therapy. If you forcefully examine this attitude, you will tackle several problems simultaneously rather than examining each one consecutively. Does that make sense? |

| | |
|---|---|
| *Client:* | It does now that I can see how they are linked. We will now work from the centre outwards rather than inwards to the centre. Is that right? |
| *Therapist:* | Precisely. |
| *Client:* | That helps me to feel less overwhelmed. |

This dialogue demonstrates the therapist switching the therapeutic focus to deeper cognitive structures to show the client the wellspring of their situationally specific rigid/extreme attitudes. This new focus allows for extensive and rapid progress as the client learns how to radically and constructively restructure their disturbance-inducing set of rigid and extreme attitudes. Though not highlighted in the excerpt, it is wise for the therapist not to assume the presence of only one core rigid/extreme attitude – a few others might also be present. In the above example, it may well be that the client has a core attitude of self-condemnation or ego disturbance (e.g. 'I'm an utter failure') because of their perceived inability to bear discomfort in their life and this attitude accounts for his depression.

### When Clients Are Reluctant to Take the Reins in Therapy

As therapist directiveness begins to fade, clients are encouraged to take the lead in using the *ABCs* of REBT for self-analysis and change and in setting and reviewing their homework tasks. However, some clients are reluctant to grasp the nettle of practising self-therapy. Reasons for this include fear of failure in their new role and attitudes of unbearability regarding the additional and more demanding work now involved. This phase heralds the beginning of the end of therapy, and some clients do not wish to acknowledge this and, instead, want to prolong therapy. Client obstacles to becoming a self-therapist often reveal that clients experience being urged to take on the therapeutic reins as the therapist abdicating responsibility for them. Whatever the reason, the therapist needs to draw out and challenge the attitudes blocking this necessary shift in therapeutic responsibility. Such attitudes will be frequently linked to clients' presenting problems, e.g. 'I can't cope with anything on my own'.

### Dealing with Client Obstacles to Client Change in the Ending Phase

During the ending phase of therapy, therapists and clients agree to work towards termination by decreasing session frequency or setting a fixed date for the final session. Clients review the course of therapy and what they have learned from it, focusing on future problem-solving as a self-therapist using REBT skills and dealing with termination issues. In this section, we address several client obstacles to client progress in the final phase of therapy.

### When Clients Want to End Therapy Prematurely

Ellis (1972) suggested that many clients leave therapy when there has been an elevation in their mood, external circumstances have improved, some measure of hope or optimism has returned, or they feel better generally. Though all of these changes are welcomed, they are likely to be relatively short-lived because clients have terminated before adequately dealing with the rigid and extreme attitudes underlying their presenting problems. REBT calls this process of change 'feeling better' but not 'getting better' (Ellis, 1972).

| | |
|---|---|
| *Client:* | I believe it's the right time to leave as I'm much better now. |
| *Therapist:* | Is that because you can accept yourself without a man and be relatively happy on your own? Or have circumstances changed in your life? |
| *Client:* | Oh yes, I believe that stuff now, but as it happens, I met this man, and the chemistry between us is perfect. We're both delighted, and I don't need therapy any longer. |
| *Therapist:* | I don't want to dampen your happiness, but you have been through the same situation several times, and when your partner leaves, you end up in suicidal despair. |
| *Client:* | This time will be different because our relationship will continue. I know it will. |
| *Therapist:* | My strong hunch is that you have paid lip service to flexible and non-extreme attitudes while still seeking the same old solutions to your problems. If the relationship does fall apart, I fear you may end up in hospital again after an overdose. I sincerely hope I'm wrong. |
| *Client:* | So, what do you want me to do – get rid of him? |
| *Therapist:* | Of course not. Enjoy the relationship and stay in therapy a bit longer. |
| *Client:* | What for? |
| *Therapist:* | To absorb and act on the idea of self-acceptance whether or not you are in a relationship. Self-acceptance is a form of protection against emotional distress. |
| *Client:* | The relationship will protect me. |
| *Therapist:* | Only when things are going right; if things go wrong, you will be exposed again to the attitudes that you're nothing without a man and that life has no meaning on your own. Self-acceptance is the genuine protection against those ideas. |
| *Client:* | Well, I'm afraid I have to disagree and, anyway, my mind is made up. |

> *Therapist:*   If you start slipping back or things are going wrong, please get in touch with me again. The door is always open for you.
>
> *Client:*   OK, I'll bear that in mind.

In this illustration, the therapist is encouraging the client to stay in therapy to understand the following:

1.  Her disturbance-producing attitudes remain intact as she has not examined and changed them. Therefore, these attitudes are likely to be reactivated if her present relationship runs into trouble or ends.
2.  By still clinging to her self-defeating ways, she has demonstrated that therapy has had little, if any, impact on her so far, hence the therapist's advice for her to remain in therapy.
3.  The rationale for this is that she can both enjoy the relationship and, at the same time, learn to develop a healthy outlook about it based on self-acceptance. This new attitude will provide emotional stability for her in or out of relationships.
4.  Although she is leaving therapy against the therapist's advice to pursue her 'love slobbism' (dire needs for love and approval), the therapist encourages her to return to therapy for further exploration of her problems if, as the therapist anticipates, they reoccur.

Some clients may wish to terminate therapy when they have achieved some progress in tackling their presenting problems. While they have identified and successfully challenged rigid attitudes in specific situations, e.g. 'I must not make mistakes when I lecture to students', it is doubtful if these REBT gains will translate into a deeper and more pervasive approach to tackling emotional distress in various life situations because core rigid/extreme attitudes have not yet been excavated, e.g. 'I have to be perfect in everything I do'. This rationale may keep some of these clients in therapy as they are excited or intrigued by the prospect of significantly reducing their general level of disturbability in life. However, if therapy is terminated at this point, these clients can be reminded that they can return to therapy if they wish to extend their therapeutic progress.

### When Clients Are Reluctant to End Therapy

Instead of prematurely ending therapy or not staying on to realise greater therapeutic benefits, some clients will want to stay in therapy as long as possible. This 'longevity in therapy' plea is clinically counterproductive as progress already made may begin to erode as clients look for ways to delay striking out on their own. This may occur because clients believe that they must feel completely confident about coping on their own, conditions in their life have to be perfect before leaving therapy, they can't cope without the regular assistance of the therapist, or their problems should be resolved entirely first.

If severing the therapeutic relationship 'does become a major issue, then the client is not ready to terminate, for this is an indication that the client relies on the therapist [or therapy] to fulfil some perceived need – perhaps approval, reassurance, or freedom from responsibility' (Wessler and Wessler 1980: 182). In the above examples, the therapist can encourage the client to examine these termination-blocking attitudes and ideas to the effect that the client can see that i) increased rather than complete confidence about problem-solving is most likely to be achieved once the client has left therapy and not remained indefinitely within it; ii) creating favourable conditions in one's life requires consistent hard work and determination that lingering in therapy will not provide – clients may be distracting themselves with Utopian fantasies rather than focusing on practical realities; iii) managing one's problems and not completely resolving them is the benchmark for decisions about terminating therapy. Frequently underlying this reluctance to leave therapy is the fear of failing as a self-therapist.

### When Clients Think that They Can't Stand on Their Own Two Feet

The ultimate aim of an REBT therapist is to become redundant as clients develop competence and confidence in tackling their present and future problems. For some clients, this new role will provide a feeling of exhilaration; for others, it will fill them with a sense of dread, particularly if they have experienced a relapse before termination. The reactivation of clients' presenting symptoms as therapy nears the end of its course

> is not a phenomenon unique to RE[B]T, nor is it anything to become alarmed about. The most useful thing for the therapist to do when these fears arise is to help clients discover what they are telling themselves to become upset and to work these notions through.
>
> (Grieger and Boyd 1980: 190)

| | |
|---|---|
| *Client:* | I was pleased with my progress, but now it's all in ruins. How can I possibly leave therapy now? This proves I won't be able to do it alone unless I can keep coming back to you. |
| *Therapist:* | How is your progress as a self-therapist destroyed because of a setback? |
| *Client:* | I thought my public speaking anxiety was under control, and then last week, I nearly died of stage fright. |
| *Therapist:* | We've often discussed that change involves both progress and setbacks. |

|  | Now, let's get to work sorting out this stage fright. What attitude was your anxiety based on? |
| Client: | Same old thing – that I've got to give a perfect performance to gain the audience's approval. |
| Therapist: | Your rigid attitudes are still fighting a solid rear-guard action. Therefore, you are still having trouble at times believing your new flexible ones. |
| Client: | They don't always feel so convincing when I'm in front of an audience. |
| Therapist: | Therefore, what needs to be done? |
| Client: | I knew you would say that. More hard work and practice: keep on forcefully examining my ideas until I only feel concerned about public speaking. |
| Therapist: | That's right. Always use the ABCs of REBT to analyse your anxiety or any other emotional problem in your life. Now you got yourself quite upset over this relapse – do you hold any rigid and extreme attitudes towards your progress? |
| Client: | I didn't think so until last week, but now I realise I'm demanding perfect progress. If things go wrong, I don't want to lose your approval or my own. |
| Therapist: | You've never had my approval or disapproval but my unconditional acceptance as a fallible human being. You don't give it to yourself all the time. |
| Client: | Well, this approval thing gets in the way. |
| Therapist: | How can you deal with it? Approval is a key theme that connects your problems. |
| Client: | Examine and change my demand for your approval. |
| Therapist: | You don't seem agitated now. What thoughts are going through your mind? |
| Client: | The setback doesn't seem so serious now it's been put into perspective. I'm feeling quite confident now about becoming a self-therapist. The dread and despair seem to have gone. |
| Therapist: | Yet another example of how your thinking creates your feelings. So, to recap: What does progress as a self-therapist mean? |
| Client: | It means lots of hard work to maintain my gains from therapy. There will be mistakes and setbacks, but these will be useful to learn from if I can keep a problem-solving focus. And as you keep telling me, don't take myself or these perfectionistic ideas too seriously. |
| Therapist: | Good. Now, shall we make the next session the last one? |
| Client: | Agreed. |

In the above extract, important points to consider are the following:

1.  The real problem is not the setback near the end of therapy but the client's awfulising attitude towards it – all their therapeutic gains have been wiped out because of the recurrence of their performance anxiety. Therefore, they conclude they cannot leave therapy at this juncture.
2.  Strengthening flexible and non-extreme attitudes while attenuating rigid and extreme ones requires consistent and persistent hard work and practice in all problem situations in the client's life. The *ABC* framework is a lifelong tool to understand and remediate emotional disturbance.
3.  Another block to the client standing on their own feet is their unrealistic notion that progress must be perfect and, like their performance anxiety, making self-acceptance conditional upon it. Even near the end of therapy, the therapist keeps encouraging the client to draw out further cognitive data to understand how they impede themself from experiencing more significant change.
4.  A positive change in the client's mood is contrasted with their earlier despair to demonstrate the thinking–feeling link. REBT therapists are always on the lookout for ways of reinforcing this link.
5.  As part of standard REBT practice, the client is asked for feedback on the issues raised in this extract to show they have understood the realistic expectations of self-therapy. This is confirmed by their ready agreement to terminate therapy at the next session.

### When Clients Struggle with Ambivalence about Therapy's End

Some clients are eager to strike out on their own but also feel sad about ending what they consider an important relationship. They may believe that feeling sad is a sign of weakness or 'not being healthy' and, therefore, attempt to suppress this emotion in the final session while struggling to put on a brave face. It is important that therapists are alert to clues that such clients are struggling with these feelings and tease out the possible irrational ideas underlying them.

| | |
|---|---|
| *Therapist:* | I'm glad you are looking forward to standing alone, but I detect a certain sadness in some of your facial expressions and the way you're interacting with me today. Would this be true? |
| *Client:* | No, I feel fine. |
| *Therapist:* | Would you tell me if you were feeling sad? |
| *Client (sighs deeply):* | I don't want to admit it, but I do feel sad. |
| *Therapist:* | What's the problem with that? |
| *Client:* | I can't be that mentally healthy if I'm sad. I should be feeling really confident about everything now. |

| | |
|---|---|
| *Therapist:* | Doesn't REBT emphasise feeling healthy negative emotions such as sadness? I feel sad about the end of the relationship, but I certainly do not see myself as mentally healthy because of it. |
| *Client:* | I know there's nothing wrong with sadness or any other healthy negative emotion. We've reviewed it enough times, but I still believe I shouldn't feel sad ... |
| *Therapist:* | Because ...? |
| *Client:* | I'm not sure. |
| *Therapist:* | You mentioned it earlier. |
| *Client:* | I've got to feel confident all the time. |
| *Therapist:* | And feeling sad is ...? |
| *Client:* | ... is a sign of weakness, failure. |
| *Therapist:* | So, you've got some lingering rigid and extreme attitudes to address, and you've shown with previous problems that you have the REBT skills to do it. Now, why is feeling sad a sign of weakness? |
| *Client:* | I must be upbeat and confident at the last session. Show the world I mean business. |
| *Therapist:* | But you're not showing the world a mentally healthy role model because you are trying to suppress your healthy sadness at the loss of an important relationship in your life. Suppressed feelings may cause trouble for you. |
| *Client:* | They already are – I'm screwing up the last session. |
| *Therapist:* | I would disagree with that. Like every other problem you've had in therapy, we're bringing a problem-solving focus to bear on it. |
| *Client:* | OK. I have a few blind spots left and some work to do on them. |
| *Therapist:* | So, what homework can you set yourself that we can review at the three-month follow-up session? |
| *Client:* | I can reread some REBT books, as I've overlooked something. |
| *Therapist:* | And your sadness? |
| *Client (hesitantly):* | Start expressing it. |
| *Therapist:* | Good. Let me get the ball rolling by expressing mine and then going on to my feelings of pleasure at the significant progress you've made in therapy. |
| *Client:* | Thanks. That will give me the push I need. |

The REBT therapist maintains a problem-solving focus right to the end of therapy and draws out the client's avoidance of expressing their sadness about termination. Their rigid/extreme attitudes underlying their avoidance are pinpointed for them to examine. Their self-assigned homework is further reading to correct their misunderstanding of REBT with regard to the expression of healthy negative emotions. Despite the emergence of these problems in the last session, the therapist does not extend therapy but suggests that these problems can be reviewed at the three-month follow-up. This will be a long enough period to indicate how the client is coping as a self-therapist. To encourage the client to express suppressed feelings, the therapist employs self-disclosure to reveal their own sadness at no longer seeing the client, thereby acting as a healthy role model for them. The therapist also wants to discuss the client's considerable progress because 'RE[B]T terminations are primarily pleasant events' (Wessler and Wessler 1980: 182).

The chapters in Part 1 of the book have focused on client-created obstacles to client change and what methods REBT therapists can employ to overcome them. Now, we turn our attention in Part 2 to therapist obstacles to client change that block or impede therapeutic progress and what remedial steps they can take.

## Notes

1 However, as the terms 'irrational' and 'rational' are frequently misunderstood and have negative connotations for many, I have replaced them when discussing attitudes. Nevertheless,1 the word 'Rational' is enshrined in the name of the therapy, 'Rational Emotive Behaviour Therapy', so I still have to address misconceptions about this term because it is present in the therapy's title.
2 Personally, I am not a fan of such exercises to test clients' reactions, but some REBT therapists (such as the one here) do advocate them.

# Part 2

# Therapist Obstacles to Client Change

# Chapter 7

# Dealing with Therapist Obstacles to Client Change in the Bonds Domain of the Working Alliance

Some REBT therapists can easily slip into blaming clients for difficulties in building a therapeutic alliance (e.g. 'They're being resistant') because they are unaware of or reluctant to look at their own ideas and behaviour which contribute to a stagnant or problematic relationship. This may be due to, among other factors, therapists holding rigid and extreme attitudes, clinical inexperience, an unvarying therapeutic style or diminishing the importance of the relationship in effecting constructive change. These and other therapist problems will now be discussed.

## When Therapists Are Overly Concerned with Getting Down to Work

REBT is generally a robust, straightforward, down-to-earth approach to emotional problem-solving which seeks to elicit and examine as quickly as possible clients' attitudes that are at the heart of the problems together with their healthy attitude alternatives. Consequently, REBT therapists usually do not feel sorry for or 'molly-coddle' their clients. Facing up to and coping with the rigours of life will bring more constructive gains for clients than lots of sympathy from therapists. However, some REBT practitioners may apply this hard-headed approach insensitively, indiscriminately or too forcefully and thereby stymie the development of a working alliance as clients shrink away from such an 'in your face' approach. A few clients might leave therapy after the first session because of it. Reinforcing these problems, therapists might start asking clients how they are upsetting themselves over this hard-headed therapeutic approach before discussing the principle of emotional responsibility (see Chapter 3). Clients may understandably feel bewildered or angry because they perceive they are being blamed for their reactions which they believe are caused by the therapist's manner.

While REBT therapists favour a 'let's get on with it' business-like approach to therapy, this has to be tempered with their clients' level of emotional distress or fragility, their expectations of therapy and preferences for a particular type of relationship. Therapists need to calibrate the pace of therapy to their clients' learning styles, allowing sufficient but not excessive time to talk about their problems. Such considerations, among others, will help to build rapport with clients and thereby

DOI: 10.4324/9781003423379-9

make therapeutic progress more likely because they believe that the therapist has a genuine interest in helping them. Therefore therapists should not be in a hurry or appear to be impatient but adopt a relaxed but focused style. As Walen et al. (1992: 44) have said, 'It is not necessary to solve the patient's problems right away'.

Instead of rushing in to tackle the clients' presenting problems, some therapists might take the opposite tack of focusing too much on nurturing the relationship at the expense of problem assessment. This may stem from their view that the client–therapist relationship is a sacred one and therefore they spend inordinate amounts of time demonstrating empathy, showing respect and offering unconditional positive regard (or, from the REBT viewpoint, unconditional acceptance). Only when the relationship has been developed through this process can therapists turn their attention to their clients' problems. Grieger and Boyd (1980) call this the 'relationship myth' and state that it has no independent existence or function. Developing a working alliance and establishing an early but unhurried problem-solving focus are not mutually exclusive activities, but complementary tasks that can convince clients of the therapist's expertise and trustworthiness.

## When Therapists Lack Empathy

Empathy is the therapist's ability to understand and communicate a client's viewpoint accurately. DiGiuseppe, Doyle, Dryden and Backx (2014) suggest that empathy is one of two factors – the other is the degree of attitudinal change that has occurred – that largely account for significant improvements in a client's mood during the course of a session. This important factor may be overlooked or paid lip service to by some REBT therapists' eagerness to impress clients with their extensive range of problem-solving techniques or clever arguments. Other therapists may see clients as merely the objects of their impersonal contemplation – another problem to unravel, another test of their clinical acumen. In both these cases, therapy is viewed as a primarily technical endeavour rather than a human one; hence the lack of empathy. Therefore clients may understandably recoil from therapists whose preoccupation is playing with their 'box of tricks' or whose manner indicates that they are being viewed through a microscope.

Empathy is an important quality that therapists need to display in order to help build rapport with clients and thereby increase the chances of effecting constructive change. REBT therapists demonstrate two kinds of empathy: affective – they communicate that they understand how clients feel (e.g., 'You must have been really hurt when you didn't get that promotion after all your years of loyal service') and attitudinal – they also show clients the probable attitudes underlying their feelings (e.g. 'Do you believe that your boss let you down or betrayed you and that he absolutely should not have treated you in this undeserved manner?'). Clients are often impressed by this double-barrelled empathic approach as the therapist has not only pinpointed the relevant feeling but also echoed their thoughts. Compassion combined with clinical competence helps to cement the therapeutic alliance.

It may be that some therapists have an emotional problem about showing empathy. They feel it, but find it hard to show it. This issue needs to be discussed in supervision and in personal therapy if it endures.

### When Therapists Need to Be Respected and Loved by Clients

Therapists are obviously not immune from rigid and extreme attitudes in general and therapy-related ones in particular. Ellis (1985, 2002) identified several rigid/extreme attitudes, including the one that therapists need to be respected and loved by their clients, that therapists may subscribe to and thereby interfere with their clients' progress. The following dialogue illustrates how therapeutic inefficiency occurs when therapists have approval.

*Supervisor:* Listening to your therapy recordings, I am constantly struck by the easy ride you're giving to the client.

*Supervisee:* I'm not sure what you mean by that.

*Supervisor:* Take homework, for example. The client said that they didn't get round to doing it and you passed up the opportunity to find out why.

*Supervisee:* I believed what they said.

*Supervisor:* But that doesn't help them or you to elicit the cognitive blocks that prevented them from doing it.

*Supervisee:* I didn't think it was important to press the client at that time.

*Supervisor:* Because to do so ...?

*Supervisee:* The client would get angry, that's why. They often get angry.

*Supervisor:* I agree that angry clients are usually difficult to deal with but you seem to be avoiding dealing with it.

*Supervisee:* I would deal with their anger if they would stop being angry!

*Supervisor:* If you did it that way, you wouldn't tap into their anger-producing attitudes. What are the client's goals for change?

*Supervisee:* To overcome their procrastination and anger.

*Supervisor:* Do you think you are making any progress with them?

*Supervisee:* A little.

*Supervisor:* I'm also aware from the recordings that you placate this client when things start to get uncomfortable and, at one point, they said you were of no help to them. What was your reply again?

*Supervisee:* 'I'm sorry you feel like that.'

*Supervisor:* What could have been a more therapeutic response?

*Supervisee:* I suppose I could have asked them why they felt like that.

*Supervisor:* Did you really want to hear their reply?

| | |
|---|---|
| *Supervisee:* | I wasn't too keen to hear it. There's no point having my nose rubbed in it if they think I'm no good. |
| *Supervisor:* | Why do you think you're soft-pedalling with the client all the time? |
| *Supervisee (hesitantly):* | I suppose, and I don't like to admit it, I'm afraid of the client not liking me. If I push them in therapy they might end up hating me. |
| *Supervisor:* | The client might hate you for the opposite reasons – that you're not helping them to achieve their goals because you're afraid to confront them. Now why do you need this client's approval? |
| *Supervisee:* | Because without it, this means I'm a bad therapist and an unlikable person. |
| *Supervisor:* | Therefore therapy is being driven for your benefit, not the client's. Do you want to retain this attitude? |
| *Supervisee:* | No, I don't. I know it's getting in the way of the client's progress and mine as well. |
| *Supervisor:* | So what are you going to do about it? |
| *Supervisee:* | Do what I should be doing with the client. In other words, helping them to examine their unhealthy and healthy attitudes from all sides and encouraging them to move forward with their flexible and non-extreme attitudes. But first getting my own house in order and developing my own healthy attitude and going forward with this in place when working with this and other clients. |
| *Supervisor:* | Which attitude would be? |
| *Supervisee:* | Self-acceptance, no matter what the client thinks of me. |
| *Supervisor:* | When you've developed that attitude, how will therapy be different? |
| *Supervisee:* | I'll be focused on encouraging the client to deal with their problems and I won't be avoiding confronting them if it seems therapeutically necessary. |
| *Supervisor:* | Good. Struggling with your problems on your own for a while may provide you with some insights as to what your clients are going through. It's a valuable learning experience. |
| *Supervisee:* | I'm already feeling more confident about the next therapy session. |

In this supervision extract, important points to consider are the following:

1. REBT practitioners are not noted for their soothing approach to problem-solving, yet the supervisee adopts it to sidestep dealing with the client's

homework avoidance, angry outbursts and any other difficult or painful issue that arises. This alerts the supervisor to the probability that the supervisee has some operative rigid and extreme attitudes.

2.  The supervisor's use of such terms as 'easy ride' and 'soft-pedalling' suggest that their hypothesis is that the supervisee has approval needs which they subsequently confirm (looking for an 'easy time' in therapy may also indicate attitudes of unbearability).

3.  In their desperation to be liked by the client, the supervisee has lost their clinical focus and thereby therapy has foundered. In making their self-devaluation attitude explicit, the supervisee now has the opportunity to put therapy back on track if they undisturb themself first.

4.  The supervisor encourages the supervisee to describe how they would act differently and efficiently in therapy if they learned self-acceptance as a further inducement to remove their own rigid and extreme thinking.

5.  Also the supervisor echoes Ellis's (1985: 170) point that 'if you try to change yourself, at first, without guidance and support from another therapist, you may be able to appreciate better the struggles of your own clients when they strive for self-change'.

## When Therapists Create an Aura of Omniscience

This occurs when therapists convince themselves that their particular brand of psychotherapy is able to explain all aspects of psychological disturbance and its amelioration rather than viewing it as an incomplete and provisional account of these processes. Armed with such an understanding of human behaviour that is not liable to be wrong, they conduct therapy with an Olympian disregard of or a condescension to clients' explanations of their problems. Here is an example not to emulate.

| | |
|---|---|
| *Therapist:* | Do you know why you get so upset when your husband pays no attention to you? |
| *Client:* | Well, it's only natural if he ignores me when I want a cuddle and a bit of affection. |
| *Therapist:* | No, that doesn't really account for it. Shall I tell you why? |
| *Client:* | I'd like to find out if I'm doing the wrong things. |
| *Therapist:* | Because you're demanding that he must show you affection in order to prove that he still loves you. For without his love you see yourself as worthless. |
| *Client:* | I don't see it like that. |
| *Therapist:* | Not yet, but you will in time. |

The therapist has no real interest in the client's replies to their questions or the client's comments: these are just used as springboards for the therapist to display their godlike wisdom. Instead of creating a genuinely therapeutic and collaborative relationship, the therapist's conception of it is that of deity and devotee.

In order to avoid developing pretensions to divinity, REBT therapists are recommended to do the following:

• Acknowledge their own frequent fallibility and, if clinically relevant, share this with their clients.
• Develop a healthy scepticism towards REBT and thereby be aware of its limitations and weaknesses.
• Employ humour against themselves if they start to yearn for infallibility.
• Show their clients that by helping them (i.e. the clients) they have gained for themselves further therapeutic skills and experience.
• Let clients arrive at their own insights into their problems through Socratic questioning and avoid handing them down on tablets of stone.

In the above dialogue, even if the therapist's hypothesis is correct, there are more client-friendly and introspective ways of confirming it.

### Guarding against Injudicious Self-Disclosure

Injudicious use of therapist self-disclosure may occur because therapists do not adhere to the 'one rule that seems inviolate … the therapist is there to give therapy, not to get it. Therapists who share problems in hopes of getting them solved cheat the clients' (Wessler and Wessler, 1980: 170). Therapists who use therapy for their own needs rather than their clients' probably subscribe to a major therapist rigid attitude: 'Because I am a person in my own right, I must be able to enjoy myself during therapy sessions and to use these sessions to solve my personal problems as well as to help my clients' (Ellis, 2002: 207). As the therapist guides the course of therapy and takes the lead in developing the therapeutic alliance, these crucial activities will be undermined as the therapist's attention and energy is diverted into exploring their own problems.

Another reason for inappropriate self-disclosure is not so much a working through of the therapist's problems, but a narcissistic assumption that the therapist's own life experiences and difficulties will be of universal interest and relevance, e.g., 'My own experiences, while not similar to yours, will nevertheless be of real help to you'. Or the therapist has been afflicted with every known problem and is quick to share this with the client but comes across as falsely empathic, e.g. 'I know exactly how you feel. I went through the same thing when it happened to me'. Clients may not appreciate being so well understood so quickly and therefore feel they are not being listened to or that the uniqueness of their problems is being devalued.

Whatever the reasons for the therapist's lack of verbal restraint, the only valid use of self-disclosure is when it is clinically relevant: therapists say that they have experienced a problem and accompanying rigid and extreme attitudes similar to those of the client and how they eventually prevailed through a variety of REBT methods. Clinical relevance is ascertained through feedback from clients – if they derive no benefit from such information, then therapists should discontinue the use of this technique. It is also good practice to ask if the client might be interested in hearing about the therapist's own experience in solving similar problems to the client.

### To Disclose or Not to Disclose

Therapist disclosure may be initiated by clients in an attempt to determine if the therapist can really understand their problems, e.g. 'Have you ever been an alcoholic?' The therapist difficulty here is that a reply of 'Yes' can cement the working alliance because the client believes he has found a kindred spirit who can help him, or destroy it because such a revelation has lost the respect of the client, who was seeking a relationship based on the therapist's expertise untainted by personal experience of their problem. On the other hand, a reply of 'No' may lose the client who wants to see a former-addict-turned-therapist but relieve the client who believes that a true professional understands but avoids the pitfalls of their clients. There is no easy answer to this dilemma except to answer honestly to such self-revelatory questions and tackle the reasons why some clients will want to leave therapy on the basis of the therapist's reply.

### Dealing with the 'Neurotic Agreement in Psychotherapy'

The 'neurotic agreement in psychotherapy' is a term used by Hauck (1966) to describe a therapist's failure or reluctance to examine their client's rigid/extreme attitudes because they hold the same attitudes, e.g., 'I must have a romantic relationship in my life, and if I don't I am not worthwhile'. Knowing that their own responses to the client's same attitudes will not be particularly convincing and wanting to avoid seeing themself reflected in the client's problem, the clinical focus is switched to other, possibly less important, issues. This results in the therapeutic alliance working at less than optimum effectiveness.

Another form of therapist avoidance which impairs the alliance is the delay in 'getting down to business' because the therapist enjoys the client's company and wants to prolong it, e.g. 'I see so many clients who I find difficult or unpleasant that when I find someone I really like, I deserve to have an easy and pleasurable time in therapy'. This easy-going approach of the therapist's may dovetail with the client's attitudes of unbearability (e.g., 'I can't bear hard work') to produce a relationship based on short-range hedonism and not on a business-like approach to problem-solving.

In both cases, the therapists are putting their own interests first and thereby leaving important client problems unexamined. By examining the rigid/extreme attitudes underpinning their own conditional self-acceptance and deservingness, the therapists will not only undisturb themselves about these issues but also return therapy to where it belongs – firmly focused on their clients' disturbances.

### When Therapists Are Intransigent

Sometimes therapists can dogmatically insist that their hypotheses or interpretations of the clients' problems are correct and therefore are not prepared to consider any disagreements from the clients, e.g. 'You're still demanding today that your parents should have stayed together when you were young and thereby none of your future problems would have occurred. You are refusing to accept this truth'. In fact, the more their clients do not accept their viewpoint, the more convinced the therapists are of their perceptual accuracy. Such conflict can obviously lead to an impasse in therapy or to early termination. The reasons for the therapist's intransigence can be uncovered in supervision.

---

*Supervisor:* Why have you turned what should be a tentative and flexible hypothesis into a rigid one?

*Supervisee:* I know I'm right about this client. I feel it so strongly.

*Supervisor:* As you know, feelings are not facts and therefore are unreliable guides to the accuracy of any particular interpretation: why must you be right?

*Supervisee:* Because it will prove that I am a highly competent therapist who can see through the client's smokescreen.

*Supervisor:* But the client does not agree with your interpretation and I doubt if they see you as highly competent.

*Supervisee:* Well, that just proves how resistant they are being.

*Supervisor:* Even if you are right, why does the client have to agree with you?

*Supervisee:* Because they are still disturbed about their parents' divorce when they were little, so why can't they admit it and be honest?

*Supervisor:* There appear to be two rigid/extreme and therapy-blocking attitudes at work here. The first one is that your hypothesis must be right and if it is not, you will see yourself as a poor or lousy therapist. The second one is that you can't bear it when clients deny their disturbances. What do you think about my hypotheses?

*Supervisee (pauses):* I notice you're offering them to me rather than imposing them. I'm reluctant to say it, but they do have the ring of truth about them.

*Supervisor:*  OK. Let's take the first idea. Who defines you as a lousy therapist if your hypothesis is wrong?

*Supervisee:*  I do.

*Supervisor:*  Is being wrong a sign of a lousy therapist or what …?

*Supervisee:*  It's actually a sign of being an open-minded, flexible, scientific REBT practitioner who is not afraid to discard their assumptions if they're wrong.

*Supervisor:*  Exactly. Your present anti-scientific stance is more likely to drive clients out of therapy rather than keep them in it. So what are you going to do about it?

*Supervisee:*  Start by admitting that my hypothesis may well be wrong and examining the data with the client in order to confirm, revise or reject it.

*Supervisor:*  Remember, hypothesis testing occurs throughout the course of therapy and not just at the beginning. Now, if you follow the actual practice of
REBT, you will more likely become a skilled therapist.

*Supervisee:*  That's what I want.

*Supervisor:*  Then it's best to keep your ego out of therapy and you'll find that you're much less disturbable and thereby of much more help to the clients. Now, your second rigid/extreme attitude – why does your client have to admit that they are disturbed over this issue?

*Supervisee:*  Because if the client admits it, then they can deal with it. By not doing so, they are pretending everything is all right. I can't stand the pretence.

*Supervisor:*  It seems you're more interested in destroying the client's supposed pretence rather than dispassionately looking for evidence that it exists. Why can't they keep up this pretence throughout therapy if they want to?

*Supervisee:*  Because it rankles so. I know they're doing it, but they won't admit it.

*Supervisor:*  It seems to me that your ego is again on the line – in order to prove you're a smart therapist and this client can't pull the wool over your eyes, you have to be the winner in this battle of wills. Does that sound plausible?

*Supervisee (sighs):*  Yeah, the ego thing is getting in the way again.

*Supervisor:*  If clients do want to play games or pretend everything is OK – and I'm not saying this client is – they lose out because they remain emotionally disturbed, but you don't have to disturb yourself over it. Now I suggest for homework that you list

> the short- and long-term advantages and disadvantages of ego-driven therapy. What do you think of that suggestion?
>
> *Supervisee:* I think that will help me to gain more objectivity about my behaviour in therapy as well as to become more clinically competent. I can see more clearly now how I'm blocking myself and therapy.
>
> *Supervisor:* Good. We'll review your progress at the next session.

In this extract from supervision, the supervisor is showing the supervisee/therapist the following points:

1. The therapist's self-disturbance arises from their rigid and extreme attitudes towards the client's problems rather than the client's purported reluctance to accept the therapist's interpretations. The therapist's insistence on proving themself right is driving therapy into a cul-de-sac, and they are displaying all the qualities that are antithetical to the practice of good REBT.
2. Hypotheses are not copper-bottomed facts but only provisional explanations that can be confirmed or repudiated. Teaching by example, the supervisor offers their own hypothesis to the therapist that each rigid/extreme attitude involves the latter nailing their credibility to the mast – to admit they might be wrong would signal their failure as a therapist.
3. The therapist agrees with the supervisor's assumptions and is encouraged to look at disinterested ways of gathering assessment information and thereby avoiding power struggles with their client. The supervisor's suggestion 'to keep your ego out of therapy' means that the therapist's fortunes will not be rising and falling like the stock exchange depending on how the client is faring, responding or behaving.
4. Becoming less disturbable will enable the therapist to improve their clinical skills and thereby become a competent therapist – the homework task (and others of similar ilk) will help the therapist to reach their goal whereas their own battering ram approach to therapy blocked them from achieving it.

### Guarding against the Inappropriate Use of Humour

Ellis (1985) frequently stated that one of the major causes of emotional disturbance is when individuals take themselves, their problems and life *too* seriously. Therefore the use of humour can be an effective intervention in helping clients to combat their disturbance-producing attitudes, but is not meant to be directed at the clients themselves. However, some therapists might believe that the general use of humour is in itself therapeutic and always aim for a 'fun-filled hour', or they become so enamoured with their putative wit that they are oblivious to its grating effect upon the client. Other therapists' inappropriate use of humour may stem from a major therapist rigid/extreme attitude that 'I must be able to enjoy myself during therapy sessions and I can't bear it when I don't' (Ellis, 1985, 2002). The net result of such behaviour is that clients may feel they are being laughed at, their problems trivialised, or they are supposed to be the admiring spectators of the therapist's comic performance.

When the therapist has made a humorous response to a client's statement, e.g., the client says that their drinking 'crept up on me' and the therapist mimics their statement by using a bottle to creep up their own body and put itself into their mouth, the therapist needs to gain immediate feedback from the client as to their interpretation of this behaviour. Did the client see the clinical relevance of this act? Did the humour help or hinder the issue of personal responsibility for one's problems? Was the humour used in a constructive or insulting way? If the client's reactions are generally negative to such questions, the further use of humour should be ruled out.

### Being Careful about the Use of Profane Language

Albert Ellis, the founder of REBT, was well known for his use of swearwords, but this is not a requirement to practise as an REBT therapist. Ellis's use of profanity is not gratuitous but serves to, among other things, build rapport with certain clients (e.g. a person whose conversation is splattered with expletives) in order to strengthen the therapeutic alliance as well as to highlight certain points, e.g. 'Why the FUCK do you always have to succeed?' As with humour, profanity is aimed at the client's self-defeating thinking and not at the client.

Some therapists may think that profanity is an important part of an REBT therapist's repertoire in their response to clients' rigid and extreme attitudes and, in a misguided attempt to emulate Ellis, arbitrarily introduce swearing into therapy in order to invigorate it, 'grab the client's attention' or indulge themself. This may well have the opposite effect upon some clients, who think they could not reveal intimate details about themselves to such 'a foulmouthed person' and consequently terminate therapy. Therapists should note whether the client uses swearwords as an indicator that profanity might be warranted or pay attention to the client's preferences for a particular type of relationship, e.g. a formal or down-to-earth one, in order to determine the content of the language they will use.

The concept of 'shithood' is frequently used in REBT and refers to individuals who see themselves as completely worthless, inadequate, incompetent etc. These epithets may be synonymous with shithood in the minds of REBT therapists but not necessarily in their clients.

| | |
|---|---|
| *Client:* | I see myself as a total failure. It's been like that for a long time. I try to fight against it but nothing works. |
| *Therapist:* | OK, so you see yourself as a complete shit. Now, what are the factors that lead you to believe … |

> *Client:*    Hold on a minute! I said I saw myself as a failure, not a shit. If I want to be insulted I can stay at home and do it myself.

To avoid such a blunder, therapists should employ only clients' terms of self-devaluation in their efforts to understand clients' perceptions and evaluations of reality. In the above example, the client may have been struggling to maintain a sense of dignity in the face of repeated failure which the use of the word 'shit' may rob them of. The concept of 'shithood' can be introduced into therapy for clients' consideration and not suddenly unleashed upon them.

### Guarding against Making Moral Judgements

Ellis (1985: 28) suggested that 'a trait that many therapists possess and that blocks them in helping clients is their moralism: the profound tendency to condemn themselves and others for evil or stupid acts'. Such moralism may lead to explicit criticism of the client, e.g. 'How in heaven's name are we supposed to make progress with your problems when you keep on turning up late?' or non-verbal signals of condemnation such as drumming one's fingers on the table, not smiling, looking impatient, not listening. This kind of therapist behaviour will often help clients to reinforce their self-devaluation tendencies and thereby they end up even more disturbed than they were at the outset of therapy. This outcome makes it highly likely that some of these clients will find it very difficult to engage fully with the REBT process. The therapist's moralistic attitudes are examined in the following dialogue in supervision.

> *Supervisee:*    The client's hopeless. We waste so much therapy time with their lateness when we could be tackling their problems.
>
> *Supervisor:*    So you think that the client must behave in the right and proper fashion by being punctual. They must act responsibly.
>
> *Supervisee:*    Exactly. If they want help, they must get to therapy on time.
>
> *Supervisor:*    Now, something strikes me as very odd: if the client is emotionally disturbed, this is obviously affecting their time-keeping, yet you demand responsible behaviour, so they will have to undisturb themself first in order to be punctual. So how is the client supposed to achieve that when by your own account they are becoming more, not less, disturbed?
>
> *Supervisee:*    I really don't know. They're pathetic.
>
> *Supervisor:*    Devaluing your client is not going to make them feel better or get to therapy on time. Your client is a fallible, not a damnable human being. Now, why does your client have to do the right thing rather than it would be preferable if they did it?

*Supervisee:*   Because I would turn up on time if I wanted help, so they too should make the effort.

*Supervisor:*   But you are imposing your moral values on your client and thereby clouding your clinical judgement. You're also depriving them of their individuality by demanding they act like you. Do you want to truly help your client or just get them to jump through your moral hoops?

*Supervisee:*   I want to help them, of course.

*Supervisor:*   Now, why does the client have to get to therapy on time?

*Supervisee:*   They don't, but I still think poor timekeeping is nothing to admire.

*Supervisor:*   I'm not asking you to admire it, and you can point out to them in a non-devaluing way that it is interfering with reaching their goals. Now, you will need to change the way you relate to this client if you want to achieve progress.

*Supervisee:*   You mean offer them unconditional acceptance as a fallible human being.

*Supervisor:*   That's exactly what REBT advocates. Now, if you work hard to achieve this, how might therapy be different?

*Supervisee:*   Well, I'd stop moralising and looking down on the client. We'd probably have a more relaxed time in therapy.

*Supervisor:*   And they may well feel you are now on their side rather than always disapproving of them. Now, what would you do about the client's timekeeping?

*Supervisee:*   Look at the reasons for the client's lack of punctuality and take constructive steps to tackle it.

*Supervisor:*   Now, how can disturbed clients suddenly undisturb themselves to get to therapy on time?

*Supervisee (laughs):*   It sounds silly now. If the client could do that, they probably wouldn't need to see me in the first place.

*Supervisor:*   Probably not. Now how would you react if I devalued you for devaluing the client?

*Supervisee:*   I'd get angry or feel bad.

*Supervisor:*   Would you be eager to come to supervision?

*Supervisee:*   I'd look for ways to avoid it or, I hate to say it, get here late.

*Supervisor:*   None of us likes to feel the moral lash across our backs, and it doesn't usually produce improved behaviour.

*Supervisee:*   Well, I'll try to keep the moralising to my own life then.

*Supervisor:*   You might find that if you brought some flexibility to your own moral standards, you wouldn't be so harsh on the client when they fall below the standards you currently demand of yourself.

| | |
|---|---|
| *Supervisee:* | That's true. I give myself a hard time as well as my client. |
| *Supervisor:* | It sounds like your client is not the only one then who needs to receive unconditional acceptance. Within such a context, you can respond to their as well as your own behaviour with acceptance, not devaluation. |
| *Supervisee:* | There's a lot to think about today. |
| *Supervisor:* | And to put into practice. We'll see how you've got on at the next session. |
| *Supervisee:* | OK. |

Important points to consider in this extract are the following:

1. The only judgements to be made in therapy are clinical, not moral ones. Judging clients on the basis of their bad or irresponsible behaviour militates against building a therapeutic alliance, but the acts themselves can be judged as to whether they help or hinder clients from achieving their goals. Demanding morally correct or healthy behaviour from disturbed individuals is in itself a sign of psychological disturbance or, at least, muddled thinking.
2. The supervisor asks the therapist (supervisee) to envisage the probable benefits that they and their client will enjoy if they offer the client unconditional acceptance rather than moral disapproval. In such a non-judgemental climate, therapy can revert to its proper focus on the client's problems starting with their poor timekeeping.
3. The supervisor encourages the therapist to see therapy from the client's viewpoint by asking them how they would react if the supervisor condemned them for condemning the client. This altered perspective prompts the therapist to begin an empathic understanding of the client's feelings.
4. Inflicting the 'moral lash' on ourselves or others does not usually lead to better behaviour as we avoid trying to understand these failings and, instead, only condemn them and ourselves. Therefore, if the therapist introduces flexibility and self-acceptance into their own moral values, they will be more likely to show compassion towards the client and thereby forge a genuine working alliance.

### When Therapists Lecture Clients

Some therapists may indulge in long or too frequent lectures on various aspects of REBT without obtaining feedback from clients. Their eagerness for didactic presentations will probably dull their sensitivity to cues that clients are not listening to them.

Clients can become resentful of such an incessant lecturing style and yearn for the end of the session or start daydreaming because they feel uninvolved in therapy.

Generally speaking, too much didactic teaching from the therapist can inhibit clients' ability to think for themselves, turn them into passive rather than active collaborators in therapy and bring about only superficial changes in their problems.

If therapists are going to give lectures, these should be small, concise and infrequent, and after each one they should obtain feedback from their clients that they have made themselves understood, e.g. 'Can you put into your own words the importance of self-acceptance?' Therapists can also monitor their therapy recordings for evidence of counterproductive lecturing.

### Guarding against Using a Monolithic Interactional Style

Some therapists use an unvarying interactional style with their clients. Instead of being responsive to their clients' preferences for a particular bond (e.g. informal and humorous; formal and serious), therapists are reluctant or unable to modulate their interactional style. This may lead to a clash of styles as their standard no-nonsense, 'let's get on with it' approach is constantly halted by their clients' requests for a quieter and more reflective manner. If clients' interpersonal behaviour is also inflexible, little therapeutic progress can be imagined.

Kwee and Lazarus (1986) suggest that therapists adopt the role of an 'authentic chameleon' which would allow them to display the most helpful facets of their personality in building rapport with a particular client while remaining genuine in the process. Flexibility is the hallmark of the 'authentic chameleon' as the therapist adapts to and blends in with the requirements of the therapeutic alliance at any given time. The only caveat to this approach is if the client's bond preferences reinforce existing problems, e.g. wanting excessive warmth from the therapist to sustain the client's approval needs. If some therapists are reluctant to adopt this role, possible rigid and extreme attitudes can be revealed and examined, e.g., 'I must practise REBT in the way that is natural to me and not have to pander to what my client wants' or 'I won't feel like myself in therapy and therefore I'll be very uncomfortable and I couldn't bear that'. For those therapists who are unfamiliar with the concept of the 'authentic chameleon' and struggle to put it into practice with clients, they can practise varying their interactional styles with their supervisor or others, e.g. family, friends or colleagues.

### Dealing with Countertransference

The term 'countertransference' is used to denote the feelings and attitudes of the therapist towards the client. These may be transferred on to the client from the therapist's reactions to significant others in the therapist's life, e.g. 'I can't stand people like my mother who endlessly whinge and whine'. The therapist's barely suppressed hostility towards or impatience with the client is highly unlikely to engender a therapeutic milieu as is shown below.

*Supervisor:* You are obviously more focused on what you despise about the client than you are on helping her.

*Supervisee:* I know. As soon as the client starts moaning, she reminds me of my mother's behaviour and this sets me on edge.

*Supervisor:* What's the rigid and extreme attitude at work here?

*Supervisee:* Well, I suppose she should bloody well stop moaning, otherwise I can't bear it.

*Supervisor:* Now if you really examined this attitude and showed yourself that you could bear the client's moaning, how would this change your interaction with her?

*Supervisee:* I'd be much calmer with her and I would pay close attention to the content of her moaning in order to uncover the attitudes maintaining it. At present, I switch off.

*Supervisor:* So you would become emotionally undisturbed and clinically focused because your attitude would be ...?

*Supervisee:* She should be that way because she is that way. As soon as I accept the reality of the situation, I might be able to help her do something about it and, if I can't, I don't have to disturb myself about that either.

*Supervisor:* Good. If you wish, you might also apply this approach to your mother. Desirable changes can then be brought about in both relationships.

*Supervisee:* I really do want to improve my performance in therapy and get on better with my mother, so I will work to develop an 'I can bear it' attitude towards both my mother and my client who reminds me of my mother.

*Supervisor:* We'll see if it's working when we next listen to your therapy recordings.

The therapist's reaction to the client may provide useful information about the impact the client may have on other people, e.g. 'I wonder if my anxiety around my client is reflected in other people's attitudes to them?' With this kind of reaction, Walen et al. (1992: 246) observe that countertransference 'enables you [the therapist] to use yourself as a monitoring device'. For example, the therapist dreads the appointment time because they will have to face the client's obnoxious behaviour; they feel as if they are walking on eggshells during therapy and experiences tremendous relief at the end of each session. The therapist's rigid/extreme attitude in this case might be: 'I must avoid at all costs my client losing their temper. If they do, it will be awful'. Once the therapist's attitude has been identified, examined and changed, they can then from a non-disturbed viewpoint disclose to the client the unpleasant effect they have on them (the therapist) and by extension the impact they may have on others in their life. Such information can help the client to develop more constructive and rewarding ways of behaving in relationships.

Therapists may develop non-countertransference relationship problems as when, for example, they find themselves sexually attracted to some of their clients. Instead of establishing an early problem-solving focus, the therapist may spend an inordinate amount of time building up the supposedly therapeutic relationship, indulging in mild flirtation and generally having a good time. Therapy is prolonged for the therapist's benefit while solving the client's problems is put on a slow track. Although the therapist may well be reluctant to, they need to give themself the attitude-examining equivalent of a cold shower:

| | |
|---|---|
| *Therapist:* | I'm their therapist, not a potential lover. It would have been nice if I had met them socially but as I didn't, too bad. I'm going to focus my mind on their problems and not on their body. If I can't make the adjustment, then I will refer the client to someone who can. |

## When Therapists Think that They Have to Be Outstanding

Ellis (1985, 2002) identified the following therapist rigid attitude: 'I must be an outstanding therapist, clearly better than other therapists I know or hear about'. Therapists who hold this attitude may be frantic to succeed with clients who have not made progress with a string of previous therapists or are deemed to be 'therapy proof'; agree to unrealistic client goals (e.g. 'I never want to experience another panic attack'); or refuse to acknowledge the limited gains that some or many clients will only achieve as they struggle to wring the last drop of progress out of them. In addition, they may deny they have any emotional problems because this is incompatible with being an 'outstanding therapist'. These various problems result in therapy being driven by the therapist's vanity and panic to succeed – the very opposite of therapeutic efficiency and possibly leading to therapist burnout.

Without encouraging such therapists to lower their standards, the supervisor can help them to transmute this rigid attitude into a flexible one, surrender their god-like pretensions and acknowledge their fallibility. With this attitude, vanity can be replaced by humility and panic by calm deliberation. Such methods will help to avoid burnout and, instead, encourage therapists to strive for the highest possible level of clinical competence.

In this chapter, I have looked at ways of dealing with therapist-created obstacles to client change in the bonds domain of the working alliance. I now turn attention to therapist-created obstacles to client change in the views domain of the alliance and particularly therapists' doubts or reservations about the REBT's *ABC* framework of emotional disturbance.

Chapter 8

# Dealing with Therapist Obstacles to Client Change in the Views Domain of the Working Alliance

I mentioned in the Preface that I added a fourth domain to Bordin's (1979) tripartite view of the working alliance. I called this domain 'views' in that they describe the ideas that therapists and clients hold about therapy (Dryden, 2006, 2011). These ideas concern:

- The practicalities of therapy (e.g. fees, frequency of sessions, the therapist's cancellation policy).
- Confidentiality and its limits.
- How the client's problems are conceptualised and how treatment of these problems is conceived.

In Chapter 3, I outlined how therapists are advised to respond to client obstacles to client change in the views domain of the alliance and in this chapter I focus on therapist obstacles to client change largely relating to their views concerning REBT's *ABC* framework and how to teach it to clients. However, I also discuss more generally about spotting and dealing with therapist obstacles to client change in the views domain of the alliance.

## Avoiding Being Dogmatic Concerning What Therapy Should Be About

REBT therapists tend to see clients as experts on their own experience and themselves as experts on REBT and the conduct of therapy. That being said, perhaps the principle that REBT values above all others is anti-dogmatism or flexibility. This means that while therapists may have a clear idea of their clients' problems and how these can best be tackled, how many sessions clients need and how often they need to meet, it is important that therapists hold and convey to clients that they hold flexible ideas on such points. Let's illustrate this point by comparing an REBT therapist who has rigid ideas about how many sessions a client needs with the same therapist who has flexible ideas about this issue.

DOI: 10.4324/9781003423379-10

| | |
|---|---|
| *Client:* | Can I ask you a question about therapy? |
| *Therapist:* | Sure. |
| *Client:* | How many sessions do you think I need? |
| *Therapist:* | Well, based on what you have told me, I would say twenty sessions would be necessary to deal with the problems you outlined. |
| *Client:* | Oh! That is quite a lot. |
| *Therapist:* | Well, that is what's required. |
| *Client (hesitantly):* | Well, I will have to think about that. |

Note here that the therapist did not even ask the client for their views on the issue. The therapist answers the question honestly, but gave themselves and the client no room for manoeuvre (a sure sign of rigidity) and no space for negotiation.

Now let's see what happens when the therapist is flexible about the issue:

| | |
|---|---|
| *Client:* | Can I ask you a question about therapy? |
| *Therapist:* | Sure. |
| *Client:* | How many sessions do you think I need? |
| *Therapist:* | Well, based on what you have told me, I would say twenty sessions would be necessary to deal with the problems you outlined. |
| *Client:* | Oh! That is quite a lot. |
| *Therapist:* | You seem quite shocked? |
| *Client:* | Well, I know I have a lot of issues to deal with, but I am concerned about the cost of therapy. |
| *Therapist:* | I can understand that. Based on what I've said and what you can afford, do you have a suggestion about the number of sessions? |
| *Client:* | Well, I think about five. |
| *Therapist:* | Well, if that is all you can afford, let's go with that. We will need to be clear what problems we can realistically tackle in the time though. |
| *Client:* | I appreciate that. Perhaps I could afford a little more ... say eight sessions? |
| *Therapist:* | Shall we agree on eight sessions? If later, you want to change that, let's discuss the issue. OK? |
| *Client:* | OK, and thanks for being flexible. |

In the second sequence, the therapist is flexible and is thus able to invite the client to give an opinion. This leads to a productive negotiation and an agreement to eight sessions which is probably eight sessions more than the client would have signed up for in the first sequence.

Let me make one important point. Being flexible does not preclude therapists from having strong views and from expressing them when called for. It also does not preclude therapists refusing to work with clients who want something unethical (e.g. therapy with absolute confidentiality when the therapist cannot offer this). However, flexibility does mean that therapists can make compromises when their ideal views on therapy are not shared by their clients.

## Dealing with Therapists' Doubts, Reservations and Objections to Accepting or Teaching the ABC Framework

The *ABC* framework represents the cornerstone of REBT theory and practice and asserts that individuals largely disturb themselves by the attitudes they hold towards life's adversities rather than by the adversities themselves, e.g. someone blames their depression on the breakup of their marriage and not on their rigid view that their partner should never have left them. This view of the causation of emotional disturbance is opposed by other therapy approaches, flies in the face of what many people would see as sheer common sense and is out-of-step with societal trends which increasingly encourage people to blame others for their problems (and sue them if possible). In Chapter 3, I discussed clients' doubts, reservations and objections (DROs) to accepting the *ABC* framework. Therapists also struggle at times in teaching the framework to their clients because they have DROs to its applicability to every human problem including their own, its lack of subtlety or complexity in explaining human behaviour and its remorselessness in uncovering self-induced disturbance through rigid and extreme thinking. This chapter examines these and other problems and suggest ways in which therapists' DROs can be addressed.

## When Therapists Think that Their Clients' Unhealthy Anger Is Self-Created, But Their Own Unhealthy Anger Isn't

Therapists can often work hard to convince clients of their self-created disturbance yet in their own lives distance themselves from this view because they consider their own problems to be of a different or higher order than those of the clients they counsel. With these therapists, the *ABC* framework usually stays in the therapy room. In the following excerpt, the supervisor attempts to understand the therapist's reluctance to apply the framework to their own problems.[1]

*Supervisor:*    You've said that when you use the *ABC* framework with your client, it has great conceptual clarity for you in understanding

|           |                                                                                                                                                                                                                                        |
|-----------|----------------------------------------------------------------------------------------------------------------------------------------------------------------------------------------------------------------------------------------|
|           | how they make themself angry. Now why does this clarity fade when you consider your own anger?                                                                                                                                          |
| *Supervisee:* | Well, the client keeps on disturbing themself because they are demanding that their train, bus, tube, whatever, should always be on time especially when they have to get to meetings. As this is not the case in life, it's easy to see what's going on. |
| *Supervisor:* | And in your case …?                                                                                                                                                                                                                     |
| *Supervisee:* | It's much more complex and can't be as easily explained by the *ABC* framework.                                                                                                                                                        |
| *Supervisor:* | How so?                                                                                                                                                                                                                                 |
| *Supervisee:* | My anger is created by the injustices in the world such as experiments on animals, racial discrimination, famine in the Third World. These are major issues in life, not whether my train is late or not.                               |
| *Supervisor:* | Well, the train being late might be a major issue for the client if they have an important meeting to attend, but you see your anger as righteous or noble rather than small-minded.                                                     |
| *Supervisee:* | Yeah, that's a good way of putting it.                                                                                                                                                                                                  |
| *Supervisor:* | These injustices do obviously exist, so what is your attitude to them? Some people wouldn't get angry over them because they couldn't care less.                                                                                        |
| *Supervisee:* | I know what you're trying to manoeuvre me to say: that these injustices absolutely shouldn't exist in the world.                                                                                                                        |
| *Supervisor:* | I'm just trying to tease out what your attitude is in order to compare it with your client's. Because as you know, REBT holds that rigid attitudes are the foundation of emotional disturbance.                                          |
| *Supervisee:* | It's hard to explain my attitude without that word 'should' getting in the way.                                                                                                                                                         |
| *Supervisor:* | Well, just say what's in your mind.                                                                                                                                                                                                     |
| *Supervisee:* | OK. These injustices should not be allowed to exist. They violate my principles of what should constitute a fair and just world.                                                                                                        |
| *Supervisor:* | Would you agree that your and your client's anger both stem from the same attitudinal source?                                                                                                                                           |
| *Supervisee:* | Yes, reluctantly. I know we're both demanding that what exists at any given time should not exist: their train being late, my injustices occurring.                                                                                     |
| *Supervisor:* | Exactly. You're both refusing to accept empirical reality. Now, if you both gave up your demandingness, obviously these things would still occur, but what might be some of the benefits?                                                |
| *Supervisee:* | Well, I'll probably generate more light and less heat.                                                                                                                                                                                  |
| *Supervisor:* | In what way?                                                                                                                                                                                                                            |

*Supervisee:* Less ranting and raving for a start. I'd spend more time collecting signatures for petitions, canvassing for support, letter writing, peaceful protests. That sort of thing.

*Supervisor:* And for the client?

*Supervisee:* They wouldn't suffer double jeopardy: not only is their train late but also they get to meetings in a foul mood and can't concentrate on them. The client could prepare on the train in a constructive way.

*Supervisor:* Good. Do you now accept that, in essence, you disturb yourself in the same way as your client?

*Supervisee:* Yes, I do but I still see my anger as more justifiable than my client's.

*Supervisor:* Well, however you describe your anger, it still has the same potentially destructive effects on you as your client. Now there is one way that you can both can use the word 'should' in your attitudes towards your respective adversities and be what we call in REBT healthily angry not unhealthily angry. Do you know how you can both do this?

*Supervisee:* I know there are different 'shoulds', but I am not quite with you.

*Supervisor:* Well, how would your client feel if they held the following attitude, 'Ideally my train should be on time, but sadly and regretfully, it does not have to do the ideal thing'?

*Supervisee:* Annoyed, but not unhealthily angry. I see what you mean.

*Supervisor:* Can you apply this to your own situation?

*Supervisee:* OK. Let me see. 'Ideally, injustices should not exist and ideally the world should be fair, but sadly and regretfully such ideal conditions don't have to exist in the world, even though I really want them to.'

*Supervisor:* How do you feel when you hold this attitude?

*Supervisee:* I'm still angry but healthily so. It's the kind of anger that will help me to do something about injustice rather than be paralysed in an angry rage.

*Supervisor:* See if you can implement this with your client and in your own life, and let's see what happens. OK?

*Supervisee:* OK. I will do that.

In this extract from supervision, the supervisor makes a number of important points:

1.  The *ABC* framework can be used to understand the causation and maintenance of anyone's unhealthy anger and whether it is labelled 'small minded' or 'noble'

is irrelevant from the REBT viewpoint. Unhealthy anger is unhealthy anger and stems from the same attitudinal roots of dogmatic musts and shoulds.

2. Even though the therapist (supervisee) believes they are being manoeuvred into saying what they believe their supervisor wants to hear, they eventually cannot avoid revealing their unhealthy anger-producing 'shoulds' about injustices in the world. This confirms their implicit rigid attitude, while the client's disturbance-creating ideas were easy to detect as they were explicitly stated.

3. Both therapist and client are refusing to acknowledge that what exists is bound to exist given the conditions that are present at that moment – this is one of two definitions of acceptance in REBT. Therefore, both of them are disturbing themselves because they do not accept empirical reality.

4. The supervisor draws out from the therapist the benefits of acceptance for themself and their client. This acts as an inducement for the therapist to work harder on both themself to change their unhealthy anger as well as with the client to change theirs.

5. The therapist still clings to the idea that their anger is more 'justifiable' than the client's, but the supervisor points out that the potentially destructive effects of sustained unhealthy anger do not discriminate between individuals or the labels they use.

6. Finally, the supervisor helps the therapist to discriminate between an ideal but non-absolute 'should' and an absolute should. The supervisor shows holding the former leads to healthy anger that can prompt constructive action while the latter leads to unhealthy anger which tends to paralyse the person and prevents constructive action.

## When Therapists Think that the *ABC* Framework Is Crudely Reductionist

Some REBT therapists believe that the *ABC* framework is an unsubtle or crude means of understanding emotional disturbance because all the therapist really wants to know is: 'Where's the must?' No matter what the presenting problem is or the level of emotional disturbance displayed, all the therapist is concerned about is demonstrating to clients the presence of an implicit or explicit rigid attitude underlying their problems. This can give the impression that REBT places all clients on a Procrustean bed and thereby discredits the idea of the uniqueness of each client and the complexity of human behaviour. These and other concerns are explored in the following excerpt.

*Supervisee:* It seems to me that we are just imposing our views on the client.
*Supervisor:* Why imposing our views rather than offering them?
*Supervisee:* Well, imposing or offering, it doesn't seem to matter really as it all comes down in the end to a 'must' or a 'should'.

*Supervisor:*   If you want to construct a working alliance then offering a viewpoint to the client, not imposing it, is a crucial step as well as asking the client what they think of your theory. Obviously, REBT does provide a clear account of emotional disturbance and sees rigid attitudes or demandingness at the foundation of it. Now why is REBT 'imposing' its view more than other therapeutic approaches?

*Supervisee:*   I don't know because I haven't trained in other approaches, but I expect they have their own theories they want clients to accept. To me, REBT seems crude and mechanistic in the way it unravels clients' problems. It seems a blunt instrument to use with clients.

*Supervisor:*   Can you think of a specific case example we can examine?

*Supervisee:*   I can. This woman had great doubts about marrying a man she had been going out with for a long time. Also she couldn't make up her mind about a career change. So she was procrastinating and experiencing a lot of anxiety.

*Supervisor:*   What was your hypothesis about her presenting problems?

*Supervisee:*   That she must be absolutely certain in both cases that she was making the right decision, otherwise her life would be awful, she would never recover from the mistakes she had made. I presented this to her halfway through the first session.

*Supervisor:*   What was her response?

*Supervisee:*   That it was too simple an explanation. REBT wasn't rich or sophisticated enough to explore her problems in sufficient depth. There were lots of nuances and subtleties to discuss.

*Supervisor:*   Did you agree with her at this point?

*Supervisee:*   I did. I felt a bit silly reducing these complex problems down to a few sentences. So I just sat back and let her explore the highways and byways of her problems.

*Supervisor:*   And where did it all eventually lead?

*Supervisee:*   Right back to my original hypothesis: that she had to be absolutely certain she was making the right decisions; hence the procrastination and anxiety.

*Supervisor:*   So, why are you not pleased that REBT was right in this case?

*Supervisee:*   It's the crude reductionism of the framework that still troubles me. I got it right, but too quickly.

*Supervisor:*   Is that because you believe that complex, long-standing problems have to have complex causes and complex solutions; otherwise you are not really doing 'proper therapy'?

*Supervisee:*   Yes, that's it. You've put your finger on it.

*Supervisor:*   Now if you believe that powerful attitudes have a tremendous influence on people's feelings and behaviours, that they are maintaining their emotional disturbance, surely by isolating, revealing and examining these attitudes with the client, you're helping to end the client's suffering as quickly as possible? Shouldn't that be the aim of all therapies?

*Supervisee:*  Of course, but the fact that I helped her to tackle her problems relatively quickly still leaves me feeling that I've provided her with only superficial solutions.

*Supervisor:*  And what did she think?

*Supervisee:*  She was pleased. She thought her demands for utter certainty were, after all, the nub of the problem.

*Supervisor:*  You see, some other therapies would inch forward through the dense undergrowth of clients' problems, so to speak, and thereby take a long time to reach the clearing or centre of their problems. Now REBT therapists, armed with their hypotheses derived from its theory, would avoid the undergrowth and parachute straight into the clearing. Hence the speed and the depth of REBT practice.

*Supervisee:*  That's assuming, of course, you've picked the right clearing or haven't drifted into the undergrowth.

*Supervisor:*  Right. If your hypothesis is wrong, then you discard it and start collecting more information in order to formulate another one. It's about being open-minded, flexible in order to confirm, revise or throw out hypotheses in the light of incoming information.

*Supervisee:*  And what happens if the client doesn't agree that there is a 'must' or 'should' implicated in her problems? Aren't REBT therapists stuck then?

*Supervisor:*  No. We certainly don't insist that there has to be a 'must' or 'should' involved, but we would assume that it's highly likely. If a therapist did translate non-devout REBT theory into rigid practice, they wouldn't be doing REBT as taught by Albert Ellis, but their own dogmatic brand of it. But to answer your question directly: if we couldn't find a 'must' or 'should' or the client disagreed with our interpretations, we would examine and help change those disturbance-creating ideas chosen by the client as heavily implicated in their problems.

*Supervisee:*  So, in terms of speed and depth, REBT therapists are quickly sorting out the ABC elements of the client's problems but particularly listening out for the rigid and extreme attitudes without insisting that they have to be there.

*Supervisor:*  Exactly. We are genuinely providing individual assessment and treatment programmes. REBT is definitely not a sausage machine.

*Supervisee:* OK, but it still seems strange that words like 'must' and 'should' can have the potential to create emotional disturbance.

*Supervisor:* It's not necessarily the words themselves but the rigid, disturbance-producing attitudes that lie behind those words that, as you correctly said, we listen out for. I am persuaded that REBT theory has great explanatory power in its view of emotional disturbance, but I hold this view non-dogmatically.

*Supervisee:* I don't have that faith yet but I'm certainly not against gaining more conviction in its theory and practice.

*Supervisor:* And how can you achieve that?

*Supervisee:* More discussions with you, other REBT therapists, reading, workshops, training, that sort of thing.

*Supervisor:* What about therapy itself?

*Supervisee:* Act in therapy as if I believe what I'm teaching.

*Supervisor:* And this will assist you to become both confident and competent in its practice without surrendering your scepticism about it.

*Supervisee:* Good. That sounds like a compromise I can live with.

*Supervisor:* If you acted in therapy like you didn't believe the *ABC* framework, how can you expect the client to believe it? You would have a self-fulfilling prophecy on your hands.

*Supervisee:* Yes, that's much clearer now. I think part of the problem is my narrow view of REBT and thereby blaming it for my deficiencies in really understanding its theory and practice.

*Supervisor:* I agree and hope we can rectify that. I look forward to our next sessions as these discussions with you help to keep me on my toes and refine my own ideas about REBT.

*Supervisee:* I've enjoyed today's supervision. It's been productive.

In this extract from supervision, important points to consider are the following:

1. Offering a viewpoint on emotional disturbance and seeking clients' opinions of it is definitely not the same thing as imposing it. The therapist's (supervisee's) inability to see this difference is due to their crude understanding of REBT theory rather than residing in the theory itself. The apparent simplicity of the *ABC* framework in quickly conceptualising clients' problems does not necessarily make it 'mechanistic' or a 'blunt instrument'; it can rapidly bring order into the chaos of some clients' lives (for a highly detailed account of the *ABC* framework, see Ellis, 1991).

2. The unease of the therapist about presenting the hypothesis regarding the client's rigid and extreme attitudes before they have heard the full story indicates that they are prey to the 'big picture trap' (Grieger and Boyd, 1980: 77)

whereby some therapists 'insist on obtaining a total picture of the client's past, present and future before beginning an intervention program'. Even when the client confirms the therapist's initial hypothesis, the therapist still believes they are therapeutically short-changing the client as rigid (musts) thinking is insufficiently credible or complex as an explanation for the client's problems. The therapist therefore subscribes to another myth that complex problems have to have complex causes and solutions in order for therapeutic justice or efficacy to be seen to be done.

3. That REBT seeks to pluck the cognitive essence (rigid attitudes) out of clients' problems, without becoming entangled in the thickets of their accounts of them, is a major feature of its therapeutic efficiency (speed and depth) as well as a target of frequent criticism for its oversimplicity (see Ziegler, 1989).

4. While REBT does aver that rigid attitudes, in the form of musts, absolute shoulds, have tos, got tos, oughts, are at the heart of emotional disturbance, it does not absolutely insist on this viewpoint. If, for whatever reason, musts and absolute shoulds are not located or the client does not resonate with them, REBT switches its focus to clients' inferences and idiosyncratic attitudes regarding their problems. This form of therapy is known as general REBT (see Ellis and Dryden, 1997). Therefore REBT does provide an individually tailored treatment programme and not a 'sausage machine' for turning out REBT clones.

5. Some REBT therapists' uncertainties and difficulties about applying the *ABC* framework arise from their own misunderstanding of or inability to grasp the tenets of REBT. While most, if not all, theoretical systems have some measure of innate confusion or contradiction, it is an easy step to blame the theory because the therapist lacks competence and confidence in its practice.

6. To rectify this problem, the therapist is encouraged to develop a more informed and balanced picture of REBT through further training, reading, discussions with more experienced therapists, etc., to enhance their practice. As the supervisor points out, this process is not meant to squeeze out the therapist's scepticism about REBT. Ellis (1983b) has argued that scepticism towards all things in life, including REBT, is an important sign of mental health.

## When Therapists Think that *B* Means Blame in the *ABC* Framework

Some REBT therapists believe that responsibility for one's disturbed feelings is synonymous with blaming the individual for having them; therefore they do not place the *ABC* framework of self-created disturbance at the centre of their interactions with clients for fear of being seen to condemn them for their disturbance-creating attitudes ideas (for a detailed discussion of emotional responsibility, see Chapter 3). Instead, to avoid any hint of condemnation, they might encourage their clients to think more positively or only challenge their inferences, e.g. 'I can understand why your wife's erratic behaviour is upsetting you and, of course, you're not to blame for the way you feel, but nothing you've said so far indicates she is going to leave you'. This obviously dilutes or undermines the possibility of clients striving for attitude change in their lives because they may leave therapy still believing that others or life events directly cause their emotional problems; in other words, they still hold to *A-C* thinking. Ironically, in the therapist's efforts to eschew assigning responsibility or blame to the client for their presenting emotional problems, the therapist may well strengthen the client' proclivities to blame others for them.

REBT powerfully distinguishes between encouraging responsibility for self-created disturbance, e.g. 'I make myself unhealthily angry because of my demands that my boss absolutely shouldn't behave in the way that he does', and avoiding any form of global condemnation of the client for having such feelings. If there is any condemnation, it usually comes from the client and not the therapist, e.g. 'I'm totally inadequate for my inability to control my anger'. When therapists have clearly understood this important distinction between responsibility and blame, they can then confidently teach it to their clients. Thus the *ABC* framework is returned to its rightful place at the centre of therapy.

## When Therapists Don't Want to Minimise Adversities at *A*

Advancing the principle of emotional responsibility when clients are still reeling from the impact of adversities may strike some REBT therapists as insensitive, if not downright callous, e.g. 'How in heaven's name can I tell him that he largely makes himself depressed over losing his job and his wife leaving him? I feel like such a cold bastard for even suggesting it'. In these circumstances, such therapists will allow clients to express their feelings at great length over adversities at *A* rather than zero in on their disturbance-inducing attitudes. In not wanting to minimise the *A* in the client's eyes, they commit the mistake of making it all-important and thereby reinforcing the client's sense of helplessness or misery in the face of such events. It is the attitudes at *B* that the client holds towards the adversity that now become minimised: *AbC*.

While REBT therapists accept the considerable impact that adversities at *A* have in contributing to the creation of disturbed emotional states, nevertheless, it is the client's appraisal of these events that ultimately determines whether the client will experience an unhealthy or healthy negative emotion, e.g. depression or sadness respectively. As Burns (1980: 207) points out:

> Sadness is a normal emotion created by realistic perceptions that describe a negative event involving loss or disappointment in an undistorted way. Depression is an illness that *always* results from thoughts that are distorted in some way.

In the above example, the client's depression largely arises from their rigid and extreme attitudes, e.g., 'This double blow absolutely should not have happened to me. My life is finished, destroyed, over'. Once the therapist has grasped this fact, they can help the client to accept and adjust to the grim reality of painful events. In this way the therapist truly helps the client to reduce or eventually remove their suffering.

## When Therapists Hold that Clients' Feelings Are Determined by Others' Abominable Behaviour

When an individual sets out to wreak as much emotional havoc as possible on a client, some REBT therapists hold that the client cannot be held responsible for their resulting emotional disturbance. For example, a woman becomes unhealthily angry (e.g. 'He absolutely should not be doing this to me') and depressed (e.g. 'I'm powerless to do anything about it. I am useless') over her ex-partner's continual allegations to her friends and work colleagues that she is a slut, is an alcoholic, has AIDS, neglects her children, etc. Such behaviour is understandably difficult to bear and therapy allows the client to vent her feelings, but the therapist does not suggest ways in which she can modify her disturbed feelings because the therapist, like the client, sees them as caused by someone else and therefore she has no control over them. The focus in therapy is on practical solutions to her emotional distress, e.g. seeking a court injunction to keep her ex-partner away from her. If the ex-partner stops what he is doing, she can feel better and 'breathe easily again'.

Although it is not an easy issue to address in therapy, the client does have some control over her emotional response to her ex-partner's thoroughly abominable behaviour – she can reduce the frequency, intensity and duration of her depression and unhealthy anger constructing flexible and non-extreme attitudes towards his behaviour, e.g. 'I am not useless. I'm giving him power over me. If I fight back instead of fall apart, I will take away his pleasure in seeing me suffer'; 'I know that his poisonous allegations are false and that's what really matters irrespective of what others think'; 'Sadly, he empirically should be doing what he is doing but I don't have to disturb myself about his disturbed behaviour. It just keeps on confirming how right I was to leave him'.

Through such scrutiny, the therapist can help the client both to develop greater emotional stability and to pursue more vigorously practical solutions in order to counteract her ex-partner's behaviour. Even if there is no cessation of his behaviour in the short term, the client's regained fortitude will allow her to withstand his rumour-mongering as well as experience some measure of happiness in her life. All these possibilities for constructive change will probably be lost if the therapist rules out any emotional responsibility on the client's part.

## When Therapists Think that the Use of the ABC Framework Adds Insult to Injury

Some REBT therapists believe there are certain adversities which are so appalling, tragic or overwhelming that not only should use of the *ABC* framework be suspended, but also even to contemplate using it would add to the violation or suffering that the client has already experienced. These adversities would include rape, attempted murder, being held hostage, trapped in a car crash or witnessing the violent deaths of others. In the face of such events, the therapist believes that the client is totally incapable of exercising any degree of control or choice over their emotional state. The *ABC* framework may have had great utility with most of the therapist's previous clients but, in this particular case, the therapist's approach is to be very supportive, let the client 'talk it through' and hope that the passage of time heals their wounds.

| | |
|---|---|
| *Supervisee:* | What else can I do? |
| *Supervisor:* | The *ABC* framework is as applicable here as anywhere else. |
| *Supervisee:* | How can it be after what he has suffered? He was savagely beaten. He spent weeks in hospital. |
| *Supervisor:* | How is he now? |
| *Supervisee:* | As you would expect, very bitter, angry, anxious, depressed. He doesn't go out very much; he is wary of people in general. |
| *Supervisor:* | Why do you say 'As you would expect'? Do you not believe that some individuals, even if only a few, might react differently to a savage attack upon them? |
| *Supervisee:* | I would feel exactly the same way if it happened to me. It seems to me that it would be a universal response to such a terrible incident. He can't help his feelings – the attack directly caused them. |
| *Supervisor:* | Your sense of fatalism, which may well be reinforcing the client's, blinds you to the obvious truth that it wouldn't be a universal response. I have been reading recently of the appalling suffering of British prisoners of war in Japanese prison camps during the Second World War. What comes across time and time again in these old soldiers' accounts is that the Japanese guards may have broken their bodies, but they fought back in their own ways and refused to let the guards break their spirit. These are awe-inspiring accounts of courage and resilience. The same theme rings out each time: the indomitability of the human spirit even under the harshest of conditions. |
| *Supervisee:* | I understand what you're saying but it seems that you're trying to trivialise his present suffering or even blame him for it. |
| *Supervisor:* | I'm certainly not trying to do that, but to point out to you that his suffering is being exacerbated or made worse by his presently held attitudes following the attack. This is definitely not to blame him for holding such attitudes, but to indicate that those attitudes are owned by him, his responsibility. |

*Supervisee:*    But he didn't beat himself up. The attack created those attitudes.

*Supervisor:*    Your client's physical injuries are totally caused by the attacker, and I hope that person gets a long prison sentence for the attack. In addition, it could also be argued that your client's initial disturbed feelings can be attributed to the attack – particularly as this attack was of a very savage nature. However, he has introduced some ideas into his thinking that, so to speak, were not present when he was attacked and are now intensifying and prolonging his disturbed feelings.

*Supervisee:*    You've lost me. What are you talking about?

*Supervisor:*    OK. Take his anxiety: what is he most anxious about?

*Supervisee:*    He's terrified of being attacked again and, from the REBT viewpoint, he's demanding it must never happen again. He's afraid to go out and has turned himself into a prisoner in his own home.

*Supervisor:*    So, this is the attitude, with regard to his anxiety, that he has constructed from the attack. Is this a realistic attitude that is going to help him live a relatively normal life again?

*Supervisee:*    Probably not.

*Supervisor:*    We know that his demands cannot be met. Even being a recluse cannot guarantee his safety – someone could break into his house and attack him. And if he doesn't modify his attitude, what might happen to him if he is attacked again?

*Supervisee:*    I expect he may well fall apart and never recover.

*Supervisor:*    Do you still believe that the *ABC* framework does not apply in this case?

*Supervisee:*    I'm beginning to be persuaded.

*Supervisor:*    OK. What is he bitter about?

*Supervisee:*    He believes that he must know that someone is trustworthy, and if not, he can't trust them. Everyone has to be held at arm's length. This has made him socially isolated.

*Supervisor:*    Did the attacker make him think that, or is that attitude his responsibility?

*Supervisee:*    Well, the attack would probably make most people more wary …

*Supervisor:*    That's understandable, and I'm not debating that, but would every person attacked hold the same attitude?

*Supervisee:*    I don't suppose they would.

*Supervisor:*    A friend of my sister was quite badly attacked a few years ago but generally speaking, she was still quite friendly and open to most people she met.

*Supervisee:*    With that example, you're trying to emphasise the *B* again in the *ABC* framework.

*Supervisor:* Of course. It's not a framework you can wheel out for use with some events and then put away in storage when other events become too distressing for you. The framework applies whatever the situation.

*Supervisee:* What about his depression, then? He feels utterly powerless to put his life back on the rails because he says the attack destroyed his dignity and self-respect.

*Supervisor:* Well, no matter what happened to him, only he can ultimately deprive himself of his dignity and self-respect. I come back to those prisoners of war: they may have walked out of those camps severely emaciated and beaten, but, for some of them, their dignity as human beings was still intact.

*Supervisee:* So when my client says the attack made him worthless, that's his conclusion about the event and, as you said earlier, not part of the event itself.

*Supervisor:* That's right. Even if the attacker explicitly told him that he wanted him to feel worthless as a result of the beating, that could only occur only if your client agreed with the attacker's intentions.

*Supervisee:* These are very difficult and contentious issues to try to convey to clients. My client might feel he is being assaulted for a second time – this time by his therapist!

*Supervisor:* That certainly is a danger. It depends on how you handle it. These issues need to be addressed with a great deal of tact and sensitivity, but addressed they have to be if you want to help your client to put his life back on the rails. In essence, your job is to help him bear what he perceives to be unbearable – show him his attitudinal contribution to making things unbearable. At present, you're not helping him do that because you are convinced that the attack is responsible for his suffering, and that's why little, if any, progress is being made.

*Supervisee:* OK. Let me try to summarise what you've been saying: my client believes the attack has rendered him thoroughly miserable, powerless to effect any constructive change in his life. My task is to teach him how to empower himself by helping him examine and change some of the disturbance-prolonging attitudes that he has brought to this event, but were not part of the event itself.

*Supervisor:* Exactly. Which, in turn, will help him to modify his present emotional disturbance. Are you now sufficiently motivated and confident in applying the *ABC* framework to this client's problems?

*Supervisee:* Well, I will admit that my own *A-C* thinking about the attack left me feeling as powerless as the client at times, so I'm more convinced now that the *ABC* framework can be applied even in this case.

*Supervisor:* Well, I hope to hear it being applied with gentle conviction in your future therapy recordings. For homework, I would suggest that you read some books about individuals who have coped with great adversity in their life. You might be more persuaded then of my arguments.

*Supervisee:* Yes, I will. That might help to remove my remaining doubts about this issue.

*Supervisor:* You can still have doubts about the framework without impairing or undermining your clinical competence. Please remember that.

In this supervision extract, the supervisor is teaching the therapist the following:

1. The therapist (supervisee) rejected the *ABC* framework in this case because of their erroneous assumption that everyone would react in exactly the same way to a savage beating – the opposite of REBT theory and practice, which the therapist is supposed to be teaching the client. Understanding the client's viewpoint is not the same thing as supporting it. The supervisor's use of the prisoner-of-war example buttresses the point that no matter how appalling the events are, the individual's reaction to them is still mediated by his attitude system.

2. If the therapist wants to help the client recover from the attack, they have to engage in the delicate and probably very difficult task of assisting him to identify those attitudes that he has constructed following the attack. These attitudes form part of the factors prolonging his suffering. This strategy runs the very considerable risk of appearing to blame the client for his emotional disturbance, which the therapist believes, at this stage in supervision, would be the case.

3. It is important for the therapist to separate the various elements involved in the attack and its aftermath in order for the client (and themself) to understand how the principle of emotional responsibility fits into this case. The attack caused the client's physical injuries, and the initial overwhelming feelings of emotional disturbance (though not all REBT therapists would agree with this latter point), but the maintenance of this disturbance is considerably helped by the client's rigid and extreme attitudes that are created after the violent assault and not part of or intrinsic to the original event.

4. The therapist should advisedly examine the long-term harmful effects upon the client if he does not modify his disturbance-prolonging attitudes, e.g., forever dreading another attack and turning into a recluse in the mistaken idea that this will guarantee his future safety, never trusting anyone again and thereby

reinforcing his social isolation. These long-term effects may turn out to be even more damaging than the attack itself.

5. The *ABC* framework of emotional disturbance is not to be used or discarded depending on the severity of the client's presenting problems. It is the centre-piece of REBT theory and practice. Avoiding its use is due to the therapist's lack of faith in its applicability to help clients deal healthily with severe adversities rather than the framework's actual ability to show clients how to reduce or remove their disturbance. Of course, how the framework is introduced to clients can be a major factor in building or breaking a therapeutic alliance. If the framework is insensitively or brusquely presented to the client, he may well think he is being assaulted again.

6. The therapist has to address the issue of emotional responsibility if the client is to empower themself and put their life back on the rails. Excessive sensitivity or tact on the therapist's part, though appearing to be the right way to behave with this client, will actually be therapeutically ineffective as this will not encourage him to 'bear the unbearable'.

7. Although the therapist still has considerable doubts about the framework's applicability in this case, this need not preclude them from teaching with 'gentle conviction' the *ABCs* of REBT to their client. The therapist does not need to be fully convinced in the *ABC* framework to help the client see how they can help themself through attitudinal change. The supervisor suggests that the therapist read some accounts of people coping with great adversity in order to underscore the arguments the supervisor has been advancing.

## When the Therapist Fears that the Client Will Leave Therapy on Being Told that They Disturb Themself

Some clients, particularly angry ones, are so utterly convinced that other people or events do cause their emotional problems that for the therapist to suggest otherwise could bring therapy to an immediate end, e.g. 'My boss makes me very angry when he insults me. I also get very angry if someone says I'm overreacting. I won't tolerate such remarks'. Those therapists who are anxious rather than concerned about this occurring face a number of difficulties: i) disagreeing with the client's view of emotional causation risks losing the client's approval as well as hastening premature termination; ii) agreeing with the client will probably strengthen the client's disturbance-producing attitudes and transform the therapist into a sycophant; iii) confronting the client will trigger the therapist's own attitudes of unbearability towards being comfortable in therapy; iv) worrying about what other therapists might think of them if their client 'storms out of therapy'; v) seeing themselves as weak and incompetent for not presenting the *ABC* framework 'come what may' and thereby sullying their integrity as a therapist. Such internal conflict is likely to lead to indecision or paralysis on the therapist's part, which will allow the client, without little interruption, to expound upon the righteousness of their anger.

Before therapists can focus their clinical attention on tackling the client's unhealthy anger, they need to examine and change their own self-defeating attitudes. By surrendering their approval and comfort needs, therapists can develop both self-acceptance and discomfort tolerance and thereby present the self-induced disturbance framework in the teeth of the client's refusal to consider it or of the anticipated client rejection of them. By keeping their ego out of therapy, therapists have no personal interest in whether the client continually rejects or eventually accepts the *ABC* framework, but they do their professional best to show the client that there might be a more constructive way of dealing with the boss without losing control. By not wilting under intimidation or shrinking from confrontation, REBT therapists can demonstrate to the client how to be assertive and determined rather than disturbed under pressure, e.g. 'Would you like to handle your boss's insults with aplomb and thereby deny them the satisfaction of seeing you crumble in their presence?' Finally, therapists can learn to rectify shortfalls in their professional integrity without condemning themselves for any shortfall. Through such methods, the therapist can maintain a non-disturbed viewpoint throughout therapy no matter how long the client stays for.

## When Therapists Think that It Does Not Matter if Clients Change Attitudes or Behaviour as It All Leads to the Same Result

Thinking that it does not matter if clients change attitudes or behaviour rests on the assumption that behavioural change is as equally effective as examining attitudes in effecting attitude change (giving up rigid attitudes in favour of flexible ones). REBT therapists who adhere to this point of view incorrectly infer that because maladaptive behaviour has been replaced with adaptive behaviour, concomitant attitude change has automatically occurred. As they do not investigate if this change has actually taken place, or do so only in a cursory way, they are in danger of terminating therapy while their clients' disturbance-producing attitudes are still intact.

*Supervisee:* My client has gotten over their public speaking anxiety. In fact, I can't keep them away from giving talks.

*Supervisor:* What was the rigid attitude they were examining?

*Supervisee:* 'I must always give a good performance. Otherwise, I'm a failure'. That attitude has been successfully examined.

*Supervisor:* What was the strategy?

*Supervisee:* The client did as many talks as possible. Everyone says how good they are at it. Their anxiety has disappeared.

*Supervisor:* How do you know that the client has changed their attitude?

*Supervisee:* The proof is in the pudding – no anxiety and lots of successful talks.

| | |
|---|---|
| *Supervisor:* | I'm glad that things are going so well for your client, but have you really searched to see if they still hold that rigid attitude? It might just be dormant. |
| *Supervisee:* | No, I haven't. It just seemed so obvious that it must have gone because the client was so happy with their progress. |
| *Supervisor:* | Well, the danger is that if your client does give a bad or poor performance, then their rigid attitude will be reactivated, and their anxiety will return, leading to avoidance of further public speaking. By not really checking to see if they still hold their rigid attitude in spite of their progress, they may still be vulnerable. |
| *Supervisee:* | But their fears may never come to pass. |
| *Supervisor:* | True, but it's better if therapy is based on enduring rather than conditional change. |
| *Supervisee:* | That's a good point. I'm only offering them the latter. Come to think of it now, their anxiety is still with them. |
| *Supervisor:* | What evidence do you have for that? |
| *Supervisee:* | I suggested to the client a few weeks ago that they did an imagery exercise in which they saw themself giving a poor speech in order to cope with it. They became very agitated and didn't want to do it. They said, 'Why spoil a good thing? Everything is going fine.' I agreed with them and felt silly for suggesting it. |
| *Supervisor:* | OK. Why not suggest it again, but this time within the context of a powerful clinical rationale. Which is …? |
| *Supervisee:* | That behavioural-based change is more limited than attitude change because it does not provide the client with any coping responses if their fears are realised. Even if they are not, I would expect that some measure of anxiety precedes every talk. |
| *Supervisor:* | Good. You can check out that last point with the client. |

The supervisor points out to the therapist (supervisee) that attitude change does not necessarily keep in step with behavioural change like an obedient dog with its owner. Because they have not changed their rigid attitude to a flexible one, they still may become anxious if they don't do well in presenting a future talk. REBT therapists should remember that behavioural tasks are used to implement attitude change and are not used on their own as the main modality of such change.

In this chapter, I have discussed therapist obstacles to client change in the views domain of the working alliance and particularly the often considerable problems and doubts that therapists have in using the *ABC* framework with their clients as well as in their own lives. In the next chapter, I will consider the obstacles that REBT therapists experience in setting goals with their clients.

## Note

1  Here and elsewhere throughout this part of the book which focuses on therapists' difficulties, supervision is conducted for educational and not therapeutic purposes.

# Chapter 9

# Dealing with Therapist Obstacles to Client Change in the Goals Domain of the Working Alliance

When clients come to therapy, they are generally in a disturbed frame of mind. They want to get relief from their psychological pain and are generally not interested in the issues that REBT therapists are concerned with when it comes to goals. Indeed, REBT therapists have a lot to consider when it comes to the goals domain of the alliance and, as such, there is much scope for therapists to founder. In this chapter, I will consider therapist obstacles to client change in the goals domain of the working alliance. In doing so, I will focus on two main areas:

- Therapist obstacles to client change due to the therapist's lack of knowledge and skills deficits
- Therapist obstacles to client change due to the therapist's personal issues.

## Therapist Obstacles to Client Change Due to the Therapist's Lack of Knowledge and Skills Deficits

What do REBT therapists need to know about goals and goal-setting to be proficient in this area of the working alliance? In my view, here are the key areas of goal-related knowledge that REBT therapists should ideally have at their fingertips.

### Negotiate Goals, Don't Set Them Unilaterally or Take Them at Face Value

When I listen to REBT therapists and trainees talk about their clients' goals, I am struck by the language that they use. Phrases like 'I got my client to see that she needed to …' and 'I set his goals …' may reveal a unilateral attitude when it comes to eliciting and setting clients' goals. It is important that goal-setting is a collaborative exercise and that goals are negotiated rather than unilaterally set perhaps on the basis of REBT theory. Therapists need to remember that REBT theory suggests interventions and it should not be used as gospel!

Some therapists may cause problems by taking clients' goals at face value. As will be seen, when clients articulate their goals for change, they may indicate a variety of problematic objectives. For example, they want others to change or they

DOI: 10.4324/9781003423379-11

wish to feel indifferent in the face of adversity. Unless therapists intervene and show their clients the difficulties with such goals, these will later be the source of obstacles to client change, albeit unwittingly.

So rather than unilaterally setting goals for clients, on the one hand, or accepting such goals at face value, on the other, it is important that therapists engage clients in process of negotiation with respect to their goals.

### Goals Should Be Specified by Clients Themselves and Not by Stakeholders

It sometimes happens that clients are 'sent' to therapy by their partners, family or employers. When this happens, it is important that REBT therapists take time to disentangle what others who have an interest (called 'stakeholders' here) want clients to achieve from therapy from what clients want to achieve for themselves. In the first vignette, the therapist accepts at face value the goal that a stakeholder has set for the client:

| | |
|---|---|
| *Therapist:* | So, what would you like to achieve by coming to see me? |
| *Client:* | Well, my partner thinks I need to spend more time with them. |
| *Therapist:* | OK, so let me help you to do that. Where shall we start? |
| *Client:* | Ummm. I don't know. |

Instead, the therapist should preferably have engaged the client in a discussion about their goals as shown below:

| | |
|---|---|
| *Therapist:* | So, what would you like to achieve by coming to see me? |
| *Client:* | Well, my partner thinks I need to spend more time with them. |
| *Therapist:* | And what do you think about their goal for you? |
| *Client:* | I can understand that from my partner's point of view. |
| *Therapist:* | What about from your point of view? |
| *Client:* | Well, I would like that too, but my partner is so angry these days. |
| *Therapist:* | How do you handle their anger? |
| *Client:* | By withdrawing from them. |
| *Therapist:* | So, on the one hand, you share your partner's goal about spending more time together, but on the other hand, you withdraw from them when they get angry. Would you like to handle your partner's anger differently? |
| *Client:* | Yes, I would. |

> *Therapist:*  How would you like to respond differently to your partner when they get angry?

In the above sequence, the therapist does the following:

1. The therapist acknowledges that in response to the question about what the client wanted to achieve, the client mentioned their partner's goal for them.
2. The therapist asked the client what the latter thought of their partner's goal and elicited ambivalence: part of the client shared their partner's goal, but another part voiced an obstacle.
3. The therapist asked the client if they wanted to deal with the obstacle and when the client responded that they did, the therapist asked for the client's goal in this respect.

Both therapist and client still have much work to do in the area of the client's goals, but they are now both focused on what the client wants rather than what the client's partner wants.

### Helping Clients to Set Goals at Two Different Goal-Setting Stages

There are usually two goal-setting stages in the initial assessment of clients' problems:

1. When clients state their problem and goal in general terms (the 'problem and goal as defined').
2. After the problem has been explored in *ABC* terms and the problem and goal have now been made specific (the 'problem and goal as assessed').

If therapists set goals only in relation to clients' problems as defined and not in relation to problems as assessed, they will not help their clients know where they are going with the latter.

> *Therapist:*  What problem are you seeking help for?
> *Client:*  My progress at work is being hampered because I don't do enough presentations. I try and find ways not to give them.
> *Therapist:*  What do you want to achieve from coming to see me?
> *Client:*  To give more presentations at work.
> *Therapist:*  What stops you from doing this?
> *Client:*  I am anxious.

| | |
|---|---|
| *Therapist:* | Anxious about what? |
| *Client:* | About being seen as incompetent by my boss. |
| *Therapist:* | What would be a constructive response to the possibility that your boss might think that you are incompetent? |
| *Client:* | To be bothered about that but not anxious about it. |

In this excerpt, the therapist does the following:

1. The therapist discovers that the goal in relation to the problem as defined is to give more presentations at work.
2. By asking the client to elaborate on the obstacle to doing that already, the therapist works with the client to identify the goal in relation to the problem as assessed, which is to be bothered about being seen as incompetent by their boss, but not to be anxious about it.

### Negotiate Goals with Reference to Clients' Psychological Problems Before Goals with Reference to Practical Problems

Clients come to therapy because they disturb themselves about the practical problems that they face in their lives. Thus, a client may have been made redundant and feels depressed about losing their job. They come to therapy with two types of problems: an emotional problem (i.e. depression) and a practical problem (i.e. they do not have a job). In cases where clients have practical problems and emotional problems about these practical problems and their therapists ask them for their therapeutic goals, they may well specify solving their practical problems as their goals rather than dealing with their emotional problems.

If therapists go along with their clients' wishes on this point, that will be laying the foundation for obstacles to client change later since the presence of emotional problems will interfere with their attempts to solve their practical problems and also, if they solve their practical problems, they may well lose interest in dealing with their emotional problems. In the present example, if the therapist goes along with the client's nominated goal with respect to their practical problem (e.g. to find a new job) and they find a job, they will not be motivated to work on their emotional problem (i.e. depression) and to set a goal with respect to this problem. This may not matter much to the client in the immediate term since they have solved their practical problem about which they depressed themself, but they have not learned to deal effectively with similar future adversities.

When clients have emotional problems about their practical problems and they nominate goals with respect to the latter but not the former, here is how REBT therapists can respond.

| | |
|---|---|
| *Therapist:* | So you have been made redundant and feel depressed about that. Is that correct? |
| *Client:* | Yes, it is. |
| *Therapist:* | What would you like to achieve by seeing me? |
| *Client:* | I would like you to help me to find a new job. |
| *Therapist:* | Do you think that your feelings of depression will help us do this or hinder us? |
| *Client:* | I think it might hinder us. |
| *Therapist:* | In what way? |
| *Client:* | Well, if I'm depressed, I may not come across well at interview and this may affect my chances of getting a job. |
| *Therapist:* | Good point. Given this, what would you like to achieve with respect to your depression? |
| *Client:* | I want to overcome my depression. |
| *Therapist:* | Well, we are now focused on your feelings, so let's look at this issue a little more clearly. |

Here, the therapist has done the following:

1. The therapist begins by acknowledging that the client has stated that they want to get a new job, which is a goal related to their practical problem.
2. The therapist then focuses the client's attention on their emotional problem and asks them Socratically if they think that the existence of this problem will help or hinder them in their quest to solve their practical problem.
3. The client can see that the existence of their emotional problem will hinder them from solving their practical problem.
4. The therapist then asks the client to nominate a goal with respect to their emotional problem.

While the client's response shows the therapist that they have more work to do on this issue with the client, the latter is now focused on a goal with respect to their emotional problem.

### Convert Vague Goals into 'SMART' Goals

When therapists ask clients at the outset of therapy what they want to achieve from the process, clients often give a vague answer such as 'to be happy' or 'to get over my anxiety'. Like other approaches within the CBT therapeutic tradition, REBT recommends that practitioners help clients specify goals that are 'SMART' (S = specific; M = measurable; A = achievable; R = realistic; and T = time-bound[1]). Therapists contribute to obstacles to client change in REBT when they do not help clients convert their vague goals into 'smart' goals or when they do not have the skills to do this. If you suspect that you fall in the latter category, we suggest that you play digital voice recordings (DVRs) of your attempts to help your clients convert their vague goals into 'smart' goals so that you can get feedback on your skills in this area from your supervisor.

Here is an example of a therapist who is skilled in helping their client convert a vague goal into a specific goal.

| | |
|---|---|
| *Therapist:* | What would you like to achieve by coming to see me? |
| *Client:* | I want to be happier than I am now. |
| *Therapist:* | What would be different in your life if you were happier? |
| *Client:* | I would have more friends. |
| *Therapist:* | What obstacle exists to you having more friends at the moment? |
| *Client:* | I get anxious around people, so I tend to avoid social gatherings or I don't speak much when I am with others. |
| *Therapist:* | What are you most anxious about when you are with people? |
| *Client:* | That they might think I'm boring. |
| *Therapist:* | If you could handle being thought boring more adaptively, would that help you with your anxiety? |
| *Client:* | Yes, it would, but is that possible? |
| *Therapist:* | Yes it is. So, if I could help you to feel concerned but not anxious about being thought boring and to be more responsive in social situations, would that be something that you would be interested in? |
| *Client:* | Definitely. |

In this interchange, the therapist helps the client in the following ways:

1. The therapist takes the client's vague goal (i.e. to be happier) and begins to make it more concrete by asking: 'What would be different in your life if you were happier?' and 'What obstacle exists to you having more friends at the moment?'
2. The client then refers to an unhealthy negative emotion at $C$ (i.e., anxiety), and the therapist immediately seeks to discover the client's $A$, 'What are you most anxious about when you are with people?'
3. The therapist takes the client's $A$ (i.e. 'That they might think I'm boring') and suggests an emotional goal (i.e., concern) and a behavioural goal (i.e., to be more responsive in social situations).
4. Note that in a fairly short period, the therapist has helped the client move from a vague goal (to be happier) to a much more concrete goal (to be concerned,

but not anxious about being thought boring in social situations and to be more responsive in social situations).

5.   While the client's behavioural goal will be clarified later, much good therapeutic work has been done in a short period of time.

The above interchange shows how REBT therapists can help clients convert vague goals into specific goals. Don't forget, though, that there are four other components to consider. Therefore, in order to minimise obstacles to client change, therapists need to do the following:

**Ensure that clients' goals are measurable ('M').** It is important that clients have clear criteria to judge whether or not they have achieved their goals and ways of determining their progress towards their goals. Helping clients to measure progress and success is important here.

**Ensure that clients' goals are achievable ('A').** If clients cannot achieve their goals, good REBT therapists will not accept them as goals and will help clients to understand why and to reformulate their goals so that they are achievable.

**Ensure that clients' goals are realistic ('R').** Sometimes, clients say that they don't want to be anxious again and want to set this as a goal for therapy. Such a goal is unrealistic since it is not within the capability of humans to reach a stage where they will not ever experience anxiety (or any other unhealthy negative emotion). Helping clients to see this and to set goals that are realistic will foster the working alliance not only in the goals domain, but across the board.

**Ensure that clients' goals are time-bound ('T').** A client's goal may be specific, measurable, achievable and realistic, but it may not meet the criterion of being time-bound. Thus, the client may wish to achieve a certain goal by a certain time, and this deadline may make the goal unachievable. In this case, the competent REBT practitioner will not accept it since doing so would be a recipe for client failure. Therefore, helping clients to be mindful of time when setting goals is an important consideration.

### Help Clients Specify Their Emotional Problems Before Helping Them Specify Their Goals

As clients' goals are closely allied to their problems, therapists can obstruct clients' progress by not helping them to specify their goals. By doing so, clients not only can see a clear connection between their problems and their goals, but also are shown the components of their goals. The therapist in the above exchange did some of this work, but in this section, we want to discuss how this can be done more formally.

*Putting a Client's Problems into the ABC Framework*

In order to help clients put their problems into the REBT framework, the therapist elicits the following information from the client:

1. The situational context in which the problem typically occurs, if relevant.
2. The client's adversity at *A*. This is the aspect of the situation about which the client is most disturbed. This will often be an inference.
3. The client's unhealthy negative emotion (UNE) at *C*.
4. The client's dysfunctional behaviour or action tendency at *C*.
5. The client's grossly distorted subsequent thinking at *C*, if relevant.

Here is an example of a client's problem that has been put into the *ABC* framework:

> *Whenever people are late for a meeting with me [situation], I get unhealthily angry [UNE at C] about their lack of respect for me [A]. I only wait for them for a minute [behavioural C] but think about how I can get my revenge on them [thinking C].*

*Putting a Client's Goals into the ABC Framework*

The therapist modifies the above schema and uses it to help the client to set goals as follows:

1. The situational context in which the problem typically occurs, if relevant.
2. The client's adversity at *A*. This is the aspect of the situation about which the client is most disturbed. This will often be an inference.
3. The client's alternative healthy negative emotion (HNE) at *C*.
4. The client's alternative functional behaviour or action tendency at *C*.
5. The client's realistic subsequent thinking at *C*, if relevant.

You will see from the above that the situational context and the adversity at *A* are common between the client's problem and their goal. What is different are the three components at *C*.

Here is an example of a client's goal with respect to their problem that has been put into the *ABC* framework:

> Whenever people are late for a meeting with me [situation], I want to feel healthily angry rather than unhealthily angry [HNE is the desired new *C*] about their lack of respect for me [*A*]. I will wait for them for twenty minutes rather than leave after a minute [new behavioural *C*], and rather than think about how

I can get my revenge on them, I will think about how to assert myself with them when they turn up [new thinking *C*].

## When Clients Nominate Understanding Goals

Clients may think that the purpose of psychotherapy is to provide them with insight into their problems, and when they have such insight, change will naturally follow. REBT puts forward a different framework of change (Ellis, 1963. Dryden and Neenan, 2004). This framework argues that there are two forms of insight: *intellectual insight*, where clients understand why and how they disturb themselves and what they need to undisturb themselves, and *emotional insight*, where they act on this understanding and get the benefits of doing so.

It follows from this that when clients nominate insight goals (e.g. 'I want to understand why I get so anxious about giving presentations'), REBT therapists need to determine if that is all they want (i.e. intellectual insight) or if they want what they see to be the psychological benefits of such understanding (i.e. emotional insight). REBT therapists who do not clarify this issue for themselves and for their clients are at risk of accepting intellectual insight goals which, if achieved, will not help clients deal effectively with their emotional problems. In such cases, REBT therapists who accept understanding goals serve as obstacles to client change. Note how the therapist in the following excerpt helps the client move from an 'intellectual insight' goal to an 'emotional insight' goal:

| | |
|---|---|
| *Therapist:* | So, you are anxious about giving presentations at work. What would you like to achieve from seeing me? |
| *Client:* | I want to understand why I get so anxious about giving presentations. |
| *Therapist:* | Would you like to have such understanding and still be anxious about giving presentations, or do you want to have such understanding and learn to overcome your anxiety? |
| *Client (laughing):* | The latter, of course. |
| *Therapist:* | Then what do you hope such insight would lead to? |
| *Client:* | Not being anxious about making the presentations. |
| *Therapist:* | What are you most anxious about with respect to giving presentations? |
| *Client:* | Saying or doing something stupid. |
| *Therapist:* | Well, I guess that is always a possibility, but if I could help you to be concerned, but not anxious, about saying or doing something stupid when you give presentations, would you be interested in that as a goal? |
| *Client:* | Definitely. |

| *Therapist:* | So let me be clear that I understand you. You don't just want to understand why you get anxious about giving presentations, you want to be concerned, but not anxious about the possibility of saying or doing something stupid while you give presentations. Is that right? |
| *Client:* | Exactly right. |

The therapist in the above interchange does the following:

1. They take the client's expressed 'intellectual insight' goal and asks them if they want to achieve this goal and still be anxious or overcome their anxiety. The therapist does this to show that there is a difference between intellectual insight goals and dealing effectively with anxiety.
2. Once the client has indicated that they want more than intellectual understanding, the therapist does a brief assessment of the client's anxiety and discovers that they are most anxious (at *C*) about the possibility of saying or doing something stupid (at *A*).
3. The therapist then puts forward concern as a healthy negative emotional alternative to anxiety as a potential emotional goal given the existence of the possibility of saying or doing something stupid at *A*, a suggestion that the client accepts.
4. The therapist closes by summarising what they have done and stresses that the client's goal will be related to emotional insight and not just intellectual insight.

Some clients may put forward intellectual insight goals related to their past (e.g. 'I want to understand what has happened in the past which has resulted in me getting so anxious about presentations'). If a client nominates such a goal, the therapist is advised to respond, as shown above, by enquiring whether or not the client hopes that such insight will lead to them overcoming their anxiety. If the client does hope to overcome their anxiety, the therapist should respond as the therapist did in the above example, helping the client to understand the REBT view on the role of the past in present emotional problems. This position is as follows:

• The past may contribute to the client's present problems, but does not cause them.
• It is possible to have the same current problem with a variety of past experiences.
• In order to overcome the current problem, the client needs to identify, examine and change the rigid and extreme attitudes that are deemed to underpin the problem and to act and think in ways that are consistent with the client's alternative flexible and non-extreme attitudes.

If the therapist does not take the above steps, it is unlikely that mere understanding of the past will help the client overcome their current problem, and an obstacle to client change will be manifest.

## When Negotiating Clients' Goals, Ensure that These Goals Are Not Contaminated by Client Disturbance

I have stressed in this chapter that a major task of REBT therapists in the goals domain of the working alliance is to help clients set goals with respect to their emotional problems. Having said that, therapists need to be mindful that clients' states of emotional disturbance may contaminate the goal-setting process. Typical examples of this would be:

• A person with anorexia who wants to set 'losing weight' as a therapeutic goal.
• A person with anxiety of losing control who wants to set 'self-control' as a goal.

While the first example is obvious, the second example is less so. People with a fear of losing self-control often think that the only way to gain self-control is to apply methods which will result in self-control. Indeed this solution is part of the problem, given that the real issue that needs to be addressed is helping them to deal with times when they do not feel in self-control. Helping such clients to set a goal such as 'being concerned, but not anxious about losing self-control' is a more productive therapeutic goal then 'gaining self-control' for such clients, given that this goal is not contaminated by the problem.

### Clients' Goals Should Be Relevant to Their Stage of Change

I have made the point above that clients' emotional state may impact negatively on goal-setting. It is also important that therapists help clients set goals according to the stage of change. I have distinguished between overcoming disturbance ('OD') goals and personal development ('PD') goals (Dryden, 2022). It is clear that therapists can create an obstacle to client change if they negotiate 'PD' goals with their clients when these clients are emotionally disturbed. For example, accepting a 'PD' goal such as 'I want to be more loving with my partner' when that person is experiencing unhealthy anger towards their partner will generally not be helpful to the client since their disturbance (unhealthy anger) will interfere markedly with their 'PD' goal (i.e. being more loving). In this case the therapist's task is to help the client see that they are much more likely to achieve their 'PD' goal once they have dealt with their emotional problem and in this respect the therapist needs to help the client to set an 'OD' goal.

However, some REBT therapists wrongly think that REBT is concerned only with helping clients deal with their emotional problems and struggle when clients want to set and pursue 'PD' goals when they have met their 'OD' goals. Such therapists tend to continue to search for problems of emotional disturbance and don't realise that they are still practising REBT when they set and help clients pursue their 'PD' goals.

It is worth remembering, then, that REBT can help clients deal with their emotional problems and help them to develop themselves in relevant areas once they have overcome these emotional problems.[2]

### When Negotiating Clients' Goals, Help Them Specify the Presence of an Emotional State, Not the Absence of One

Often when clients have been helped to identify their emotional problem and are asked what their goals are in respect to this problem, they reply that they don't want to experience that problem. If therapists accept this answer uncritically, they are again laying the foundations for obstacles to client change later in the process.

---

*Supervisor:* I noticed that when you asked your client what she wanted to achieve with respect to her anxiety about being criticised, she replied that she did not want to be anxious and you seemed to accept this as a valid goal.

*Supervisee:* That's correct, I did.

*Supervisor:* Can you see any problems with accepting it?

*Supervisee:* No, it seems OK to me.

*Supervisor:* OK, bear with me if you will and I will demonstrate what's wrong with it. I want you to imagine that you are a train ticket seller and I am a passenger wishing to buy a ticket. OK?

*Supervisee:* Good afternoon. Where would you like to travel to?

*Supervisor:* I don't want to travel to Bath.

*Supervisee:* OK. But where do you want to buy a ticket for?

*Supervisor:* I don't want to buy a ticket for Bath.

*Supervisee (laughing):* OK, I get the point.

*Supervisor:* Which is?

*Supervisee:* When a client indicates that they do not want to feel anxious, neither of us knows what they do see as their emotional goal.

*Supervisor:* And therefore?

*Supervisee:* And therefore, it's my job to help them to specify that goal.

---

1. In the above interchange, the supervisor resists the temptation to make two points didactically to the therapist, as follows:

   a. 'Not feeling anxious' is not a viable goal in REBT since it lacks a specific direction.

   b. It is the therapist's responsibility to help the client to specify such a direction.

2. Instead, the supervisor uses an analogous role-play situation which helps the therapist to understand both points.

### Goals in the Face of Adversity Need to Be Negative and Healthy (Not Indifference, Happiness or a Less Intense Version of a Disturbed Emotion)

One of the aspects of REBT theory that clients and therapists new to REBT struggle with is the concept of healthy negative emotions (HNEs). These healthy negative emotions (at *C*) are deemed to stem from flexible and non-extreme attitudes (at *B*) held towards adversities (at *A*). Thus, when clients are disturbed (i.e. experience unhealthy negative emotions, or UNEs) about these adversities, the task of REBT therapists is to encourage their clients to work towards experiencing HNEs about the same adversities.

However, clients often have other ideas. Thus, instead of HNEs, clients might nominate emotional goals that are characterised by:

- *Indifference*: this is problematic because in order to achieve it, clients would have to believe: 'I don't care that this adversity happened'.
- *Happiness*: this is problematic because in order to achieve it, clients would have to believe: 'I am pleased that this adversity happened'.
- *A less intense version of a disturbed emotion (e.g. less anxious)*: this is problematic because it still involves clients holding rigid and extreme attitudes, albeit with less intensity than hitherto.

Therapists who uncritically accept such unrealistic goals serve only to create obstacles to client change later in the therapy process. Here is an example of a therapist who does not uncritically accept a goal of indifference.

| | |
|---|---|
| *Therapist:* | So to recap, you feel unhealthily envious whenever your friends have something that you want but don't have. Is that right? |
| *Client:* | Right. |
| *Therapist:* | And what is your goal when you are faced with friends having something that you want but don't have? |
| *Client:* | To be indifferent about this. |
| *Therapist:* | OK. Let me ask you something that may seem off track, but isn't. OK? |
| *Client:* | OK. |
| *Therapist:* | On Saturday, Albion Rovers are playing away to Caledonian Braves in the Scottish Lowland League. Who do you want to win? |
| *Client:* | I really don't care. |
| *Therapist:* | Because it doesn't matter to you who wins? |
| *Client:* | That's right. |

| | |
|---|---|
| *Therapist:* | Now does it matter to you if you don't have something that you prize that your friends have? |
| *Client:* | Yes, it does. |
| *Therapist:* | So, in order for you to be indifferent about this, you have to persuade yourself that it does not matter to you when it does. How are you going to do that? |
| *Client:* | I don't know. I don't think I can do that. |
| *Therapist:* | Well, you could lie to yourself. |
| *Client:* | But I still won't believe it. |
| *Therapist:* | I guess your choice then is to feel unhealthily envious about your friends having something that you prize but don't have, or to feel healthily envious about this. Which would you like? |
| *Client:* | Healthy envy ... I think, but what is the difference between the two? |

Here, the therapist helps the client in the following ways:

1. Having established that the client feels unhealthy envy about their friends having something that they prize but do not have, the therapist asks the client to nominate an emotional goal about this adversity. The client nominates 'indifference' as their feeling goal.
2. The therapist then goes about showing the client in a Socratic manner that when one is truly indifferent about something, the object of indifference is of no consequence to the client.
3. Given this, the therapist shows the client that they can choose to feel healthy envy about their friends having something that they prize but do not have, or to feel unhealthy envy about it.
4. The excerpt closes at the point at which the therapist is about to show the client the difference between healthy envy and unhealthy envy.

### Emotional Goals Should Preferably Be Accompanied by Behavioural and Thinking Goals at C

As we have seen above, one of the tasks of REBT therapists is to help clients to make keen discriminations about salient items such as unhealthy negative emotions and healthy negative emotions. One of the ways of doing this is to invoke the behavioural and thinking accompaniments of both sets of negative emotions. It follows from this that clients' goals about adversities should preferably specify not only the presence of healthy negative emotions but also their behavioural and thinking accompaniments (for a formal way of doing this, see pp. 143–144).

### Goals Need to Be within the Control of Clients

When therapists ask their clients what they want to achieve from REBT, it often happens that clients nominate goals that are, in fact, outside of their sphere of control. These often refer to changes in others or to changes in life's circumstances. In providing an example of each below, we will comment on what is problematic about them from an REBT perspective.

• 'My goal is for my mother to be more loving to me'

This goal implies a change in the mother's behaviour which the client would infer as more loving. As their mother's behaviour is under her control and not theirs, this is a problematic goal.

• 'My goal is to get promotion'

While getting promotion will be partly down to factors within the client's control (e.g. their performance in their present role, how they prepare their application form for promotion and how they perform at interview), it also involves factors outside the client's control (e.g. what the promotion appointments board thinks about the person's current job performance, application form and performance at interview and what criteria they choose to set concerning who is to be promoted). Given the latter, the client's goal is problematic.

Therapists who accept such goals uncritically will be promising more than REBT can deliver and, thus, the foundation for later obstacles to client change is set.

When clients nominate goals that are outside their control, therapists should respond to this, show them the problematic nature of such goals and refocus clients' attention on factors that are within their control. The following excerpt shows an REBT therapist doing this.

| | |
|---|---|
| *Therapist:* | What would you like to achieve from therapy? |
| *Client:* | My goal is for my mother to be more loving towards me. |
| *Therapist:* | If she was more loving to you, what would she be doing that she is not doing now? |
| *Client:* | She would phone me more often and show a genuine interest in what I'm doing. |
| *Therapist:* | Knowing your mother as you do, what's the best way you can bring this to her attention so that you increase the chances of getting what you want? |
| *Client:* | By being nice to her myself, buying her a present and then bringing the matter up with her gently. |

| | |
|---|---|
| *Therapist:* | Have you done that? |
| *Client:* | No. |
| *Therapist:* | Why not? |
| *Client:* | Because I am angry with her for not being loving. |
| *Therapist:* | I see. Here's my thought about your goal and what you've just said. I think the main problem here is that you are waiting angrily for your mother to change before you do anything that will increase your chances of getting what you want. |
| *Client:* | Put like that, I can see what you mean. |
| *Therapist:* | So, does it make sense that we address your anger so that you can do what may result in your mother being more loving? |
| *Client:* | Good idea. |
| *Therapist:* | I'll help you to specify your goal with respect to this in a minute. One other thing, if you are nice to your mother, buy her a present and then bring up the issue up with her gently, does that increase your chances of her being loving or does it guarantee success? |
| *Client:* | It increases the chances, but doesn't guarantee it. |
| *Therapist:* | Why is that? |
| *Client:* | Well, even if I do all those things, my mother may still decide not to be loving. |
| *Therapist:* | That's right, that's why in REBT we help clients set goals that are within their control. In your case, this is the obstacle that you have to doing what would increase your chances of success. But as you rightly note, there will be no guarantee of success. Incidentally, how would you feel if your mother continues to be unloving despite your attempts to influence her? |
| *Client:* | I'd be devastated. |
| *Therapist:* | What's your goal here? |
| *Client:* | Not to be devastated. |
| *Therapist:* | But to feel what instead? |
| *Client:* | Sad. |
| *Therapist:* | So to recap, you have two goals that are within your control. First, you want to address your unhealthy anger that stops you doing certain things that will increase your chances of getting a more loving response from your mother, and second, you want to feel sad, but not devastated, if your mother continues to be unloving despite your best efforts. Is that accurate? |
| *Client:* | Yes. |
| *Therapist:* | OK. Shall we first talk about your goal with respect to your anger about your mother not making the first move? |

In the above excerpt, the therapist has done the following:

1.  The therapist helps the client to be more specific about what would constitute 'loving' behaviour from their mother. The therapist asks the client what's the best way they can bring this to their mother's attention to increase the chances of getting what they want. In doing this, the therapist focuses on what is in the client's control, i.e., their behaviour.
2.  The therapist then discovers that the client has not done what they think will best influence their mother and enquires as to the reason. Having ascertained that the client is angrily waiting for their mother to make the first move, the therapist agrees with the client that this is an obstacle to changing their own behaviour and that this needs addressing, and notes that they will set a goal with respect to this problem shortly.
3.  The therapist then helps the client to see that even if they act in a way designed to influence their mother to be more loving towards them, the mother may still decide not to respond in the desired manner. This is an important point. While the therapist may accept as a goal behaviour designed to influence another person to change, because such behaviour is within the client's control, it is important that the client realise that such influence attempts may fail. The therapist in the above interchange does this and elicits the client's feelings about their mother not changing. Realising that their response represents an emotional problem, the therapist helps the client to set a goal with respect to the problem there and then. The fact that the therapist has not helped the client to set a concrete goal with respect to their anger is that doing so requires more work than setting a goal with respect to the client feeling devastated about their mother not changing. At the end, the therapist suggests goal-setting with respect to the client's anger.

### Helping Clients to Get a Good Balance Between Short-Term Goals and Long-Term Goals

REBT argues that we are likely to be at our happiest when we achieve a balance between enjoying the pleasures of the moment and planning constructively for the future (known as long-range hedonism). Clients often pursue short-term goals (e.g. avoidance of discomfort) which sabotage their long-term goals (e.g. overcoming their anxiety). On the other hand, some REBT therapists, particularly trainees, focus only on long-term goals, thereby implying that short-term goals are unimportant or self-defeating.

| | |
|---|---|
| *Trainee:* | You're falling behind with your studies because you go to too many parties. Is that right? |
| *Client:* | Yes. |

| Trainee: | So, pleasure always first, then work a distant second, and sometimes you never get down to it at all. |
|---|---|
| Client: | A good party versus studying alone on some boring subject. No contest. |
| Trainee: | Do you want to pass your exams? (client nods) Then I would suggest you stop all party-going and concentrate on hard study. When the exams are out of the way, then go to parties. Does that sound like a worthwhile goal to work for? |
| Client: | Stop all party-going? |
| | *[The client does not seem to be interested in the goal as it is extreme (i.e. all work and no play) and hardly likely to motivate them to change.]* |

In the following extract, the therapist looks at a goal that involves both work and play:

| Therapist: | What about study during the week and parties only at the weekend, but you don't go to the parties when you don't study? |
|---|---|
| Client: | Yes, I can live with that. |
| Therapist: | So, let's look at developing an attitude that will help you to get a better balance between studying and partying. |

When REBT therapists help their clients to reach a balance between pursuing both short- and long-term goals, they minimise obstacles to client change. If they expect clients to delay gratification completely, they will help create such obstacles.

### Monitoring Goals with Clients

I hope I have conveyed so far the intricacies and complexities of negotiating goals with clients. To this has to be added one even more complicating factor: clients' goals change over time. Therapists who assume that goals properly negotiated at the outset of therapy remain unchanged over the course of therapy are more likely to foster obstacles to client change than therapists who monitor clients' goals and deal with changing goals.

Therapists can monitor clients' goals formally at agreed review sessions or informally when it appears that their goals may have shifted. In whichever way clients' goals are monitored, REBT is more effective when geared towards clients' current goals than when geared towards goals identified at the outset of therapy.

There is one rider to this. Some clients claim that their goals have changed in order to avoid working towards any particular goal because they fear failure, for example. Given this, it is important for therapists to assess why clients modify their goals.

### Eliciting from Clients a Commitment to Achieve Their Goals

Stating a goal is not the same as being committed to achieving it. To be committed to change means undertaking willingly the hard work involved in reaching the goal and seeing clearly the benefits to be gained when the goal is achieved. Therapists who assume that clients will, as a matter of course, put in the effort and hard work to achieve their goals once they have agreed these goals with their therapists are likely to be naive.

A commitment to achieve a therapeutic goal involves the following stages.

1. A clear statement of the goal and its benefits. If one is ambivalent about achieving the goal, it is important to carry out a cost-benefit analysis to increase motivation to change.
2. A plan of what one needs to do to achieve the goal. This includes the realisation that repetition of the activities made explicit in the plan is an integral part of change.
3. A verbal declaration that one will execute the plan.
4. Executing the plan.

Seasoned REBT therapists realise that difficulties can occur at each of the four stages listed above and deal with them when they become manifest. Novice and naive REBT therapists assume, for example, that if clients declare that they will execute their plan, then they will do so. Sadly, this is a recipe for creating or encountering obstacles to client change.

### Obstacles to Client Change in the Goals Domain of the Working Alliance Due to Therapists' Personal Issues

So far in this chapter, I have discussed the knowledge and skills that therapists need in order to minimise the existence of obstacles to client change in the goals domain of the working alliance. It is a premise of this book, however, that knowledge and skills do not guarantee that these will be implemented by REBT therapists. Practitioners may have a number of personal issues, the existence of which may well impede them from carrying out what they know is good practice in negotiating clients' goals using the skills that are in their skill repertoire. Thus, in this section of the chapter, we will consider some of these impeding personal factors.

### Dealing with Attitudes of Unbearability

As should be apparent from the discussion of the knowledge and skills that REBT therapists need to minimise obstacles to client change in the goals domain of the working alliance, negotiating effective goals with clients in REBT can be a lengthy and painstaking business. Therapists with attitudes of unbearability towards therapy may well decide to opt out of the fray and go along with poor client goals (if indeed they ask clients about their goals at all!) all for an easy life.

While this can be picked up in supervision, it is recognised by seasoned REBT supervisors that therapists who have attitudes of unbearability towards therapy may well also have attitudes of unbearability towards supervision. The latter results in taking to supervision cases where one is doing well and therapy is going smoothly, so that supervisors tend to give positive feedback and certainly do not challenge supervisees since they have nothing to challenge them on!

One way round this for supervisors is to implement a technique I call the 'lucky dip' technique, although it can easily be called the 'unlucky dip' technique for reasons that will soon become clear. In this technique, the supervisor asks the therapist to bring to therapy digital voice recordings (DVRs) of a number of therapy sessions, and the supervisor picks one at random to play in the supervision session.[3]

In the following session, the supervisor has, for a while, harboured the suspicion that the therapist they are supervising has 'faked good' in presenting only cases and recordings of sessions that are going well and smoothly. They have asked the therapist to bring in fifteen of their DVRs on a USB drive and has selected one to play. In playing the recording, it is clear that the therapist has accepted a goal put forward by his client that indicates the absence of an unhealthy negative emotion rather than the presence of a healthy negative emotion. The therapist is an experienced practitioner and certainly has the knowledge and skills to deal with this common problem in the goals domain in the working alliance. The supervisor handles the situation in the following manner:

| | |
|---|---|
| *Supervisor:* | When your client said that their goal was not to feel anxious about sitting exams, I'm puzzled as to why you let that go. What error have you made in letting that issue go? |
| *Supervisee:* | I have not helped her to set a specific healthy negative emotion about sitting exams. |
| *Supervisor:* | I was sure that you knew that and that you know how best to address it. Am I right in that? |
| *Supervisee:* | Yes, you are. |
| *Supervisor:* | So, I'm curious why you didn't do it? |
| *Supervisee:* | I guess it didn't occur to me. |
| *Supervisor:* | So, if you had thought about it at the time, you would have done it? |

| | |
|---|---|
| *Supervisee:* | I'm not sure. |
| *Supervisor:* | How so? |
| *Supervisee:* | Well, it's hard work negotiating appropriate goals with clients and it was the end of a long hard day and … |
| *Supervisor:* | So what conditions would have had to be present for you to have negotiated an appropriate goal with your client? |
| *Supervisee:* | OK. I get the point. I was saying that it was too much of a pain to do it. |
| *Supervisor:* | Would you do the same all over again? |
| *Supervisee:* | Well, I might if I don't deal with my attitude of unbearability. |
| *Supervisor:* | So, I guess the issue is whether you are going to do that? |
| *Supervisee:* | You know I have been resting on my laurels too much recently. When you asked me to bring me to bring in a big sample of my recordings, I felt myself really not wanting to do it. But now the issue is out in the open, I am going to address my attitudes of unbearability and develop attitudes of bearability. |
| *Supervisor:* | How can I best help you do that? |

In this interchange, the supervisor has helped the therapist (supervisee) to realise that the reason that they did not help the client to set a suitable goal was not because they lacked the knowledge or the skill to do it, but because they held an attitude of unbearability towards the effort and discomfort that doing so would have entailed. The therapist realises that this is a more general issue for them and decides with determination to address it. Note that throughout this sequence, the supervisor took a Socratic, non-challenging stance. They did so because the therapist is experienced and does not need an active-directive approach. The supervisor helped the therapist understand what was happening, and when the latter did so their commitment to change was apparent. If the supervisor needed to be more challenging, they would have been, thus modelling an attitude of bearability.

### Dealing with the Need for Clients' Approval

Helping clients to reformulate their initially stated goals for change not only is hard work, but also may antagonise some clients no matter how delicately the therapist may raise and discuss the issue. In order to practise REBT effectively, practitioners not only need to do so while tolerating the discomfort of the 'slings and arrows of outrageous therapy fortune', but also need to show themselves that they don't have to have their clients' approval while doing REBT. In the first excerpt below, the therapist backs away from staying with the goal negotiation process when the client gets cross, while in the second excerpt they persist.

---

**Excerpt 1**

*Therapist:*   So you are anxious about being boring when you are out on dates? How would you like me to help you with this problem?

*Client:*   I want you to help me to not be anxious about this.

*Therapist:*   Given that being seen as boring is a negative event for you, you need to feel something, and not being anxious means that you would not have any feelings.

*Client:*   Why are you being so pedantic? You know what I mean, you are just being picky.

*Therapist:*   Sorry about that. It's not my intention to be picky. OK, let me help you to not be anxious about being thought boring.

---

**Excerpt 2**

*Therapist:*   So you are anxious about being boring when you are out on dates? How would you like me to help you with this problem?

*Client:*   I want you to help me to not be anxious about this.

*Therapist:*   Given that being seen as boring is a negative event for you, you need to feel something, and not being anxious means that you would not have any feelings.

*Client:*   Why are you being so pedantic? You know what I mean, you are just being picky.

*Therapist:*   Sorry about that. It's not my intention to be picky. However, if I don't help you to set a goal that you can see and work towards, you may well not deal as effectively with your anxiety problem as you would if I did help you to set a suitable goal. Can you see that?

*Client:*   Well, I still think you are being picky.

*Therapist:*   But are you prepared to bear with my pickiness as you see it, if doing so helps me to help you more effectively?

*Client:*   OK.

---

Therapists who believe that they need to have their clients' approval tend to give in to clients' wishes without much of a struggle (as demonstrated in the first excerpt above). In doing so, they fail to persist with a useful therapeutic strategy as the therapist did in the second excerpt. It follows, therefore, that REBT therapists should advisedly practise REBT preferring but not needing their clients' approval.

Unless doing so will unduly threaten the working alliance, I recommend that REBT therapists prioritise good REBT over getting client approval if the two are likely to conflict.

### Dealing with Shame

Novice REBT therapists are often over-concerned about showing their clients that they are incompetent. They think that if they say to clients that they are not sure how to respond for the best in therapy and that they need to get advice from their supervisor, the client will look down on them and they will feel shame as a result. Consequently, they tend to go along with their clients' problematic goals because although they know that they are problematic they don't know why, or because they know why these goals are problematic but don't how best to deal with them.

When learning REBT, it is important to do so from the standpoint of an attitude of unconditional self-acceptance (USA). Trainees who say to clients, in effect, 'At my stage of training, I am not sure about how to set a goal with you on this problem, but I will find out and get back to you' are doing the following:

- They are getting the most out of the learning process. Hiding one's ignorance does not promote learning and growth as a therapist.
- They will learn how to set goals and thus will be less likely to create obstacles to client change than trainees who try to bluff their way through therapy.
- They serve as a good role model for clients who believe that their own self-esteem is based on knowing all the answers.
- If a client does openly mock them for displaying ignorance, they can practise maintaining their USA attitude in the face of this adversity.

In short, practising REBT to avoid shame will tend to promote obstacles to client change, while practising REBT from the standpoint of USA will help to minimise the occurrence of such obstacles.

Clients and therapists have tasks to undertake if clients are to achieve their goals. In the next chapter, I outline and discuss the many therapist obstacles to client change that can occur in the tasks domain of the working alliance and how these can best be addressed.

### Notes

1  'Time-bound' means that the client has an agreed timeframe within which to achieve the goal.
2  Some would call this activity Rational Emotive Behavioural Coaching (see Dryden, 2018).
3  Of course the therapist can choose to bring only recordings of good sessions, although if they have to bring along a large sample of such sessions, this self-selection bias is minimised.

# Chapter 10

# Dealing with Therapist Obstacles to Client Change in the Tasks Domain of the Working Alliance

In Chapter 5, I examined the blocks that clients have in carrying out their goal-directed tasks. While REBT therapists may continually remind clients of their therapeutic responsibility in effecting constructive change (e.g. 'If you don't put into practice what is taught in the sessions you won't make much progress'), these therapists may forget, ignore, fail to understand or pay lip service to the fact that they have their own form of therapeutic responsibility to adhere to. This comprises a number of tasks throughout the course of therapy which are designed to help clients to achieve, ideally, the highest possible degree of change in their lives. The reasons for therapists' lack of diligence in applying themselves to these tasks will now be explored.

## When Therapists Don't Investigate Clients' Anticipations of and Preferences for Therapy

Some REBT therapists might automatically assume that providing clients with rapid relief from their presenting problems is the main order of business and spending time on teasing out clients' expectations of therapy is holding up the momentum of therapy. Also, they may believe that exploring such issues is largely irrelevant because no matter what the clients say, they are still going to be taught the *ABCs* of REBT. Therefore, sounding confident and authoritative is what really counts in clients' eyes and, as this approach will impress them, they will quickly 'fall into line'. A few therapists might resent dwelling on clients' anticipations of and preferences for therapy because 'they [clients] should be grateful that someone is prepared to help them. I'm not pandering to their whims'. This take-it-or-leave-it approach may alienate more clients than it attracts. The aforementioned therapist attitudes can leave clients confused, overwhelmed, indignant or thinking that they have been devalued – hardly the basis for building a working alliance.

By discovering clients' anticipations of therapy, important misconceptions can be corrected, e.g. 'You will be able to cure me'; 'I do all the talking, you just listen and that's how I get better', thereby reducing the potential for obstacles to client change when therapy unfolds in a way they did not envisage. Encouraging clients to express their preferences for a particular therapeutic relationship

DOI: 10.4324/9781003423379-12

helps 'to establish and maintain an appropriately bonded relationship that will encourage each individual client to implement his or her goal-directed thera-peutic tasks' (Golden and Dryden, 1986: 368–9). Such idiosyncratic prefer-ences might include a formal, no-nonsense relationship based on the therapist's expertise or a relaxed, informal one with the therapist seen as a confidant. The point of gathering this information is to create a client-friendly environment which encourages them to address their problems within the *ABC* framework – the manner in which this is done is more important than the speed with which it is carried out.

## When Therapists Don't Take Care When Socialising Clients into REBT

It is important for clients to understand both what is expected of them and what lies ahead if they are to participate effectively in REBT, e.g. collaborating with the ther-apist in the trial and error of emotional problem-solving rather than submissively absorbing the therapist's 'insights'. Instead of detailing what the therapist's and client's respective responsibilities and tasks are as part of structuring the therapy process, the therapist may sum it up ominously: 'There's lots of hard work ahead for both of us'. The therapist's guarantee of hard work but delivered without an accompanying clinical rationale makes the clients' understanding of their expected role in therapy much harder to grasp – like groping forward in the dark. Not pro-viding clients with a general design of therapy might be due to the therapist's own inability to think strategically and, instead of offering guidance, therapy unfolds in an inchoate fashion, e.g. tasks are foisted on clients as the therapist thinks of them, rather than integrated in a systematic way into therapy.

Socialising clients into REBT makes their responsibilities and tasks explicit and lessens the chances of them receiving any unexpected 'shocks'. This approach helps to buttress rather than rupture the working alliance. This process can be car-ried out in the form of a direct address to the client.

---

*Therapist:*    Our job in therapy is to identify your key attitudes that are at the base of a great deal of your present emotional disturb-ance. By examining these attitudes, we can work out ways of developing more helpful ones, which will, in turn, reduce your emotional disturbance. In order to bring this about, you will be required to carry out homework tasks designed to increase your confidence and skill in problem-solving. The ultimate aim of therapy is for you to become a self-therapist and thereby increase the likelihood of successfully tackling your problems of today, tomorrow and the future.

---

Instead of letting clients swallow undigested their 'job description', it is important for therapists to obtain feedback in order to clarify points and deal with clients' doubts, reservations or objections about it. Some therapists may not wish to be so blatant in outlining the client's role in therapy and, instead, signal the collaborative and task-orientated nature of the endeavour by an early problem-solving focus, e.g. 'OK, what problem shall we look at first?' However, as Dryden and Yankura (1993) point out, clients could become confused if their tasks are introduced into therapy without a supporting rationale.

## When Therapists Are Too Active and Too Directive

REBT therapists usually adopt an energetic and forceful approach to therapy that guides clients to the salient aspects of their presenting problems and is deemed to be more effective in helping clients change than a passive or non-directive style of intervention. Thus, they are active in, among other clinical responsibilities, asking questions, gathering information, limiting extraneous material, problem-defining, goal-setting and assessing problems using the *ABC* framework – all with the express purpose of directing clients to the attitudinal centre of their emotional disturbance. Some therapists might pursue the active-directive style too zealously and thereby overlook or pay no attention to their clients' interactional and learning requirements.

*Supervisor:* How do you think therapy is going for the client?

*Supervisee:* We're really getting down to business. Things are moving along well.

*Supervisor:* I can believe that. Your recording sounds as if you're roaring through therapy at a hundred miles an hour. Is your client keeping up with you though?

*Supervisee:* I haven't had any complaints from the client.

*Supervisor:* You may not have heard any, but have you asked them? In fact, I haven't heard the client say much at all. Have they been flattened by your juggernaut?

*Supervisee:* What do you mean?

*Supervisor:* I get the impression that the pace of therapy is much too fast for the client, and they have been left behind.

*Supervisee:* They seem compliant. Nodding in agreement with the points I'm making.

*Supervisor:* In REBT, we look for genuinely collaborative clients, not compliant ones. You're failing to get feedback in order to establish if the client really understands the points you are making, if they are happy with the pace you're setting, if your approach is best suited to their learning needs, and what kind of preferred relationship they would like with you. All these things will help to create an optimal learning environment for your client.

*Supervisee:* But it's my natural pace and style in therapy.

*Supervisor:* But is it theirs? Unless you adjust your pace and level of verbal activity to suit your client's, you will probably have a high attrition rate among clients through boredom, confusion, hostility.

*Supervisee:* What's the problem with my 'verbal activity' as you call it?

*Supervisor:* Instead of asking one question and waiting for an answer, you ask half a dozen and often end up answering them yourself. Therapy sounds like a monologue rather than a dialogue.

*Supervisee:* It seems like my sessions are a catalogue of disasters.

*Supervisor:* You're obviously trying to help the client, but this would be done better if you slow down, ask one question at a time and follow the other suggestions I've already made.

*Supervisee:* Well, it does make sense: people generally tell me that I talk too fast and show impatience when things are dawdling along.

*Supervisor:* OK. So, you will need to monitor your speedometer in therapy.

Working too fast in therapy is a common problem, particularly among novice REBT therapists. They may have seen on video such expert REBT therapists as Albert Ellis, Raymond DiGiuseppe, Janet Wolfe and Richard Wessler set a fast pace with some of their clients and incorrectly assume that this is the standard speed to conduct therapy. What they overlook is that these clients profited from a faster rather than a slower pace, and that is why these recordings were selected for demonstration purposes. REBT is primarily a psycho-educational therapy approach and therefore, as the supervisor puts it, the therapist needs 'to create an optimal learning environment for them'. This is achieved by using the client's reactions to therapy to build a learning profile of them, e.g. a slow pace if they keep on saying 'I'm not sure' after each question, examples to illustrate each point if they are a concrete thinker, diagrams on the board 'as I'm not too good with ideas', the therapist as a friendly face rather than a forbidding one 'to help me feel more at ease when I don't understand what's being said to me'. An active-directive approach means a certain style of therapy, not a predetermined speed at which to conduct it.

## When Therapists Accept Vague Terms as Disturbed Emotions

When clients are asked how they feel about life's adversities, they frequently say things like 'terrible', 'bad', 'screwed up', 'rejected', 'a failure', 'stressed out'. Clients may consider these terms to be apt descriptions of their feeling states, but for REBT therapists they are a vague collection of *A*, *B* and *C* factors which need to be sorted out and slotted into their appropriate places within the framework. Some therapists may believe that 'bad' or 'stressed out' are sufficiently precise or descriptive terms to indicate which unhealthy negative emotions the client is suffering from, e.g. 'It sounds to me by what the client is saying that they are depressed and angry'. Also, these therapists may be reluctant to 'push' clients to be more specific about their feelings when they are so obviously distressed or unsure themselves, e.g. 'How do I know if I'm depressed or guilty? I just know that I feel terrible'. Lack of specificity in identifying an unhealthy negative emotion may mean, for example, that the therapist is grappling simultaneously with several disturbed emotions and their different attitude structures; the therapist is tackling a healthy negative emotion instead of an unhealthy one, e.g. sadness and depression respectively, or the therapist is mistaking an activating event ($A$) for a feeling ($C$), e.g. 'I feel frustrated over things'.

Specifying a disturbed negative emotion is the starting point for therapeutic intervention as it provides important clues to what the client's operative rigid/extreme attitude might be, e.g., pursuing the central idea or theme in hurt of a perceived injustice to oneself which is totally undeserved eventually leads the therapist to the client's disturbance-inducing attitude, such as 'He forgot my birthday and this proves I'm not that important to him. I must be as important to him as he is to me and if I'm not, I'm worthless'. Each disturbed emotion that the client has can be tackled in a similar and consecutive fashion. Distinguishing between unhealthy and healthy negative emotions reveals that the client's 'pissed off' state is actually healthy, not unhealthy anger, and therefore valuable therapy time is not wasted on trying to change the client's healthy feeling. By learning REBT's emotional vocabulary, the therapist can see that frustration is not listed and therefore is usually to be treated as the client's $A$. Then, the therapist can ask how the client feels about being frustrated – 'Angry!' ($C$) – which then sets the stage to uncover the $B$.

By teaching REBT's taxonomy of unhealthy and healthy negative emotions, the therapist now replaces vagueness with precision in identifying the client's $C$. Clarifying 'hard to get at' or unclear emotions through various techniques (e.g. the empty chair technique, imagery exercises) enables the clients to uncover their suppressed feelings or bring specificity to their amorphous emotional state. All these techniques, among others, usually allow therapists to pinpoint rapidly clients' disturbed feelings so that their amelioration can occur as early as possible in therapy (see Dryden 2022).

## When Therapists Wrongly Assume that They Know What Clients Are Disturbed About

In assessing the client's adversity at $A$, the therapist is trying to locate what the client was most disturbed about in the problem-related situation which triggered the client's rigid/extreme basic attitude at $B$ which, in turn, largely created the client's disturbed feelings at $C$. REBT therapists often use a method known as inference chaining to discover $A$ which is a skilful and often complicated procedure to carry out (see Dryden, 2024). Therapists who fail to be thorough in assessing $A$ and fail to locate the adversity are not helping their clients to discover what they are most disturbed about in the problem-related situation. For example, a therapist who states that the client's anxiety is due to the possibility of making factual errors in front of colleagues does not help the client to pursue the implications of such errors in order to come face-to-face with what the client is most anxious about. Such an inadequate analysis often leaves clients thinking that 'something is still missing' and the problem remains unresolved.

Burrowing into the *A* rather than scratching about on the surface of it should be the guiding principle of inference chaining (though, of course, the first inference in the chain could be the critical one).

| | |
|---|---|
| *Therapist:* | Let's assume that you do make factual errors in front of your colleagues. Then what? |
| *Client:* | I'm supposed to be an expert on the subject and I'm showing myself up as a fool in front of them. |
| *Therapist:* | OK. Let's assume that they do see you as a fool rather than as an expert. Then what? |
| *Client:* | My professional reputation would be in tatters. Everything I've worked for would be destroyed. |
| *Therapist:* | And what would happen next if your reputation was shattered? |
| *Client* *(crying):* | Oh God! I'd want to kill myself. I've never seen it so starkly before. I couldn't stand the humiliation and shame of failure. |
| *Therapist:* | So what are you most anxious about – your reputation being shattered or the suicidal thoughts that would occur if this happened? |
| *Client:* | My reputation. I must preserve it at all costs and that's why I can't allow myself to make any errors. |

The therapist's 'Let's assume ... Then what?' questions lead the client to uncover what they are most anxious about if they make factual errors in front of their colleagues and the verbalisation of her rigid and extreme attitude, 'I must preserve my reputation at all costs. I couldn't stand the humiliation and shame of failure'. By pinpointing the adversity at *A* and 'springing' the implicit rigid/extreme attitude, the therapist will now be tackling the root of the client's anxiety rather than probing at its periphery.

## When Therapists Don't Attend to Clients' Meta-Problems

One of the distinctive features of REBT is its routine searching for clients' meta-problems i.e., their secondary emotional problems about their primary ones (e.g.

anxiety about anxiety; shame about feeling depressed; guilt about displaying anger). This procedure is carried out to determine if clients are preoccupied with or distracted by these meta-problems thereby interfering with them focusing on their first-order ones, e.g. someone who presents with a history of panic attacks is deeply ashamed of his 'unmanly' behaviour and focuses on his self-disgust rather than on the therapist's explanation of the cognitive model of panic. Some therapists may overlook this important aspect of assessment because, among other reasons, they are too eager to get to work on the primary problem, only give cursory attention to any secondary problems that may exist, readily agree when clients deny they exist or do not help them to understand the important role of meta-problems in the perpetuation of their emotional disturbance.

A routine question for teasing out meta-problems is to ask, for example, 'Are there any other feelings that you experience in relation to your panic attacks?' If the client is unsure what the therapist means by this question, the therapist can present a brief explanation of the reasons they are probing for meta-problems. If none is uncovered at this point in therapy, the therapist can remain alert to clues that the client is experiencing them, e.g., the client seems distant, their attention wanders or the client isn't making expected progress on their primary problem. If meta-problems are identified and deemed to be more clinically significant to work on first, it is important that the therapist presents a rationale to the client for this approach, but without insisting upon it.

## When Therapists Imply that Preferences Can Be Equated with Passivity

In encouraging clients to surrender their rigid attitudes in favour of flexible attitudes, inexperienced REBT therapists often imply that embracing a preferential outlook means being passive, indifferent or resigned in the face of unpleasant events. Needless to say, many clients will be hostile to this suggestion and get the wrong impression of REBT philosophy, e.g. 'You mean I'm just supposed to roll over and play dead when he insults me?'; 'Achieving very high standards is no longer important?' Such therapists may wonder what the 'problem' is when clients do not readily accept their viewpoint.

| | |
|---|---|
| *Supervisee:* | The client doesn't seem to grasp how preferences will help them. |
| *Supervisor:* | I'm not surprised. Listening to your digital voice recording, I can't hear you advocating preferences, particularly strong ones, in this client's case. |
| *Supervisee:* | But I have been – I keep on reminding the client that it doesn't matter if they don't reach her high standards. |
| *Supervisor:* | That isn't a powerful preference but a statement of indifference. Look at it from the client's viewpoint: they are continually |

*Supervisee:* I suppose mediocrity.

striving to achieve high standards, and by giving up their rigid demands, what have you left her with?

*Supervisor:* Exactly. No wonder the client is giving you a hard time in therapy. Now, how can you state a really strong flexible preference which does not advocate that the client drops their standards?

*Supervisee:* 'I passionately want to achieve my very high standards but I don't have to'.

*Supervisor:* So, you are encouraging the client to introduce flexibility into their thinking about their standards without implying that they have to lower them. What are the benefits of a flexible, preferential approach?

*Supervisee:* Well, the client can keep on striving to maintain their standards but is no longer anxious about falling below them. If they do fall below these standards, they can bring a problem-solving focus and examine what went wrong. With their rigid attitude, they usually plunge into doom and gloom and take longer to achieve their standards again.

*Supervisor:* Good. That should help to put therapy back on track. Now remember that the preference part of a flexible attitude can be mild, moderate or powerful, but don't confuse them with statements of indifference or resignation.

*Supervisee:* OK. I've really got the difference now.

*Supervisor:* I'll look forward to listening to your next recording with this client then.

Therapists are advised to pay close attention to how they phrase the preferential part of a flexible attitude and ensure that they convey the correct message of healthy alternatives to rigid attitudes. Feedback from clients will confirm how successful they have been in this task.

## When Therapists Don't Deal with Clients' Doubts, Reservations or Objections to REBT

It is highly likely that many, if not all, clients will have some DROs to REBT theory or practice, e.g. 'I can't see what's the problem about me demanding that my husband must love me? After all, that's why he married me'. Because such DROs are not openly expressed, some therapists may not search for them, and they may see such probing as an onerous or potentially anxiety-provoking task or blithely believe that therapy is 'progressing nicely'. The danger in not testing for the existence of DROs is that if the client has them, they will likely increase to the extent that the client is focused on them rather than on the therapy itself or they may overwhelm the client and lead to premature termination.

REBT therapists need to encourage their clients to express openly any DROs they have about any aspect of therapy. This 'invitation' can be part of clients' induction into REBT. Of course, once this invitation has been issued, therapists should handle such DROs in an open, respectful and non-defensive manner – therapists who take umbrage at a client's comments display hypocrisy and are likely to undermine their stance as a flexible and non-extreme role framework. Therapists' reluctance to engage in this task may reflect attitudes of unbearability (e.g. I must be free from the onerous task of dealing with clients' doubts about REBT. Therapy is hard enough without having to do this') or self-devaluation attitudes (e.g. 'What if I can't come up with good answers, as I must do, to remove her doubts? It would prove that I am competent as a therapist and less worthwhile as a person'). Unless such therapists examine and change these attitudes, clients' unexamined doubts may well prove a source of obstacles to client change later in therapy.

## When Therapists Conclude the Examination of Clients' Attitudes Too Quickly

Helping clients to examine their rigid/extreme and flexible/non-extreme attitudes is a major activity of REBT therapists. The degree of skill, persistence and creativity shown in doing this often means the difference between clients achieving enduring rather than superficial change in their lives. Ellis (1979, 1985) emphasised the role of force and energy in helping clients to examine often deeply rigid/extreme attitudes and their flexible/non-extreme attitudinal alternatives. Some therapists, often novice ones, incorrectly believe that a few tilts at a rigid and flexible attitude, for example, will bring about a change of attitude. More commonly, therapists can become disillusioned about making any therapeutic headway when their clients show no signs of making such a change.

| | |
|---|---|
| *Supervisee:* | It's so difficult. Nothing seems to work with this client. |
| *Supervisor:* | Remind me of her attitude. |
| *Supervisee:* | 'I must be in control at all times; otherwise, I'm totally inadequate.' |
| *Supervisor:* | So, what attitude examination strategies are you using with her? |
| *Supervisee:* | The usual ones of logic, empiricism and pragmatism. |
| *Supervisor:* | 'How does it logically follow …?', 'Is it consistent with reality?' and 'Where is it going to get you?' You haven't cracked the case yet? |
| *Supervisee:* | I keep on going over these arguments but the client won't budge. They won't adopt the alternative flexible/non-extreme attitude. |

*Supervisor:*   Remember, they don't have to budge in order to prove what an outstanding therapist you are. If they remain disturbed, too bad! Also, they may have a different conception of what flexible and non-extreme means, so you will need to check that out. Now, listening to your digital voice recording, your attitude examination strategies are presented in a monotonous and lacklustre fashion – no matter what the client says, you ask them the same three questions.

*Supervisee:*   I thought that's what I'm supposed to do?

*Supervisor:*   You can use a wide array of attitude examination strategies underpinned by those three criteria and also vary your style. For example, the client sounds lively and humorous.

*Supervisee:*   They are.

*Supervisor:*   Well, I would inject some humour into the sessions. I would drop books, fall out of my chair, walk into the bookcase, that sort of thing, and then ask the client if I'm totally inadequate because I lost control.

*Supervisee:*   It might not work.

*Supervisor:*   That's true, but try it anyway. Take risks, be inventive, creative. Don't be afraid to experiment …

*Supervisee:*   … rather than be a stick-in-the-mud, which is what I am.

*Supervisor:*   But you don't have to stay like that. Look for lots of ways of contradicting their attitude, such as what are they doing in therapy if they have total control? If they really were in complete control of themself, they wouldn't need to demand it of themself as it would be patently obvious to themself and others.

*Supervisee:*   Those arguments seem so obvious when you say them, but they haven't occurred to me. I'm just asking the same three questions mechanically without any flair or imagination.

*Supervisor:*   Have you really brought out the heavy price the client has to pay for keeping up this facade of total control when the reality is imperfect control? All the strain and anxiety created by this tension? The depression and anger when things go wrong?

*Supervisee:*   Well, I do ask the client about the practical consequences of hanging on to this attitude, but we don't pursue it very far. No, we haven't really spelt it out.

*Supervisor:*   What about homework tasks?

*Supervisee:*   To deliberately make a mistake at work and learn to accept themself as a fallible human being.

*Supervisor:*   What happened?

*Supervisee:*   The client said they wouldn't do it.

*Supervisor:*   Individuals who demand infallibility don't like those feet of clay homework tasks. I would have suggested that the client record the mistakes they will inevitably, not deliberately, make to reinforce the point about their fallibility.

How old is the client?

*Supervisee:* 40.

*Supervisor:* I would keep on pointing out that they have had 40 years of evidence which conclusively disproves their total control attitude. How many more years do they need before the point sinks in?

*Supervisee:* The client is hard going.

*Supervisor:* Well, you need to be equally persistent in encouraging them to examine both their rigid/extreme and their flexible/non-extreme attitudes. How are you getting on helping them to develop the flexible/non-extreme alternative?

*Supervisee:* I'm still helping the client to examine their rigid and extreme attitude.

*Supervisor:* Building up the greater benefits of flexible/non-extreme attitudes beliefs is part of the attitude examination process. So how could you try and interest the client in them?

*Supervisee:* Well, self-acceptance would be a good thing for the client.

*Supervisor:* Why?

*Supervisee:* Well … I'm not sure, really.

*Supervisor:* With self-acceptance, they would not be anxious about not being in control at all times. When they did make mistakes, they could quickly bounce back from them because they have kept a problem-solving focus and avoided becoming mired in depression and anger. They would be learning from their mistakes how to develop greater control rather than wasting time and energy on maintaining this facade. That would be a real and realistic sense of control. When you are not afraid of losing control, that's when you really are in control. Keep on showing them why you believe these are good ideas to acquire.

*Supervisee:* I'm sure I'll forget all this in the session.

*Supervisor:* Then, write these points down on cards to act as prompts during the session. Have you found out if they have had other deeply held ideas they eventually discarded?

*Supervisee:* No, I haven't thought of that. Obviously, if that has occurred, this might give me some information on how to structure my present interventions.

*Supervisor:* Exactly. Are you any the wiser now?

*Supervisee:* Yes, I am. I've got to wake my brain up to the great possibilities in helping clients to examine their attitudes.

In this extract from supervision, important points to consider are the following:

1. The goal of helping clients examine their attitudes is to encourage them to see the superiority of flexible/non-extreme attitudes over rigid/extreme ones in emotional problem-solving. It is not about a power struggle between the therapist and client where the former has to convince the latter of the usefulness of REBT's concepts.

2. The logical, empirical and pragmatic arguments advocated in the REBT literature (Ellis and Dryden, 1997; Dryden, 2024) are only the starting point of the attitude examination process and not equivalent to this process itself. Hauck (1980) suggested that one's credibility and strength as an REBT therapist is partly due to the ease with which the therapist can employ a wide range of arguments to prompt a shift in the client's thinking.

3. Effective examination of clients' attitudes involves creativity, humour, risk-taking, persistence, repetition and force and energy, in order to provide the client with persuasive arguments to change their attitudes. Promoting such attitude change needs to be regarded as an ever-improving skill, and it would be unwise for any REBT therapist to claim that they have totally mastered it.

4. As a general point, those therapists, novice or experienced, who find helping clients to examine their attitudes unusually difficult to do, are advised to practise as much as possible with friends and colleagues, join a debating society, watch videos or read transcripts of highly proficient REBT therapists at work, learn how to develop a genuine enthusiasm for analysing argument rather than a programmatic approach to it. In this way, attitude examination might become more of a pleasure and less of a chore.

## When Therapists Don't Establish a Criterion for Client Coping

The coping criterion is the point at which clients manage their problems, but not always smoothly or easily. This criterion is used by therapists to determine the right time to switch from one client problem to another. However, some therapists may switch too quickly because they inaccurately infer that once a rigid/extreme attitude associated with a particular problem has been identified, then 'the problem is almost solved'. Therapists may also, in a single session, switch rapidly between the ego and discomfort aspects of a particular problem without properly investigating either. Jumping from problem to problem in quick succession can leave clients feeling confused, unaware of the crucial role of attitudes in their presenting problems, and inadequately prepared to tackle their emotional difficulties.

In order to establish a genuine coping criterion, therapists need to elicit from clients that they understand and agree with the REBT view that rigid/extreme attitudes lie at the foundation of their emotional problems, ensure that clients are equipped with the skills to carry out multimodal tasks in order to examine and change these attitudes, troubleshoot actual or potential blocks to working through their problems, and establish that clients can act according to their flexible/non-extreme attitudes. When these conditions have been met, it would be clinically appropriate for the therapist to focus on another client problem. The previous problem does not at that point slip out of the therapist's vision but continues to be monitored for signs of obstacles to client change or backsliding.

## When Therapists Leave Clients Marooned at the Level of Intellectual Insight

Ellis (1963) wrote of the distinction between intellectual and emotional insight as it pertains to REBT. The former type of insight refers to flexible/non-extreme attitudes lightly and intermittently held but with rigid/extreme attitudes still exerting a powerful influence; the latter type relates to flexible/non-extreme attitudes strongly and consistently held with rigid/extreme attitudes now attenuated. Getting from intellectual to emotional insight means putting REBT theory into daily hard work and practice. Some therapists may leave clients stranded at intellectual insight (e.g. 'I understand it in my head how these new attitudes will help me to overcome my problems ...') because they believe that insight alone is sufficient to effect enduring change. Therefore, therapy slips into a discourse on flexible/non-extreme attitudes rather than an enactment of them.

In order for clients to reach emotional insight ('... and I also now feel these attitudes in my gut'), therapists need to encourage them to undertake and experiment with a wide range of homework tasks (e.g. 'stay-in-there' assignments, shame-attacking exercises, rational emotive imagery) in order to internalise a flexible/non-extreme outlook. This stage of therapy also involves removing client obstacles to achieving emotional insight, such as the 'I won't be me' syndrome (Grieger and Boyd, 1980), whereby clients believe that they will lose their identity in the change process and attitudes of unbearability, e.g., 'I want to change but the work involved is too damn hard!' Hard work and continual practice will eventually bridge the 'head–gut' divide.

## When Therapists Negotiate Homework Tasks that Are Not Therapeutically Potent

As discussed above, homework tasks represent the bridge between intellectual and emotional insight. Some clients may not get very far along this bridge, or they may take an inordinate amount of time to cross it because the tasks that the therapist has negotiated with them are insufficiently challenging to promote substantial or rapid constructive change. For example, the therapist agrees with the client's 'tiny steps' approach to overcoming their social anxiety, thereby prolonging it rather than encouraging them to stay in social situations as long as possible in order to habituate themself to the discomfort involved. Any therapeutic potency that the task could offer is undermined by the therapist colluding with and probably reinforcing the client's attitudes of unbearability instead of encouraging them to argue forcefully against them.

In planning homework tasks, it is important for the therapist to consider if the designated tasks will help clients to come appreciably closer to their goal, but without discouraging them from undertaking the tasks because they appear too difficult to execute, e.g. clients agree to enter and stay in social situations on alternate nights rather than every night in order to banish their social anxiety. I call this principle of homework negotiation 'challenging, but not overwhelming' (Dryden, 1985). Each task selected should be aimed at weakening clients' rigid/extreme attitudes while strengthening their flexible/non-extreme ones. In this way, homework becomes the real crucible of change rather than anything that happens in the therapist's office.

## When Therapists Fail to Identify Core Rigid/Extreme Attitudes

As a client's situation-specific rigid/extreme attitudes are revealed and examined (e.g., 'I must give a perfect presentation to my work colleagues'; 'I must not let a friend down when they ask me for a favour'; 'I must not show any weaknesses in front of my children'), they usually suggest common themes which frequently coalesce into core rigid/extreme attitudes which link the client's problems across a range of relevant situations. In the above example, a core rigid/extreme attitude might be 'I must have the approval of significant others in my life; otherwise, I'm worthless'. Working at this fundamental attitudinal level can help clients to effect enduring and widespread change in their lives as many problems are tackled simultaneously rather than consecutively. Some therapists may assume that removing or 'knocking down' each rigid/extreme attitude is profound attitude change of a sort, but obviously remains a haphazard way of achieving it and leaves clients vulnerable to emotional disturbance in problematic contexts that have not been examined. Also, plodding through each problem may give clients tunnel vision rather than offering them a panorama of their problems by tapping into their rules of living or core attitudes.

When clients start working through their problems, it is important for therapists to encourage them to probe for central ideas or themes that recur in each problem dissected.

---

*Therapist:*    Can you see any connection between giving the perfect work presentation, not letting down a friend and not showing weaknesses in front of your children?

*Client:*    Yes, I can. I'm always demanding approval from people I consider important in my life. I wish I could stop doing it.

*Therapist:*    What would be the value of working on this core rigid attitude rather than asking for more similar problems to explore?

> *Client:*    If we look at other problems, it will be the same old story of me having to behave in the right way each time. Let's get to the heart of the problem: my need for approval – and the sooner the better.

If clients are unable to identify core attitudes in their problems, the therapist can suggest what they might be and seek feedback in order to confirm, modify or reject them.

## When Therapists Hold Clients Back from Becoming Their Own Therapists

As clients develop greater confidence and competence in tackling their problems, the therapist should begin to diminish the level of active-directiveness in order to encourage clients to become their own therapists for present and future emotional problem-solving. Hence, clients take on more responsibility for, among other things, agenda-setting, undertaking an *ABC* assessment of their problems, eliciting disturbance-inducing attitudes, selecting attitude-examining strategies and devising homework tasks. However, if the therapist does not pull back and continues to play a dominant role in directing therapy, some clients are likely to remain dependent on the therapist to promote therapeutic change and thereby increase the chances of relapse when they leave therapy, remain at the level of intellectual insight rather than internalise a new flexible/non-extreme attitudinal outlook, or prolong therapy to delay standing on their own feet.

Dryden and Neenan (2021) suggest that it is important that therapists give their clients an opportunity to serve as their own therapist as early in the process as is clinically indicated. This can be determined by monitoring how quickly clients accept and act on the principles of emotional and therapeutic responsibility, e.g. a client acknowledges that they make themself anxious by demanding that they must have the right answer if they speak up in class and suggests that their first homework task is to reply to questions when they are unsure of the answer. As clients take over more of the reins of therapy, the therapist can slip into the role of their consultant or trainer and provide advice on how to improve their problem-solving skills. If a client's progress falters significantly, the therapist can temporarily resume a more active role until the client's obstacles to change have been addressed, e.g., the client experiences panic in class when they get an answer wrong and is reluctant to return; the therapist shows them how to re-establish cognitive control over their panic and encourages them to return to class.

## When Therapists Take Too Much Credit for Clients' Progress

As therapy moves towards termination, it is important for therapists to help their clients attribute the majority of their progress to their own efforts rather than to

their therapist, e.g. 'I taught you how you mainly created your self-induced disturbances, but you did all the hard work between sessions to overcome them. Without
that tremendous determination on your part, therapy would have been stuck in the
mud'. This kind of summary puts the locus of control and change within the client
and is usually a powerful stimulus for clients to maintain their gains after therapy
has ended. Some therapists may baulk at giving too much credit to the clients for
their progress and diminishing their own contributions to it; instead, these therapists convey to their clients how 'dazzling' they were in orchestrating the process
of change and thereby relegating the clients to the sidelines of therapy. Such therapist self-adoration is likely to communicate to the clients that 'you can't do it
without me' and, if believed, greatly increase their chances of relapse once therapy
has ended.

Therapists who feed their vanity as the omnipotent force of change in others'
lives usually have considerable ego problems that they bring into therapy, e.g. 'I
need the client to see and acknowledge how great I am in getting them better'.
By examining and changing such attitudes, therapists can remove their ego from
therapy and refocus their clinical attention where it belongs – making sure their clients are equipped to be effective problem-solvers. The real satisfaction for REBT
therapists is not in blowing their own trumpet but in seeing their clients acquire a
flexible/non-extreme attitudinal outlook that can help to guide them for the rest of
their lives.

In this chapter, I have explored therapist blocks to carrying out their various
assignments and have suggested methods for addressing these obstacles. In
Chapter 11, I will discuss a diverse collection of therapist problems that usually
inhibit or undermine the client's progress in therapy.

# A Compendium of Therapist Problems

This chapter presents a collection of therapist problems that are driven by ideological rigidity and shows how therapists can often experience more obstacles than their clients to changing rigid and extreme attitudes. These problems if not addressed successfully may pose significant obstacles to client change. As will be seen, some of these rigid and extreme attitudes are easy to uncover, e.g., an unhealthily angry therapist who demands that his clients must carry out their homework tasks, while others are harder to detect because they are subtly expressed, e.g. a therapist's pleasure in seeing a client every week masks their fear that the client's absence would prove that they are a bad therapist. Also therapist rigidity may masquerade as force and energy in the process of constructive change: clients are pushed to overcome their problems in order to rescue therapists from their own sense of a 'crushing defeat' if their clients remain emotionally disturbed. These and other issues will now be discussed.

## When Therapists Think that They Must Have an Easy Time in Therapy

A succession of clients who experience obstacles to change whom the therapist finds troublesome, who are complex or otherwise self-sabotaging, can put a considerable strain on the therapist's resilience or equilibrium, so it is understandable when a therapist desires 'a few easy clients' to usher in a more tranquil period in therapy. However, trouble arises when the therapist transmutes a desire into a rigid attitude, e.g., 'Because I want an easy time in therapy, therefore I absolutely must have one' and thereby rapidly diminishes their tolerance for coping with the next client whom the therapist finds difficult. The therapist may signal their attitude of unbearability to such a client with, among other ways, visible displays of anger when the client 'steps out of line', perfunctory examination of attitudes, indifference to whether the client carries out their homework tasks. The therapist will probably also experience great relief when a client who is experienced as difficult drops out of therapy – this may confirm from the therapist's viewpoint that the client lacked commitment to change rather than was discouraged by the therapist's

DOI: 10.4324/9781003423379-13

negative attitude towards them. The client's absence now provides the therapist with the easy time in therapy they have been demanding.

Although a clutch of 'easy' clients may provide a welcome interlude in the seemingly never-ending stream of clients whom the therapist experiences as difficult, REBT therapists need to keep on reminding themselves that there is no reason why they must have an easy time in therapy even though they may think that they deserve one. Their own disturbed behaviour may reinforce that of such a client and thereby make therapy even tougher than it was already. Such clients present a formidable challenge as they are liable to test the limits of the therapist's competence and patience. This can be viewed by the therapist as a valuable learning experience in order to improve clinical skills and strive for an attitude of bearability. Even though the therapist will generally work much harder with clients whom they find difficult, accepting the reality of the often highly disturbed behaviour of such clients will allow the therapist to have an easier time in therapy than would be the case if the therapist continually railed against such behaviour. An easy time in therapy is likely to produce complacent rather than competent and creative therapy. As Hauck (1980: 248) pointed out, no matter how badly clients behave, 'they are there to stimulate you, to enrich your life, to broaden your horizons ... [they] are the key to your therapeutic success'. So welcome them into your office!

## When Therapists Hold that They Must Encourage Their Clients to Examine All Their Rigid and Extreme Attitudes

While a client may express many rigid and extreme attitudes during the course of therapy, it does not mean that all of these attitudes are implicated in the client's presenting problems or all of them have to become the focus of clinical attention simply because they are rigid and extreme. The experienced REBT therapist keeps in focus the client's key rigid and extreme attitudes that are implicated in the problems for which they are seeking help and generally avoids examining less important or peripheral ones.

Some REBT therapists, usually novice ones, mistakenly believe that it is their devout mission to uproot all the client's rigid and extreme attitudes – or what they perceive to be rigid and extreme. Any sentence that contains a 'must' or 'should', an 'it's awful' or 'I can't stand it', etc., is immediately examined, e.g., 'Why must you wash your hair just because it is greasy?'; 'Prove that traffic jams are awful?'; 'Where's the evidence that you can't stand sugar in your coffee?' These are hardly the issues that the client wants to discuss in therapy, and they may well become confused by and frustrated with the therapist's relentless questioning every time they mention one of the aforementioned words or phrases. In attempting to remove all the client's putative rigid and extreme thinking, the therapist ends up reinforcing their own genuine rigidities and diminishing their chances of helping the client to overcome the problems they really want addressed in therapy.

Such 'knee-jerk' examination of client rigid and extreme attitudes misrepresents REBT. As Walen et al. (1992: 212) point out: 'Remember that these words [and phrases] are harmful because of the concepts that they stand for, not their face value'. Such words and phrases are part of our daily vocabulary and are frequently used in a harmless way – there is usually no absolutist ideas lurking behind these terms. Even if the client did mean, in the REBT sense, that they cannot stand sugar in her coffee, it is highly unlikely to be clinically relevant to their presenting problems or an issue that they have come to therapy to discuss. By surrendering their own dogmatic approach to therapy – 'I must get my clients to examine all of their musts!' – the therapist gradually gains clinical acuity in determining which terms used by the client are implicated in the emotional problems they wish to address and therefore are legitimate targets for examination.

## When Therapists Hold that They Must Always Be Flexible and Non-Extreme in Outlook

Acquiring a flexible and non-extreme attitudinal outlook means reducing one's general level of disturbability, but not completely removing it. This is the message to convey to clients in order to counter any misconceptions they may have that REBT will teach them how to be in emotional control at all times because each problem they have will be solved by impeccable logical analysis. Therefore, human fallibility is an inseparable part of a flexible/non-extreme attitudinal outlook. However, some REBT therapists equate being flexible and non-extreme with never again holding rigid/extreme attitudes or experiencing unhealthy negative emotions. Instead of posing as healthy role models for their clients, they are actually exhibiting psychological disturbance in their presence.

---

*Supervisor:* Listening to your digital voice recordings, I'm greatly struck by your notion of flexibility and a non-extreme outlook, which seems to imply that all emotional disturbance has been banished for good. Is this true?

*Supervisee:* Well, once you've learned how to think in a flexible and non-extreme manner, there's no reason or excuse for disturbing yourself again.

*Supervisor:* That's a pretty harsh doctrine. Are you teaching that to your client?

*Supervisee:* I'm attempting to, but they are not very receptive to it. They see it as something cold and alien to them. I'm hoping to win them over by acting as a role model.

*Supervisor:* As an uncompromising rather than a flexible one. I don't think your client is going to be persuaded.

---

*Supervisee:*   We'll see. Anyway, why do you call it harsh? Being flexible and non-extreme means establishing permanent cognitive control of one's reactions to life events.

*Supervisor:*   The reason I call it harsh is because you are not allowing for human fallibility – that human beings from time to time will slip back into self-defeating patterns of thinking, feeling and behaving. Being flexible and non-extreme in REBT terms includes accepting human fallibility. Your view of flexibility and being non-extreme is not the REBT one, and therefore you are misleading the client and yourself.

*Supervisee:*   I'm not misleading my client or myself. I am trying to teach them to be flexible by surrendering all their demands and expressing their goals only in terms of desires and preferences.

*Supervisor:*   And are you also trying to teach your client how to cope constructively when they transform desires into demands and start disturbing themself again?

*Supervisee:*   But that's the point – when the client stops making demands all over the place, then they will stop disturbing themself for good.

*Supervisor:*   If only it was as simple as that. You've fallen into the same trap as some other REBT therapists have done; namely, now that you are an REBT therapist, you have to be flexible and non-extreme at all times. You said earlier that there is no excuse for becoming disturbed again once you've learned how to think in a flexible and non-extreme manner. Doesn't sound to me as if you're expressing that idea as something that is a flexible preference.

*Supervisee:*   I suppose it does sound rather harsh, but I'm trying to follow this philosophy myself as well as offer it to the client.

*Supervisor:*   Well, you had better examine what it is you're offering the client. By demanding that you must be flexible and non-extreme in outlook at all times you are, in fact, being what?

*Supervisee:*   Rigid and extreme. The opposite of what I preferably should be teaching them.

*Supervisor:*   And yourself. When you are disturbed, do you tell yourself, for example, that you are only annoyed or concerned when you are actually feeling unhealthily angry or anxious?

*Supervisee:*   I don't like to admit it but that does happen sometimes. If I admit that I'm unhealthily angry, this means that I'm disturbing myself, which means, in turn, I'm being rigid and extreme which I prefer not to be.

*Supervisor:*   Well, you're not expressing it as a preference, but as a demand that you must not be rigid and extreme.

*Supervisee:* How do you work that out?

*Supervisor:* Because if you really followed the flexible preference, you would acknowledge that you still experience unhealthy negative emotions but want to limit their frequency, intensity and duration in your life. Instead you're denying that you feel them because ...

*Supervisee:* ... that would mean I'm not thinking in a flexible and non-extreme way, which I must do at all times.

*Supervisor:* Exactly. Now, are you going to teach your client the REBT view of flexible and non-extreme thinking once you've sorted it out in your own mind?

*Supervisee:* I can see now where I've been going wrong, but I'm worried about what the client will think when I admit my mistakes.

*Supervisor:* Because you'll be displaying what as a therapist and human being?

*Supervisee (laughs):* My dreaded fallibility.

*Supervisor:* Which forms part of a ...?

*Supervisor:* A truly flexible and non-extreme outlook.

*Supervisor:* You might find your client is now more receptive to REBT as they won't feel you're trying to turn them into Mr Spock from 'Star Trek'.

*Supervisee:* I can see now how the client probably does think that.

*Supervisor:* OK. So in your next DVRs let me hear you teaching your client proper REBT.

Throughout their training and beyond, REBT therapists are repeatedly taught that a flexible and non-extreme philosophy of living is an anti-musturbatory one that includes human fallibility – accepting oneself as a fallible human being is often the phrase that rings the loudest in the clients' ears. Yet some therapists remain deaf to this message and demand that they must be flexible and non-extreme at all times and thereby deny their own fallibility. In order for this rigid and extreme view to be detected, examined and changed, it is important for therapists to have regular supervision. Left unchecked, this anti-REBT stance will help some clients to develop more rigid and extreme ideas rather than fewer.

## When Therapists Base Their Self-Worth on Keeping Clients in Therapy

A plaintive but silent plea is sometimes made by those therapists who judge their clinical competence on the basis of clients attending therapy every week, e.g. 'My clients must come back to therapy regularly in order for me to see myself as a good and effective therapist'. Attendance is the yardstick of competence, not outcome.

Because of their need to ensure that clients return, these therapists make therapy as easy and as pleasant as possible for their clients. Therefore, hard work is not on the session agenda. Clients may leave therapy feeling better because of all the positive strokes they have received, but they are highly unlikely to be getting better as their disturbance-creating attitudes have been left unexamined and therefore intact.

Clinical competence in REBT is assessed by the reduction in or elimination of the client's emotional disturbance and not by the length of time spent in therapy. When therapists have understood this distinction by tackling their ego problems, they can then focus their clinical attention on teaching their clients to be problem-solvers. This is achieved by clients becoming collaborators in therapy to identify, examine and change their rigid/extreme attitudes to flexible/non-extreme ones through a variety of homework tasks. This usually involves clients experiencing the discomfort of hard work and the dogged persistence of the therapist in pushing, persuading and encouraging them to change. Some clients may drop out of therapy as the non-disturbed therapist is no longer bending over backwards to help them feel comfortable or worthwhile. While premature termination is regrettable, help-ing those clients who remain to realise enduring therapeutic gains is more important than trying to retain all clients in order to achieve only palliative benefits for them.

## When Therapists Think They Must Examine Immediately Their Clients' Rigid/Extreme Attitudes

REBT is a highly active-directive form of psychotherapy and seeks to elicit as early as possible the client's rigid and extreme attitudes for examination. Although REBT does have a 'let's get on with it' message to convey to clients, it does rec-ognise that some or most clients will need time to settle into therapy. For them, having a rigid/extreme attitude examined as soon as it is uncovered is likely to impair the development of a good working alliance as they feel under attack from the therapist, e.g. 'Why won't my therapist listen to what I have to say instead of examining my attitudes all the time?' For some REBT therapists, zeroing in on a rigid/extreme attitude once it is detected is the hallmark of a highly proficient ther-apist; not a moment must be wasted in getting to grips with the client's emotional disturbance and rapidly ameliorating it. Also some of these therapists may have self-esteem problems: to hold back on examining a client's attitudes might indicate to the client that they are unsure of themselves and thereby let the client gain the upper hand.

Immediate examination of the client's rigid/extreme attitudes and their flexible/non-extreme alternatives is not necessarily a sign of a proficient REBT therapist but, more usually, of a hasty and ill-prepared one. Care needs to be taken in con-structing a working alliance, inducting clients into REBT, gathering background information, assessing accurately clients' presenting problems, gaining feedback, and pinpointing the relevant rigid/extreme attitudes to examine rather than the first ones the clients utter. Once these activities have been accomplished, it is much more likely that the clients will be amenable to having their attitudes examined.

Setting the stage for attitude examination rather than a headlong rush into it will usually create the impression of clinical competence and remove the need for power struggles, real or imagined. Examining a client's attitudes is not for the therapist's self-satisfaction but to enable the clients to feel healthy negative emotions as their goals for change.

### 'It Doesn't Feel Comfortable': When Therapists Believe that They Must Be Comfortable in Therapy

The comment that therapists must be comfortable in therapy seems to be widely expressed by therapists from all kinds of therapy disciplines. The 'it' (in 'it doesn't feel comfortable') refers to any difficulty, obstacle, problem, conflict, tension, discomfort, etc. that threatens to destabilise or impair the relatively smooth or harmonious functioning of therapy. In order for therapists not to feel uncomfortable, they implement measures (e.g. placating the client, not discussing painful issues) to defuse or sidestep any looming difficulties. Although REBT therapists are generally a hard-headed and unsentimental bunch who do not usually flinch from dealing with whatever occurs in therapy, some are not immune from the need for comfort in their therapy practice:

*Supervisor:* Listening to your digital voice recordings, you seem not to deal with some of the issues that the client wants to talk about.

*Supervisee:* I don't agree. We put on the agenda whatever they want to talk about.

*Supervisor:* Such as …?

*Supervisee:* We're exploring their depression, which is related to losing their job, their diminishing social circle, nothing seeming to go right in their life. So it's all being covered.

*Supervisor:* It seems to me there are issues the client is not going to offer up easily for discussion but wants them addressed anyway. They refer several times to something that happened with a former partner, but on each occasion, you let it pass.

*Supervisee:* Well, the reason I do that is because when they are ready to tell me, I expect they will.

*Supervisor:* And you think it is as straightforward as that?

*Supervisee:* You obviously don't.

*Supervisor:* That's true. My hypothesis about your behaviour is this: that you are aware of avoiding the partner issue because exploring it may detonate all sorts of painful issues that would turn therapy into a very uncomfortable experience for you.

*Supervisee:* There may well be an element of truth in that. On the other hand, I've had very uncomfortable experiences in therapy and haven't tried to run away.

*Supervisor:* I'm sure that's perfectly true in other cases, but we're trying to find out why this case is different. What do you think the partner issue might be?

*Supervisee:* Well, I suppose it might be rape or some form of sexual abuse.

*Supervisor:* Let's suppose you're right. Now, what prevents you from exploring these issues with the client?

*Supervisee:* I'm worried about opening this can of worms of emotional pain and not being able to close it again.

*Supervisor:* Well, you don't want to close the can, but help her to deal with the problems that emerge from it.

*Supervisee:* I don't feel I'd be able to cope with it.

*Supervisor:* What's the 'it' you believe you can't cope with?

*Supervisee:* The uncertainty whether I'll be really able to help her. Week after week I'll be listening to this outpouring of unhappiness but not knowing if she's going to get better. That's what I'd feel really uncomfortable about: having to tolerate this uncertainty.

*Supervisor:* So, this uncomfortable feeling is actually discomfort anxiety: which is about getting into these areas with her and not knowing what the outcome will be and having to tolerate this uncertainty.

*Supervisee:* Yeah, that's right.

*Supervisor:* How would you state the anxiety-producing attitude?

*Supervisee:* Something like 'I absolutely must be certain that I can help her otherwise I won't be able to stand the uncertainty that I might be getting therapy hideously wrong'.

*Supervisor:* OK, Which therapist has a guarantee that they will have a successful outcome in dealing with these issues?

*Supervisee:* I know there are no guarantees …

*Supervisor:* Well, you're demanding one.

*Supervisee:* What I mean is that more experienced, confident and skilful REBT therapists would know how to handle rape and sexual abuse cases.

*Supervisor:* And how did they acquire these capabilities?

*Supervisee:* I know – they had to go through a learning process.

*Supervisor:* Which never stops. You apply REBT to this case as any other. I'll assign you reading which covers these areas and, of course, you're in regular supervision, so I'll be keeping a close eye on your progress or lack of it.

*Supervisee:* I really do want to help them. I'm just worried about whether I actually can help them or not.

*Supervisor:* Neither you nor the client will know that until you start finding out. While you delay, their suffering continues.

*Supervisee:* OK. I'll start in the next session.

*Supervisor:*   Good. Now one last thing to say: your assumption is that the partner issue is related to rape or sexual abuse. It could be something else like their previous partner lied to them about being in love with them. We want to develop a treatment programme based on empirical data, not hunches. So, what are you going to do with that assumption of yours?
*Supervisee:*   Check it out with the client.
*Supervisor:*   Right. I would suggest that you don't actually present it to them, but let them tell their story and silently check it out. It might be the more tactful thing to do in the circumstances. I'll look forward to supervising your next recording.
*Supervisee:*   I feel more confident now about bringing it.

Important points to note in this excerpt from supervision are:

1. The supervisor suggests that there are two kinds of agenda setting: the explicit kind, where the client readily offers problems for discussion, and a more tacit form that is hinted at by the client. As the therapist (supervisee) is reluctant to acknowledge the client's tacit agenda, this prompts the supervisor to explore the possible reasons for it.
2. The supervisor's hypothesis is that the therapist's avoidance is based on their worry about feeling very uncomfortable when confronted with the client's highly painful emotional issues related to their tacit agenda. The therapist gingerly accepts this hypothesis and suggests that these issues might relate to rape or sexual abuse and therefore 'I don't feel I'd be able to cope with it'.
3. In order to determine what lies at the heart of the therapist's anticipated discomfort in dealing with these issues, the supervisor asks them to clarify what the 'it' refers to – the therapist having to bear the great discomfort of not knowing whether they have the clinical ability to help the client. Then, the therapist's discomfort anxiety is crystallised into a rigid/extreme attitude for examination.
4. The supervisor points out that the therapist's uncertainty creates one certainty: the client's suffering continues while the therapist searches for a guarantee that their clinical intervention will be successful. In order to develop greater clinical competence and confidence, the therapist needs to tolerate the uncertainty of treatment outcome while preparing themself to deal as best they can with the problems that arise from tackling the client's tacit agenda.
5. The therapist's assumption that the 'partner issue' refers to rape or sexual abuse is just that – an assumption and therefore needs to be corroborated by the client. Therapy driven by assumption is a poor basis for developing a treatment programme.

## When Therapists Think They Know What Is Best for Their Clients

While REBT therapists encourage their clients to strive for attitude change in their lives (surrendering rigid and extreme attitudes and developing flexible and non-extreme attitudes), they acknowledge that some clients will fall short of this goal. Clients will frequently terminate therapy as soon as they feel better because their presenting symptoms have now been reduced or removed. Tracing the largely attitudinal roots of these symptoms may seem irrelevant, arduous or too time-consuming to many clients to warrant prolonging therapy. From a pragmatic viewpoint, some change is usually better than no change. However, some REBT therapists may see mere symptom reduction or removal as no change at all and issue dire warnings about the client's imminent relapse, 'skating on thin cognitive ice' or only applying a Band-Aid to the psychic wound rather than treating the wound itself.

Such therapist arrogance is based not only on a 'do as you're told because I know what's best for you' approach but also on the disdain they feel for those clients who waste the therapist's precious time by entering therapy only to feel better instead of getting better, e.g. 'If you just wanted reassurance, you should have spoken to a friend rather than come to therapy. I'm here to offer you real solutions to your problems, not to placate you'. These attitudes will probably hasten the client's departure from therapy; they are highly unlikely to encourage the client to reconsider their decision to terminate.

Such therapists easily forget that the elegant solution in REBT is the preferred goal, not the only goal. Clients are not to be despised because they seek palliative solutions to their problems. To insist that all clients must stay in therapy until their dogmatic thinking has been removed creates the great possibility of the therapist being more disturbed than the clients; therefore the therapist would be attempting to keep clients in therapy in order to teach them a flexible/non-extreme attitude system. The therapist's 'I know what's best for you' diktat would now carry a heavy charge of irony.

While REBT therapists would certainly not object to only helping clients to feel better, they can also present to them a persuasive clinical rationale to keep them longer in therapy:

---

*Therapist:*   I'm glad that the reassurance you've received has helped to reduce your anxiety, but the next and even more important stage in therapy is to deal effectively with that anxiety by showing you how to cope if your fears ever turned out to be true. This stage takes longer but the benefits are usually lifelong. Would you be interested in entering this next stage?

---

Even if some therapists do believe that they know what is best for their clients, it is the clients who remain the final arbiter of the degree of change they wish to effect in their lives.

## When Therapists' Personal Problems Cloud Their Clinical Judgement

REBT therapists strive to keep their egos out of therapy and refrain from making moral judgements about their clients (but not always of their actions or traits). We have already looked at examples where this does not occur. In a similar vein, REBT therapists try to prevent their personal problems from infiltrating into and adversely affecting their clinical practice. When this does happen, the client becomes the target of the therapist's hidden agenda.

*Supervisor:* In listening to your session recordings with this client, you seem to be giving them a very hard time in therapy.

*Supervisee:* In what way?

*Supervisor:* Well, when they turn up late for appointments, don't do homework, disagree with you, provide inadequate feedback and have trouble understanding REBT concepts. That sort of thing.

*Supervisee:* The client is lazy, argumentative and inattentive. They want to make progress with their problem but without doing any work, so I have to push them.

*Supervisor:* I agree that some clients require pushing, but you seem to be persecuting this client. You can barely contain your anger with them.

*Supervisee:* When you say 'persecuting this client', you obviously have some hypothesis you're going to present to me about my behaviour.

*Supervisor:* Correct. From what I can tell, there seems to be a personal issue involved which you're taking out on the client.

*Supervisee:* Where's your evidence for that assumption?

*Supervisor:* Well, you brought to supervision a couple of months ago a client with very similar behavioural problems, and I commented on how well you were handling that person. You certainly were not hot under the collar then about their behaviour.

*Supervisee:* Well, this client is different, that's why.

*Supervisor:* Is it the client or is it that your attitude is different this time?

*Supervisee:* I don't know. Maybe I had a bad day or something.

*Supervisor:* You seem to be getting angry with me asking you these questions. What's going on?

| | |
|---|---|
| *Supervisee:* | You're implying that I'm being less than professional with this client. I told you, they are very difficult! That's the reason. |
| *Supervisor:* | If I'm wrong about it, am I allowed to imply it as your clinical supervisor? My role as your supervisor is to help you develop your therapeutic skills as well as to monitor what goes on between you and your client. If I'm right, denying what's actually going on in therapy is not going to help you resolve it. The client receives a double whammy: they are not helped to sort out their problems, and they are on the receiving end of your anger. |
| *Supervisee (sighs):* | Yes, I am angry. I'm angry that you're right about the personal issue. |
| *Supervisor:* | And therefore ...? |
| *Supervisee (mock anger):* | You absolutely shouldn't be right! |
| *Supervisor:* | Because as I am ...? |
| *Supervisee:* | Well, this means that I have to admit reluctantly that I am being unprofessional with this client and a few others whose recordings you haven't heard yet. Then I'm angry with myself for being unprofessional in the first place. |
| *Supervisor:* | OK. Thanks for being honest. As you know, I'm not here to provide personal therapy for you, but obviously I need to consider the impact that your problems are having on your clinical practice. Now let's find out what the attitude is that arises in your private life that you bring into your professional one. |
| *Supervisee:* | Well, my partner and I are arguing all the time, tense silences, doors being slammed, no peace at home at all. I'm glad to come to work for a bit of peace and quiet. |
| *Supervisor:* | And if you don't get it because your clients are giving you a hard time, what then? |
| *Supervisee (emphatic):* | I'm not prepared to put up with it! At work as well as at home. You must be joking. |
| *Supervisor:* | So what's the demand you're making, just to be clear? |
| *Supervisee:* | If I'm having hassle at home, I must have a quiet time at work. I can't bear it when my clients start messing me about. If they make me suffer, then I'm going to make them suffer. |
| *Supervisor:* | Your use of the word 'suffer' reflects your present emotional disturbance.<br><br>You're supposed to be creating a therapeutic environment and not a torture chamber. |
| *Supervisee (wearily):* | Yes, I know. I shouldn't be taking it out on them. |

*Supervisor:* So how are you going to stop doing it then?

*Supervisee:* By disconnecting my private life from my professional one. Every day I come to work, I can forcefully remind myself that just because I have turbulence at home, there is no reason why I must have tranquillity at work, though, of course, it would be preferable to have it. If things are tough at work and at home, too damn bad.

*Supervisor:* How can you make things less tough for yourself if your clients are 'messing you about' as you call it?

*Supervisee:* By accepting the reality of their present behaviour and looking at constructive ways of tackling it by examining the reasons why one keeps on turning up late or another doesn't do their homework. In other words, not use my anger to try and bludgeon them into submission, which isn't working anyway.

*Supervisor:* Now imagine that you have dealt with your anger: how different will your day be?

*Supervisee:* Well, I won't be disturbed in the sessions or while waiting for the next client to show. I won't be consumed by my anger any longer and will have more energy at work for other things.

*Supervisor:* And how will you be on the way home?

*Supervisee:* I won't be wound up as much and therefore less likely to start sniping as soon as I get home. I'll be much more inclined to try to sort out our relationship. It was good talking about it with you.

*Supervisor:* OK. Now, let's see if you begin to put this new attitude into practice in your next recordings. Remember, there's no evidence that supports your attitude that you must have what you want either at home, work or anywhere in life, so deal with that 'must'. It's not compatible with effective problem-solving.

Important points to note in this excerpt from supervision are the following:

1. The supervisor is alerted to the possibility that the actions of the therapist (supervisee) are driven by personal motives in the way they attack the client for the latter's recalcitrant behaviour. The supervisor's hypothesis is quickly challenged by the therapist, but the supervisor does not become defensive and simply presents their evidence for the therapist to consider.

2. Even though the therapist admits that the supervisor's hypothesis is correct, and is angry at the latter's accuracy as well as their own unprofessional conduct, the supervisor is not sidetracked into examining these secondary issues but continues to probe for the attitudinal source of the therapist's primary anger. This starts in their domestic life and spreads into their professional one.

3. The supervisor's role is not to provide the therapist with personal therapy, but to deal with the clinical impact of their domestic problems. The supervisor uses

Socratic questioning in order to allow the therapist to suggest how they can undisturb themself and the likely therapeutic benefits that will be gained.

4. In order to provide an added encouragement to change, the supervisor nudges the therapist to speculate on the possible advantages they may experience in their private life if they act in a non-disturbed way. The supervisor points out as a summation of the session that rigid thinking is an ineffective cognitive tool for solving problems in any sphere of our lives.

5. If the therapist is unable to change their disturbance-inducing ideas, then a period of personal therapy is advisable. The therapist would be referred to another REBT therapist so that, as a client, their presenting problems can receive undivided clinical attention.

## When Therapists Believe that They Must Crush Their Clients' Obstacles to Client Change to Prove What Strong and Determined Therapists They Are

Ellis (1985, 2002) wrote a book describing common forms of what he called 'client resistance'[1] and the wide range of multimodal techniques that can be used to overcome it. While providing an excellent resource for therapists whose patience and problem-solving skills are sorely taxed by such clients, Ellis acknowledged that for some clients, no amount of therapeutic effort appears to moderate their emotional disturbance. Instead of accepting this grim reality, some REBT therapists see such obstacles as the client throwing down the gauntlet, which they are compelled to pick up to prove how omnipotent they are. Instead of employing creative persistence to overcome or bypass these obstacles to client change, they seek to crush these obstacles as an end in itself to prove 'who is the boss in therapy'. Actually, working on the client's problems is often an afterthought or anticlimax for these therapists, while clients who linger in therapy may do so in a state of sullen dejection or obedient passivity. Power without therapeutic purpose is a hollow victory that these therapists are unable to see.

Therapists should remember that tackling obstacles to client change is usually a significant learning experience for them – the more difficult the case, the more that therapists have to stretch themselves to find the right combination of skills and techniques to produce therapeutic movement. Inevitable failure with some clients is not linked to self-devaluation but unconditional self-acceptance as a fallible therapist. Therefore, it is vital that therapists do not see therapy as a power struggle which they have to win because their ego is on the line. Instead, they can focus their energies where they clinically belong – overcoming clients' obstacles to client change in order to empower them to realise their goals for change. That is the real power that therapists can achieve.

## Therapists Who Think that the Concept of Fallibility Applies to Clients and Not to Themselves

A key teaching of REBT is to encourage clients to accept themselves unconditionally as fallible human beings. If they choose, they can judge, rate or condemn their actions or traits but not themselves. Self-acceptance is the basis for enduring emotional stability in their lives. Although some REBT therapists may be persuasive in urging clients to embrace this concept, they fail to act on it themselves. They refuse or are reluctant to admit they have personal problems or display any perceived weaknesses. This may occur because, among other reasons, they rigidly hold that as a therapist, they must be free from problems or flaws, that understanding and practising REBT is a kind of amulet against emotional disturbance or refrain from potentially painful self-examination.

While the client may accept the undeniable truth of human fallibility, the therapist flees from their fallibility by projecting an image of a calm, controlled and superior being. This is diametrically opposed to what the therapist is supposed to be teaching the client, who may come to view the therapist as more of a fraud or hypocrite than a role model.

'Practise what you preach' is the guiding principle for such therapists. If clinically relevant, they should use judicious self-disclosure to discuss with clients similar problems they experienced and how they coped with them or poke fun at their own behaviour to deflate their pretensions to superior status. Being a psychotherapist may provide greater insight into the wellsprings of human disturbance, but it does not and cannot eradicate our own disturbance-creating tendencies. Certainly, REBT makes no claims to do this, but it can show individuals how to reduce significantly their general level of disturbability. Self-examination does not have to be too painful a procedure if therapists are prepared to admit their problems and flaws rather than condemn themselves on the basis of them. What therapists can demonstrate to their clients is a kind of highly efficient fallibility, i.e. rapidly correcting mistakes, resolving problems and examining disturbance-creating attitudes in order to reach their short- and long-term goals. Clients are more likely to respond favourably to this framework of human behaviour than the unattainable one that the therapist is fixated with.

In this chapter, I have discussed various forms of ideological rigidity that undermine or impair the progress of therapy. In Chapter 12, the final chapter of this book, I focus on therapist difficulties that occur in the various stages of the therapeutic process.

### Note

1  See the Preface for a discussion of the term 'resistance' and why I have chosen not to use it in this edition of the book.

# Chapter 12

# A Process-Orientated View of Therapist Obstacles to Client Change

In Chapter 6, I discussed the obstacles that clients experience during the beginning, middle and ending phases of therapy that can largely be attributed to themselves. Now, I will consider some of the problems or pitfalls that therapists experience that can obstruct client change in these same phases. How therapists can make a relatively smooth transition from one phase to another by tackling such obstacles will now be addressed.

## When Therapists Are Their Own Obstacles to Client Change in the Beginning Phase

In the beginning phase of REBT, the therapist starts to construct a working alliance, undertakes an early problem assessment, teaches the *ABCs* of REBT and negotiates initial homework tasks. While this seems straightforward therapists can get in their own way and thus serve as an obstacle to client change in a number of ways.

### When Therapists Believe that They Have to Make Sense of It All

When clients are asked to talk about the problems that brought them to therapy, they often do so in a verbose, rambling and emotionally charged way. It would be very surprising if clients described in an orderly fashion the series of events which led to their current predicament. Usually, the *ABC* elements of the clients' presenting problems are intricately interwoven and it is the therapist's task to tease them apart in order to bring clarity to confusion, make order out of chaos. The quicker this is achieved, the quicker that clients can tackle their rigid and extreme attitudes and gain relief from their emotional disturbance. However, some REBT therapists may unnecessarily delay this process because they are reluctant to interrupt clients as they elaborate upon their problems because this might appear insensitive, or they encourage clients to keep on talking as they are unsure when to intervene, or they believe that clients will start to feel better as they 'let it all out' and thereby a natural resolution of their problems will get underway. Such inaction on the part of these therapists may actually increase the time clients spend in problem-exploration

DOI: 10.4324/9781003423379-14

mode rather than in problem-solving mode. Instead of enlightenment beginning to dawn after the early sessions of therapy, the clients may be none the wiser about what is ailing them.

It is important for therapists to realise that in the beginning phase of REBT, the client follows the therapist's lead rather than vice versa. This is necessary if the client is to learn the *ABC* framework of emotional disturbance and change in order to become a self-therapist. Therefore, the therapist getting to grips with the client's troubles as early as possible is a good role model for clients to follow in their own attempts at problem-solving. The perceived insensitivity that may occur by interrupting the client can be lessened by giving a rationale and asking for permission to do it, e.g. 'If you are providing more information than I require to understand your problems, may I interrupt you so that we can begin to work on actually tackling them?' If therapists are unsure when to intervene this may require further skills training in what Grieger and Boyd (1980: 59) call 'listen[ing] for the *As*, *Bs*, and *Cs* of client problems', particularly the all-important rigid and extreme attitudes. The idea that allowing clients to talk endlessly about their problems is somehow curative does not really hold water, as the clients may have been doing this for years and still remain emotionally disturbed. Helping clients to make sense of themselves and their problems through the *ABC* framework begins as soon as they step into the therapist's office and not at some unspecified time later in therapy.

### When Therapists Think that They Have to Understand Their Clients' Past in Order to Understand Their Present

REBT is largely an ahistorical approach to emotional problem-solving in that it focuses on how clients are maintaining their problems rather than on how they were acquired. REBT therapists who undertake a lengthy historical examination of the clients' problems may well create the impression that the past and not the present is the true focus of therapy.

| | |
|---|---|
| *Supervisor:* | I've listened to a few of your digital audio recordings now and the majority of your time is spent dwelling on past events. Is this the best way to help your client? They are still experiencing the guilt today no matter how it started. |
| *Supervisee:* | Well, I suppose if I can understand as fully as possible how the guilt originated and how it developed over the years, fifteen years in fact, only then can I focus on the here-and-now. The client certainly wants to talk about the past. |
| *Supervisor:* | I'm sure the client does, but how long will it take before you arrive in the present? |
| *Supervisee:* | It's a complicated process – who knows? |

*Supervisor:*   You're making it too complicated. You've trained in REBT yet you're barking up the wrong tree. What do you think I mean by that?

*Supervisee:*   I suppose you mean that I should focus on the client's current attitudes towards past events that explain why they feel guilty. Instead, I'm excavating the past as if I'm convinced that's where the answer lies.

*Supervisor:*   Exactly. In REBT, you don't cut the past adrift but link it to the present. The client has held the same attitude for the last fifteen years and therefore the solution to their problems is in surrendering their guilt-inducing attitudes today.

*Supervisee:*   I do see that, but I'm worried that the client will think I'm minimising or trivialising past events if I keep on bringing them back to the present.

*Supervisor:*   Have you presented a clear rationale to the client why you would be doing this? In essence, are you teaching him REBT?

*Supervisee:*   No, I haven't done that. I suppose I'm just following where the client leads.

*Supervisor:*   Well, if you haven't, then they will believe that the past is all-important and continue to go on about it. Now let's get the both of you into the present. What is the client guilty about?

*Supervisee:*   They left their partner about fifteen years ago when they were both going through a crisis. They had debts, the house was going to be repossessed, the client lost his job, the two of them were rowing all the time. It was a real mess. The client says that if they can find out why they left their partner, this might ease their guilt.

*Supervisor:*   But not fully address it. Why do you think the client left their partner?

*Supervisee:*   They already hinted at it several times – they couldn't cope with all the pressure. Thinking about it now, the client's guilt seems to be getting worse as they keep on condemning themself as weak and spineless for running out on their partner.

*Supervisor:*   So running out on their partner is the client's A or adversity. What do you think the attitude might be that's maintaining their feelings of guilt?

*Supervisee:*   Something like 'I absolutely shouldn't have run out on my partner and left them to face all those problems on their own. Because I did, I'm a worthless and rotten person'.

*Supervisor:*   So, how do you propose to tackle this attitude without slipping back into the past?

*Supervisee:* I'll start by providing the client with the clinical rationale that I've failed to do so far.

*Supervisor:* You'll probably need to do it more than once. Then what?

*Supervisee:* Teach the client how to accept the grim reality of what they did fifteen years ago without condemning themself for it.

*Supervisor:* Does that mean the client gets off scot-free?

*Supervisee:* No. They can take responsibility for their perceived bad behaviour and, from a non-disturbed viewpoint, try to understand the reasons for the way they acted. In this way, they are more likely to feel remorse rather than guilt. So, the client may experience a painful regret for their bad behaviour but will have removed the crushing burden of guilt.

*Supervisor:* Good. You're doing REBT again. You'll also be showing the client that by tackling their rigid and extreme attitudes in the present, this will change the way they will tend to view the past as they begin to understand how they created and maintained their guilt. So the past is being addressed but without being locked into it.

*Supervisee:* That does make a lot of sense. I've got my bearings back again.

*Supervisor:* I hope so. In your next recordings, then, I want to hear some here-and-now therapy.

This excerpt from supervision focuses on what Grieger and Boyd (1980) call 'the past history trap'. This is the widespread view among therapists (and the wider public) that past events in themselves have an irrevocable and often malign influence upon our present feelings and behaviour. The only way for individuals to break free of this influence is to revisit the past in order to gain insight into the origins of their problems. While not wishing to diminish the impact of unpleasant or adverse past events, REBT argues that the real insight into these events is the rigid and extreme attitudes that individuals have constructed from them and carried forward into the present. Therapists can help clients to identify, examine and change these presently held attitudes 'so that tomorrow's existence can be better than yesterday's. In a sense, the person each day chooses to either hold onto disturbed beliefs or to give them up' Grieger and Boyd (1980: 76–7).

### When Therapists Fail to Help Clients to Distinguish Between Healthy and Unhealthy Negative Emotions

REBT divides negative emotions into unhealthy and healthy states with attitudinal correlates of, respectively, rigid extreme attitudes and flexible non-extreme attitudes. For example, guilt, depression and anxiety are underpinned by the former attitudes, while their healthy alternatives of remorse, sadness and concern are based on the latter. Clients are encouraged to adopt this emotional vocabulary in order to reduce or avoid misunderstanding and confusion in describing their feelings and the ones they wish to change (of course, the therapist and client can devise their own taxonomy of negative emotions). Some REBT therapists, particularly novice ones, automatically assume that clients understand the differences between these feeling states and therefore do not investigate the attitudinal content of their supposedly non-disturbed emotions.

---

*Client:*      I get so annoyed with my boss's obnoxious behaviour. I don't like feeling this way.

*Therapist:*   You don't have to like it, but what's wrong with feeling annoyed? It's a healthy and natural feeling. You don't want to feel indifferent about your boss's obnoxious behaviour, do you?

*Client:*      No, I suppose not. I would like to handle my emotional reaction in a more positive way, if that's possible.

*Therapist:*   Feeling annoyed is fine, that's positive. Maybe it needs a bit of fine-tuning. Probably you're feeling too annoyed.

*Client:*      Maybe that's it, though I'm not convinced.

*Therapist:*   Now let's get down to the real business of REBT, which is tackling emotional disturbance. Now when do you feel angry? *(emphasises word)*.

*Client:*      When I'm annoyed. It's the same thing.

*Therapist:*   No, you can't feel annoyed when you're angry or vice versa. You're getting confused. I said 'when do you feel angry?' not annoyed.

*Client:*      I'm not confused. Are you telling me what and how I should feel?

*Therapist:*   Well, no ... but in REBT there is a difference between anger and annoyance.

*Client:*      I don't know the difference. Anyway, I don't see any difference.

*Therapist:*   Oh, I'm sorry for my blunder. I just thought you would realise the difference, that's all.

---

The therapist makes a cardinal error in not checking the client's understanding of these emotional states and thereby brushes aside the client's desire to focus on their annoyance with the glib assurance that 'it's a healthy and natural feeling'. The client believes that anger and annoyance are one and the same emotion and resents the therapist's fiat on how they should feel. The therapist's manner is unlikely to be conducive to building a working alliance. In REBT, nothing is taken for granted and therefore its emotional vocabulary is compared with and contrasted to the client's. Seeking an agreed emotional language not only helps to clarify the client's goals for change but also provides them with genuine reassurance that their feelings have not been hijacked by the therapist.

### When Therapists Put Words into Their Clients' Mouths

REBT theory asserts that rigid attitudes lie at the foundation of emotional disturbance. These attitudes are usually explicit or implicit in clients' statements about their presenting problems. Stating this view of disturbance is not the same as clients agreeing with it. Like every other concept in REBT, it is offered to clients for their consideration and not their compliance. Because REBT therapists know in advance the rigid form of the clients' self-defeating thinking (the assessment will reveal the specific content of this thinking), some therapists cannot resist the temptation to tell clients how they disturb themselves rather than let clients decide for themselves if this is indeed the case. Such misguided eagerness often stems from therapists' urgent needs to display their 'superior' insights into the clients' problems, their notion that proficiency is equated with didacticism, and their impatience to hurry therapy along as they assume that 'getting to the rigid attitudes' is the overriding imperative. The following dialogue illustrates some of these points.

| | |
|---|---|
| *Client:* | I'm always a little anxious when I meet new people. Maybe it's because they might find me a bit boring and not like me. |
| *Therapist:* | You are more than a little anxious. You have a specific statement in your head which goes something like this: 'I absolutely must not be seen as boring, otherwise I will lose people's approval. It would be terrible to be rejected'. That's what you're probably telling yourself and which is driving your anxiety. |
| *Client:* | I can't hear myself saying that in those situations. |
| *Therapist:* | Only because it's outside of your current awareness, but I'll help you to find it quickly. We don't want to waste time beating around the bush when I've already given you the answer. |
| *Client:* | So, that's what I'm saying to myself then? |
| *Therapist:* | Yes, that's your statement you need to address immediately. Everything else is secondary. |

The therapist might as well hold up cue cards for the client to read. Their behaviour in therapy is more prescriptive than proficient. There is no evidence of the therapist encouraging the client through Socratic questioning to develop greater awareness in order for them to discover if a rigid attitude is at the root of her anxiogenic thinking. It is far better for the client to reach their own insights than for the therapist to tell them what these are. Of course, some clients will not be persuaded of or agree with the disturbance-producing potential of rigid attitudes and therefore this is no insight for them. In that case, therapists should focus on the key ideas that these clients think are the real source of their problems. The idea that telling clients how they are disturbing themselves will produce quicker progress is usually counterproductive, because the clients may pay only lip service to the therapist's pronouncements, respond negatively to their patronising manner or feel excluded from what should be a collaborative endeavour. If therapists refrain from putting words into their clients' mouths, they will be better able to defend themselves against the accusation that all they want to do is turn out REBT clones and not independent thinkers (see Chapter 5).

## When Therapists Are Their Own Obstacles to Client Change in the Middle Phase

During the middle phase, the therapist helps clients to internalise their newly acquired flexible and non-extreme attitudes and weaken their lingering but often still powerfully held rigid and extreme ones. This is carried out by the therapist encouraging clients to face relevant adversities and act in ways that are consistent with and strengthen their flexible and non-extreme attitudes. Also, the therapist will be on the lookout for the presence of core rigid and extreme attitudes that link the client's problems. Therapist difficulties encountered in this phase will now be explored.

### When Therapists Do Not Warn Clients about the Possibility of Lapse and Relapse

Clients can often make quick, even spectacular, progress in the early stages of therapy and therefore conclude that their problems are 'solved'. Some REBT therapists might be so enamoured with their own 'brilliance' for effecting such rapid change that they fail to mention to the clients that progress is usually accompanied by lapses and, if these are not dealt with, relapse (going back to square one). On the other hand, this point may well be deliberately overlooked as these therapists do not want to introduce a discordant note into a, so far, highly successful and enjoyable therapeutic alliance. When clients typically experience a re-emergence of their emotional disturbance, the shock and despair they may feel could have been lessened (or even removed) if the therapist had properly instructed them in the likely process of change.

Discussing the probability that there will be some lapses in a client's overall progress allows the therapist to inject a note of realism, but not fatalism, into therapy:

*Therapist:*    As I'm sure you're aware, progress is very often two steps forward and one step back. This certainly does not mean that you can never overcome your problem. What it does mean is that

> every time you step backward you will need to redouble your efforts to move forward again.

As with every problem considered in REBT, therapists encourage their clients to use the *ABC* framework to pinpoint the cognitive source of their backsliding (see Dryden, 2024). If clients are making good or excellent progress, therapists should be exploring the factors that account for it and not be distracted by self-admiration as an 'outstanding therapist'; this can quickly turn to self-devaluation if clients encounter obstacles or their progress starts to unravel. Therapists should be mindful that an enjoyable relationship is not necessarily a therapeutic one, as difficult or contentious but important issues can be skirted in order to keep therapy 'upbeat'. Also while therapeutic success is to be applauded, it needs to be tempered with caution as progress is rarely sustained indefinitely.

### When Therapists Find It Difficult to Hold Their Tongues

While greater use of short didactic presentations of REBT concepts are usually made in the early stages of therapy as clients are socialised into REBT, their frequent use during the middle phase of therapy is contra-indicated, because this may undermine or impair the development of the client's role as a self-therapist. A client's ability to think through problems usually varies in inverse ratio to the amount of lecturing that the therapist does. Too much of it can help to turn clients into passive partners in therapy who parrot REBT tenets rather than active and increasingly independently-minded problem-solvers.

Dryden and Neenan's (2021) advice to REBT therapists to 'let your clients' brains take the strain' means a corresponding decrease in their own level of verbal activity. Instead of lectures, therapists should use Socratic dialogue as much as possible, e.g. 'What are the implications for you if change is based on self-esteem rather than self-acceptance?'; 'How were you able to stay in that situation when only a few weeks ago you would have fled from it?' Therapists cannot do the thinking for their clients once they have left therapy, so while they remain in it, clients need to be encouraged to take control of the change process. If the client leaves at the end of a middle phase REBT session complaining that their brain hurts, this is a good sign that have been made to think. If the therapist leaves complaining that their throat hurts then they have been doing too much speaking and need to learn to hold their tongue.

### When Therapists Are Intimidated by How Much Clients Know about REBT

Some clients, perhaps only a small number, become erudite in the theory and practice of REBT and give unfailingly 'correct' answers to every question posed by the therapist. This may convince the latter that therapy is on track for a highly successful outcome.

---

*Supervisor:*  Listening to the digital voice recordings, it sounds like you have an REBT expert on your hands.

*Supervisee:*  They are brilliant. They've read lots of books on REBT, listened to all of Ellis's CDs. I can't catch them out on anything. They always knows the right answer. They even point out mistakes I make in applying REBT.

*Supervisor:*  What's the client's presenting problem?

*Supervisee:*  They are afraid of being rejected if they enter into romantic relationships, but they've worked it out logically in their own mind, so they are really over the problem.

*Supervisor:*  Well, I'm not so sure. Has the client carried out any homework tasks to face their fear of rejection?

*Supervisee:*  No, but then you see, they don't really need to as they have worked out why they are afraid of rejection and thereby resolved it.

*Supervisor:*  How have they done that?

*Supervisee:*  By convincing themself that they don't need other people's approval or love and, therefore can accept themself under all conditions. Obviously, you don't agree.

*Supervisor:*  I'm suspicious. The reason I'm suspicious is because they know all the theory but are not putting any of it into practice.

*Supervisee:*  But they know more about REBT than I do!

*Supervisor:*  This might be true on the theory side but as I said they are not acting on it. That's where your clinical focus should be. What's blocking them from carrying out the homework tasks?

*Supervisee:*  I'm not sure really. I suppose I've let myself be dazzled by their vast knowledge of REBT.

*Supervisor:*  Vast, but empty, as no action appears to flow from it. Let's consider some hypotheses. First, the client genuinely believes that insight alone is sufficient to promote enduring change.

*Supervisee:*  So they can solve problems without getting out of their armchair.

*Supervisor:*  Right. Second, they had attitudes of unbearability.

*Supervisee:*  That change is too hard, uncomfortable, frustrating. That sort of thing.

*Supervisor:*  That's right. Third, and this is more uncommon, they have a kind of narcissistic reluctance to be judged by others as they think they are superior to them. By not entering into relationships and the possibility of rejection, they thus preserve their self-image.

> *Supervisee:* Now that the dazzle is fading, I can see more clearly their homework avoidance. They always opt for further reading but no action.
>
> *Supervisor:* Continually remind them what the B in REBT stands for: behaviour, forcefully acting against their rigid and extreme attitudes if they truly wish to live by a flexible and non-extreme attitudinal outlook. It doesn't mean more beavering through REBT books. If they are such an expert, why haven't they followed through on it?
>
> *Supervisee:* It's been a very eye-opening session. Thanks.

Because the therapist (supervisee) is overawed by the client's impressive grasp of REBT theory, they fail to notice that the client is, in fact, not crossing the bridge between intellectual and emotional insight, i.e. REBT principles are understood in the client's head, but not acted upon. The supervisor suggests several hypotheses that may underpin the client's behavioural avoidance as a way of changing the therapist from admirer to sceptic. The therapist has forgotten to ask the most basic question, namely, 'If the client is so incredibly knowledgeable about REBT, why aren't they acting according to their flexible and non-extreme attitudes?' The therapist needs to focus on the client's behavioural avoidance and the attitudes that underpin it order to help them internalise the REBT view of therapeutic change. This is based on knowledge of REBT plus experience of applying it, not just on the impressive knowledge of REBT that the client has.

### When Therapists Hold Attitudes of Unbearability Towards Their Clients' Attitudes of Unbearability

After some initial success in confronting their problems, many clients begin to realise that the path of progress is much longer and rockier than they had expected. Disillusionment can begin to set in along with a marked reluctance to work hard to maintain current progress and deal with other problem areas in their lives. Also, lapses and even relapses are experienced. Clients can endlessly complain about how difficult and uncomfortable therapy is. The danger is that the therapist becomes so fed up with the client's constant complaining that they display behaviour consistent with their own attitude of unbearability towards the behavioural products of their clients' attitudes of unbearability.

> *Therapist:* You seem to be complaining every week. Does it help you to complain?
>
> *Client:* I can't help it. Nothing is going right at the moment. I didn't think that sorting my problems out would be this hard. Things were going well for a while.

| | |
|---|---|
| *Therapist:* | Well, that's what change is all about. What did you expect – an easy ride? |
| *Client:* | It would help. Anyway, you're supposed to be more sympathetic. You're supposed to be helping me! |
| *Therapist:* | You're not exactly helping me to help you with all this complaining, are you? |
| *Client:* | I can't help it if I find things difficult. I can't cope without a drink. You know what happens to me when I'm under any pressure. That's why I'm in therapy. |
| *Therapist:* | God, give me strength!! |

The therapist's attitude of unbearability is as evident as the client's. Therapy has ground to a halt. Each is looking to the other to get it moving again: the client expects the therapist to be more sympathetic to their plight while the therapist believes that the proper focus of therapy is problem-solving and not complaining. The proper focus of therapy is tackling all problems that occur, including the client's complaining behaviour and the therapist's accusatory tone. Therefore the therapist needs to undisturb themself first about the client's complaining and thereby begin to develop an attitude of bearability to the client's displays of unbearability:

| | |
|---|---|
| *Therapist:* | Empirically, the client should be complaining as that's the way he undoubtedly is at the moment. I certainly don't like listening to it but I can certainly bear it. The client can learn to develop an attitude of bearability, as I can and therapy can become more productive again. |

Instead of appealing to a higher power for forbearance, the therapist has found it closer to home by following the principles of REBT that presently elude the client.

### When Therapists Engage Too Much in Intellectual Discussion with Their Clients

As clients begin to develop a greater understanding of REBT, their questions, criticisms or observations of its theory and practice can have a corresponding level of sophistication, e.g. 'Surely if our actions are an indivisible part of ourselves, then in judging the action we are also judging ourselves? This undermines the notion of unconditional self-acceptance'. While these and other questions obviously need to be addressed, for some therapists they become the trigger for turning therapy into a seminar on the philosophical foundations of REBT (and possibly satisfying their need to display their true vocation as a professional philosopher or be seen as a 'deep thinker'). While the client's intellect might be stimulated by such discussion, it is also highly likely that therapy will get bogged down in overly lengthy theorising rather than acting as a platform for concerted action against the client's emotional disturbance.

Philosophical discussion should be relatively brief and, whenever possible, directly related to the client's presenting problems:

---

*Therapist:*   Your actions can never represent or equal your true complexity as a human being. Judging yourself on the basis of your actions is an insult to this complexity and a potential pathway to emotional disturbance. In your case, condemning yourself as an utter failure for losing your job largely accounts for your present depression.

---

It is important that feedback is obtained to determine if the client not only understands the points made but also agrees with them. Philosophical discussion can be a highly enjoyable aspect of therapy, but abstraction should not replace action as the main focus of collaboration.

### When Therapists Use a Limited Repertoire of Techniques

As therapists seek ways of encouraging clients to deepen their conviction in their newly acquired flexible and non-extreme attitudes (promoting emotional insight), they usually experiment with a wide range of multimodal techniques to facilitate this process. They are not afraid of going back to the drawing board to devise new techniques when their present ones have produced little, if any, change in the client. However, some therapists have a limited number of techniques they employ and believe that as they are tried-and-tested they will be effective with all clients, e.g. 'Jump in at the deep end straightaway. This means stay in the uncomfortable situation until your anxiety abates. Then you'll prove to yourself that you can bear it'. If the task is unsuccessful because the client would not stay in the situation or refuses to undertake it, such therapists will usually claim that the client is at fault rather than conclude that the technique is inappropriate for the client.

One of the chief characteristics of effective REBT therapists is their ability to be creatively persistent in seeking solutions to the clients' problems. This involves risk-taking: a particular technique may provide a therapeutic breakthrough or turn out to be a damp squib. If the latter is the case, the therapist refrains from blaming the client or making excuses. By role modelling the use of trial and error, the therapist hopes that the client will adopt it for present and future emotional problem-solving. In the above example, if implosion (flooding) techniques are ineffective, the therapist can suggest a range of 'challenging, but not overwhelming' assignments that are sufficiently stimulating to promote constructive change but not so daunting as possibly to inhibit clients from carrying them out (Dryden,

1985). Therapists are advised to remember that what worked for a previous client may not work for the present one.

## When Therapists Are Their Own Obstacles to Client Change in the Ending Phase

In this stage of therapy, therapists consider that their clients have made significant progress towards resolving their problems by using REBT skills. They now agree to work towards termination by decreasing session frequency or setting a fixed date for the end of therapy. Therapists encourage their clients to review the course of therapy, what they learned from it and how they will tackle future problems as self-therapists. Termination issues are addressed. Therapist obstacles to client change in this phase will now be discussed.

## When Therapists Terminate Their Clients Abruptly

When therapists believe that their client can now stand alone as a competent and confident self-therapist, they begin to signal to their client that the end of therapy is approaching, e.g. 'Now that you're managing your problems, I think two or three more sessions are sufficient to deal with some remaining issues. Would you agree?' This allows both parties time to express their feelings about and review their therapeutic relationship and, sometimes, for the client to discuss any difficulties in disengaging from it. Some therapists, out of boredom, lack of planning, sheer bloody-mindedness or a mistaken idea that 'this is the hard-headed way to do it', suddenly announce that the present session is the last one. If the client protests about this abrupt termination, the therapist views it as a sign of continuing disturbance and suggests that the client 'find out how you are disturbing yourself about termination'. The client may think rightly that they have been unceremoniously thrown out of therapy.

While REBT therapists do not turn termination into an elongated affair, they are mindful that care and consideration need to be used in deciding the date of the final session. Boredom should not be a factor in this process and when it is, it reflects the therapist's impatience 'to get this client and their problems out of therapy as soon as possible as I can't take much more of it'. Spontaneously ending therapy because 'it feels the right thing to do' is no substitute for premeditation based on the facts of the client's progress and not the therapist's feelings about it.

If ending the therapeutic relationship does become a major problem for the client, 'then the client is not ready to terminate, for this is an indication that the client relies on the therapist to fulfil some perceived need' (Wessler and Wessler, 1980: 182). It is far better for the therapist to explore this perceived need than end therapy unilaterally and tell them it is time to deal with their problems on their own.

The best way to end therapy is in collaboration with the client, and quite often, this is after increasing periods between sessions have occurred so that the client can get used to dealing with their issues by themselves. In one sense, since the client is welcome to come back for one or more sessions in the future, therapy is never terminated once and for all. Indeed, knowing that they *can* book another session to see their former therapist often means that the client doesn't need to do so.

## When Therapists Urge Their Clients to Remain in Therapy Longer than Is Necessary

REBT therapists do not usually attempt to keep clients in therapy once the latter have proved their mettle as self-therapists. To do so might be counterproductive as clients begin to doubt their hard-won abilities as the therapist 'still doesn't believe I'm ready to go it alone'. Their doubts would be misplaced because the real problem lies with the therapist's reluctance to let them go.

---

*Supervisor:*  In listening to the digital voice recording of your sessions, your client seems very confident, bright and capable of striking out on their own. They say several times that they are ready to leave, yet you urge them to stay longer in therapy Why is that?

*Supervisee:*  Well, the client is all those things you have suggested but sometimes a little too confident for their own good. I think there are pitfalls ahead that they haven't seen yet.

*Supervisor:*  That may be true, but isn't it up to the client to locate those pitfalls? If they do get caught up in them, why can't they use their obvious REBT skills to get out of them?

*Supervisee:*  Surely there's nothing wrong with trying to make the client as ready as possible before they leave therapy?

*Supervisor:*  It seems to me they are ready now. The real test of their degree of change is when they leave therapy and not while they remain within it. They can't stay in therapy for the rest of their life.

*Supervisee:*  Well, of course not. I'm not suggesting that at all. You're being very persistent with this issue, which usually means you've got a hypothesis to present to me.

*Supervisor:*  Correct. How would you feel if they left therapy now?

*Supervisee:*  A little annoyed. Only because, as I've said, there's still more work to be done.

*Supervisor:*  How would you describe the other clients on your caseload? Are some of them, for instance, making the great progress that this client is?

*Supervisee:*  No, this client stands head and shoulders above the rest of them. The other clients are a mixture of those making limited progress, those who are stuck, those who attend sporadically and those with personality disorders, that sort of thing. But what's the point you're going to make?

---

*Supervisor:*   That you're keeping this client in therapy for your own needs and not because they truly require further therapy. While they continue to make excellent progress, this proves what a competent and worthwhile therapist you are. Your other clients don't give you this glow of success and that's why you have to hang on to this particular client.

*Supervisee (rather irritably):*   Well, I don't see what's wrong with feeling this glow.

*Supervisor:*   Because the client is being detained in therapy to keep your glow burning. You have made your clinical competence dependent on their continuing success. What's best for the client has been subordinated to your needs. That won't do.

*Supervisee (sighs):*   OK. You're right. That's what I'm doing. I know it's not very therapeutic.

*Supervisor:*   So, what's the next step then?

*Supervisee:*   Release the client from therapy as I'm detaining them, as you call it. They are ready to leave, as you shrewdly pointed out.

*Supervisor:*   But before you do that …?

*Supervisee:*   Stop making my competence as a therapist conditional upon client success or failure. That doesn't mean that I won't try my therapeutic best with all my clients.

*Supervisor (mock surprise):*   I should hope not! Another issue to consider is that you define therapeutic success narrowly, which helps to fuel your rigid and extreme attitude.

*Supervisee:*   What do you mean by that?

*Supervisor:*   Well, when you said that some of your clients were making limited success, you didn't seem impressed at all. Success is success, whether or not it's limited, dull or boring. Not all, not even most, clients will make spectacular progress as this client has done. Helping clients deal with obstacles to change and encouraging people who attend spasmodically to attend more regularly are successful endeavours. Do you get my point?

*Supervisee:*   I do. I always try to latch on to the high-flyers in therapy. That's the only kind of success I really identify with.

*Supervisor:*   Which brings self-esteem problems for you and captivity for the client. So what will I hear in your next recording with this client?

*Supervisee:*   The final session and a non-disturbance-producing goodbye from me.

*Supervisor:*   Great.

In this excerpt from supervision, important points to consider are the following:

1.  The client's confidence in their ability to be an independent problem-solver and the decision of the therapist (supervisee) to delay termination alert the supervisor to the possibility that the therapist is harbouring rigid and extreme attitudes. Something is amiss when the therapist implies that their client has to attain an almost unnatural state of readiness before leaving therapy.
2.  The supervisor asks how the therapist would react if the client left therapy now and what the other clients on their caseload are like in order to gather further data to support the supervisor's hypothesis that the therapist needs continual evidence of the client's progress in therapy in order to accept themselves as a competent clinician.
3.  The therapist confirms the supervisor's hypothesis. The supervisor asks the therapist to suggest ways of undisturbing themselves about their competency needs. This is an example of 'letting the therapist's brain take the strain' of problem-solving (clients are not the only ones to suffer 'brain strain' in REBT).
4.  The supervisor points out that the therapist's narrow definition of therapeutic success is part of their rigid/extreme attitude. Success can be measured on a continuum from spectacular at one end to dull and boring at the other end. Success is whatever degree of progress is being made by the client at any particular moment in therapy.
5.  Just to ensure that the therapist will be acting in a more constructive way towards the client, the supervisor asks the therapist how they will conduct the next session with the client. The therapist's reply that it will be 'the final one' is a none-too-soon liberation for the client and the start of one for the therapist.

## When Therapists Think that the Elegant Solution Is the Only Solution

The REBT therapist's preferred client goals for change are often more ambitious than the client's. The ideal REBT goal is for clients to minimise their rigid thinking, strive to accept themselves and others unconditionally as fallible human beings and develop an attitude of bearability towards life's hardships. This is known as the 'elegant solution' to emotional problem-solving. Some clients will not be interested in achieving these ends and will want to leave therapy as soon as their problems recede. Some REBT therapists usually panic at this suggestion because, in their eyes, they are short-changing the clients if they leave too soon as they have not done 'correct' REBT with them yet. The client, however, has reached a plateau of change and does not want to be prodded, pushed or persuaded to ascend to the peak of 'what could be'. Because the therapist is rigidly adhering to the preferred REBT practice, they are more likely to view themself as a failure if the client does not pursue the elegant solution; hence their pleas with the client to stay in therapy.

| | |
|---|---|
| *Therapist:* | You need further help with your anxiety. |
| *Client:* | No, I don't. I feel less anxious now. I'm better. |
| *Therapist:* | But it's a deceptive kind of improvement. Those ideas that produce your anxiety are still lurking around. Remember those 'musts'. |
| *Client:* | Look, you've helped me to be less anxious about failing and I thank you for that. That's all I wanted when I came here. |
| *Therapist:* | But you haven't properly learned REBT yet. You're only feeling better at this stage, but not getting better because you haven't completely got rid of those demands about failure. Your self-acceptance is still conditional. These issues are still to be resolved. |
| *Client:* | I've done all the resolving I want to. This is going to be my last session. |
| *Therapist:* | All I'm asking you is to please stay in therapy so you can see how REBT will bring about a fundamental change in your attitude. There would be less human disturbance generally if people got rid of their 'musts'. |
| *Client:* | Thank you, but no! |

Therapists can change their rigidity to flexibility if they remember that the elegant solution is a choice to be offered to clients and not to be imposed upon them. It is not a sign of therapist failure if some clients choose not to pursue this solution, but a salutary reminder to presumptuous therapists that REBT is not the panacea for all psychological ills, and that people can still be happy even if they hold on to some of their rigid attitudes. That the degree of change is to the client's satisfaction, though maybe not containing much depth to it, should be the source of the therapist's congratulations rather than their despair over the client's lack of ideological purity in tackling their problems. Even if the client was tempted to stay longer in therapy, the therapist's behaviour is not much of an encouragement for them to do so or the best advertisement for the flexible and non-extreme approach that REBT is based on.

In this and the other chapters, I have drawn on my experience as an REBT therapist and supervisor of long standing to identify and deal with a variety of obstacles to client change that afflict both clients and therapists. I hope that the guidance offered in this book will assist REBT therapists in enhancing their therapy practice and deepening their understanding of REBT. The two usually go hand in hand.

# References

Beck, A. T. (1976). *Cognitive Therapy and the Emotional Disorders*. New York: International Universities Press.

Bordin, E. S. (1979). The generalizability of the psychoanalytic concept of the working alliance. *Psychotherapy: Theory, Research and Practice*, *16*: 252–260.

Burns, D. D. (1980). *Feeling Good: The New Mood Therapy*. New York: William Morrow.

DiGiuseppe, R. A., Doyle, K. A., Dryden, W. and Backx, W. (2014). *A Practitioner's Guide to Rational Emotive Behavior Therapy*. 3rd edn. New York: Oxford University Press.

Dryden, W. (1985). Challenging but not overwhelming: A compromise in negotiating homework assignments. *British Journal of Cognitive Psychotherapy*, *3(1)*: 77–80.

Dryden, W. (1991). *A Dialogue with Albert Ellis: Against Dogma*. Buckingham: Open University Press.

Dryden, W. (2006). *Counselling in a Nutshell*. London: Sage.

Dryden, W. (2011). *Counselling in a Nutshell*. 2nd edn. London: Sage.

Dryden, W. (2018*). Rational Emotive Behavioural Coaching: Distinctive features*. Abingdon: Routledge.

Dryden, W. (2021). *Rational Emotive Behaviour Therapy: Distinctive Features*. Abingdon: Routledge.

Dryden, W. (2022). *Reason to Change: A Rational Emotive Behaviour Therapy (REBT) Workbook*. 2nd edn. Abingdon: Routledge.

Dryden, W. (2024). *Fundamentals of Rational Emotive Behaviour Therapy: A Training Manual*. 3rd edn. Chichester: John Wiley.

Dryden, W. and Ellis, A. (1997). Dilemmas in giving warmth or love to clients (interview). In W. Dryden (ed.) *Therapists' Dilemmas*, revised edn. London: Sage.

Dryden, W. and Neenan, M. (1995). *A Dictionary of Rational Emotive Behaviour Therapy*. London: Whurr.

Dryden, W. and Neenan, M. (2004). *The Rational Emotive Behavioural Approach to Therapeutic Change*. London: Sage.

Dryden, W. and Neenan, M. (2021). *Rational Emotive Behaviour Therapy: 100 Key Points and Techniques*. 3rd edn. Abingdon: Routledge.

Dryden, W. and Yankura, J. (1993). *Counselling Individuals: A Rational-Emotive Handbook*. 2nd edn. London: Whurr.

Ellis, A. (1958). Rational psychotherapy. *Journal of General Psychology*, *59*: 35–49.

Ellis, A. (1963). Toward a more precise definition of 'emotional' and 'intellectual' insight. *Psychological Reports*, *13*: 125–126.

Ellis, A. (1972). Helping people to get better rather than merely feel better. *Rational Living*, *7(2)*: 2–9.

Ellis, A. (1979). The issue of force and energy in behavior change. *Journal of Contemporary Psychotherapy*, *10*: 83–97.

Ellis, A. (1980). Rational-emotive therapy and cognitive behavior therapy: Similarities and differences. *Cognitive Therapy and Research*, *4*: 325–340.

Ellis, A. (1983a). The philosophic implications and dangers of some popular behavior therapy techniques. In M. Rosenbaum, C. M. Franks and Y. Jaffe (eds) *Perspectives on Behavior Therapy in the Eighties*. New York: Springer.

Ellis, A. (1983b). *The Case against Religiosity*. New York: Institute for Rational-Emotive Therapy.

Ellis, A. (1985). *Overcoming Resistance: RET with Difficult Clients*. New York: Springer.

Ellis, A. (1991). The revised ABC's of rational-emotive therapy (RET). *Journal of Rational-Emotive and Cognitive-Behavior Therapy*, *9(3)*: 139–172.

Ellis, A. (1994). *Reason and Emotion in Psychotherapy*, revised and updated edn. Secaucus, NJ: Carol.

Ellis, A. (2002). *Overcoming Resistance: A Rational Emotive Behavior Therapy Integrated Approach*. New York: Springer.

Ellis, A. and Dryden, W. (1997). *The Practice of Rational Emotive Behavior Therapy*. 2nd edn. New York: Springer.

Golden, W. L. and Dryden, W. (1986). Cognitive-behavioural therapies: Commonalities, divergences and future developments. In W. Dryden and W. L. Golden (eds) *Cognitive-Behavioural Approaches to Psychotherapy*. London: Harper & Row.

Grieger, R. and Boyd, J. (1980). *Rational-Emotive Therapy: A Skills-Based Approach*. New York: Van Nostrand Reinhold.

Hauck, P. (1966). The neurotic agreement in psychotherapy. *Rational Living*, *1(1)*: 31–34.

Hauck, P. (1980). *Brief Counseling with RET*. Philadelphia, PA: Westminster Press.

Horney, K. (1950). *Neurosis and Human Growth*. New York: Norton.

Kwee, M. G. T. and Lazarus, A. A. (1986). Multimodal therapy: The cognitive-behavioural tradition and beyond. In W. Dryden and W. L. Golden (eds) *Cognitive-Behavioural Approaches to Psychotherapy*. London: Harper & Row.

Maslow, A. (1968). *Toward a Psychology of Being*. 2nd edn. Princeton, NJ: Van Nostrand.

Rogers, C. R. (1957). The necessary and sufficient conditions of therapeutic personality change. *Journal of Consulting Psychology, 21,* 95–103.

Walen, S. R., DiGiuseppe, R. and Dryden, W. (1992). *A Practitioner's Guide to Rational-Emotive Therapy*. 2nd edn. New York: Oxford University Press.

Wessler, R. A. and Wessler, R. L. (1980). *The Principles and Practice of Rational-Emotive Therapy*. San Francisco, CA: Jossey-Bass.

Young, J. (2024). *No Bullshit Therapy: How to Engage People Who Don't Want to Work with You*. Abingdon: Routledge.

Ziegler, D. J. (1989). A critique of rational-emotive theory of personality. In M. E. Bernard and R. DiGiuseppe (eds.) *Inside Rational-Emotive Therapy: A Critical Analysis of the Theory and Practice of Albert Ellis*. San Diego, CA: Academic Press.

# Index